Middle Class Meltdown in America
Causes, Consequences, and Remedies

In accessible prose for North American undergraduate students, this short text provides a sociological understanding of the causes and consequences of growing middle class inequality, with an abundance of empirical supporting data. The book also addresses what we, as individuals and as a society, can do to put middle class Americans on a sounder footing.

Kevin T. Leicht is professor and chair of the Department of Sociology at the University of Iowa. His research examines the relationship between globalization, economic change, and social inequality in a variety of contexts. His work has appeared in the *American Sociological Review, American Journal of Sociology, Social Forces*, and the *Academy of Management Journal*, and he is former editor of *The Sociological Quarterly* and *Research in Social Stratification and Mobility*. He currently serves as president-elect of the Midwest Sociological Society.

Scott T. Fitzgerald is associate professor and director of graduate studies in the Department of Sociology at the University of North Carolina Charlotte. His research examines social and economic inequality, social movements, public policy, and religion, and has appeared in *Social Forces; Mobilization: An International Journal; Sociological Spectrum*; and *Policy Studies Journal*. He is currently the political sociology co-editor of *Sociology Compass*.

Titles of Related Interest

The Stupidity Epidemic: Worrying about Students, Schools, and America's Future
by Joel Best

Who Lives, Who Dies, Who Decides?: Abortion, Neonatal Care, Assisted Dying, and Capital Punishment
by Sheldon Ekland-Olson

Outsourcing the Womb: Race, Class and Gestational Surrogacy in a Global Market
by France Winddance Twine

Disposable Youth: Racialized Memories and the Culture of Cruelty
by Henry A. Giroux

Geographies of Privilege
by France Winddance Twine and Bradley Gardener

Unequal Prospects: Is Working Longer the Answer?
by Tay McNamara and John Williamson

Middle Class Meltdown in America

Causes, Consequences, and Remedies

Second Edition

Kevin T. Leicht
and Scott T. Fitzgerald

Routledge
Taylor & Francis Group

NEW YORK AND LONDON

Second Edition published 2014
by Routledge
711 Third Avenue, New York, NY 10017

and by Routledge
2 Park Square, Milton Park, Abingdon, Oxon, OX14 4RN

Routledge is an imprint of the Taylor & Francis Group, an informa business

First published 2006 by Worth Publishers.

Library of Congress Cataloging-in-Publication Data
Leicht, Kevin T.
[Postindustrial peasants]
 Middle class meltdown in America : causes, consequences, and remedies / by Kevin T. Leicht and Scott Fitzgerald. — Second edition.
  pages cm
 Includes bibliographical references and index.
 1. Middle class—United States. 2. Financial crises—United States. 3. United States—Economic conditions—2009– 4. Consumer credit—United States. I. Fitzgerald, Scott T. II. Title.
  HT690.U6L45 2014
  305.5'50973—dc23
  2013030892

ISBN: 978-0-415-70951-4 (hbk)
ISBN: 978-0-415-70952-1 (pbk)
ISBN: 978-1-315-88550-6 (ebk)

Typeset in Minion
by Apex CoVantage, LLC

Printed and bound in the United States of America by Publishers Graphics, LLC on sustainably sourced paper.

Brief Contents

Contents

Preface

This is a book about the American middle class—people who are arguably the cultural, economic, and political bedrock of modern society. The "American dream" is essentially a dream of becoming solidly middle class—of owning a home, having a steady job, and providing educational and other opportunities for your children—and one that has inspired millions of people as they sacrifice and toil. In the following pages, we tell the story of the struggling American middle class by weaving together sociological and economic research, personalized portraits and examples, and an abundance of figures and graphs providing accessible documentation of important social, economic, and political trends. By telling this story, we hope to demonstrate the continued relevance of sociological investigation into contemporary social problems by focusing on the interconnections between economics, politics, and civil society. And we seek to help students become engaged citizens and encourage broad public discussions and action directed toward improving the future prospects of all—including the American middle class.

We began our 2007 book *Post-Industrial Peasants: The Illusion of Middle Class Prosperity* with a pronouncement: "Before you read our book, we'll give away the ending: The American middle class is in trouble." At the time, the argument that we developed there seemed bold enough to warrant an opening disclaimer. For decades, the American public had been told that the U.S. economy was consistently growing stronger, more productive, and more efficient. Ordinary Americans watched as the value of their retirement accounts and personal wealth soared due to skyrocketing home values and the seemingly unstoppable upward tick of the Dow Jones. To claim that the American middle class was in trouble seemed to fly in the face of these and other cherished economic indicators.

While it was indeed a bold pronouncement even at that time, we were not alone in sounding the alarm. Our work brought together a wide range of extensive data and analyses generated by academics (including economists, sociologists, political scientists, and anthropologists), policy analysts, and journalists documenting and illuminating the plight of the middle class in contemporary society. However, prior to 2008, those of us claiming that something was wrong—that the economic prosperity generated by the massive U.S. economy was driven largely by risky procedures in the financial sector; that consumer spending and confidence was being supported not by growing wages but by increased personal debt; that the record number of homeowners and levels of real estate wealth came from a growing housing bubble and questionable lending practices—were clearly in the minority, and collectively we spent considerable time simply documenting the various macro-level trends and individual stories that bore out our nagging suspicion that something was wrong.

Much has happened since 2007 that has fundamentally shifted the focus of discussion on the American middle class. In the past few years, we have witnessed the longest recession since the Great Depression of the 1930s, the near-catastrophic collapse of global finance, unprecedented numbers of personal bankruptcies and home foreclosures, and major government interventions into the economy: the 2008 Troubled Asset Relief Program, the 2009 American Recovery and Investment Act, and the 2010 Tax Relief, Unemployment Insurance Reauthorization and Job Creation Act. Tellingly, in 2009, President Barack Obama established the first ever Middle Class Task Force.

In the following pages, we argue that the changes to the middle class over the past forty years are a big deal. While the story is complex, our telling of it is not. Through news accounts, personalized stories, and charts and graphs that are accessible to non-specialists, we show that:

- The middle class has experienced a decline in real purchasing power due to the stagnation of real incomes since the late 1970s.
- The gaps between the stagnant incomes and consumption aspirations of the middle class are made up through easily available credit—credit that almost magically appeared just as middle class incomes were stagnating.
- The use of debt as an instrument for maintaining consumption created an illusion of prosperity that masked important shifts in power and control within society. Workers and families who are living off borrowed money that they promise to pay back later are in a fundamentally different place than those who are able to pay for current consumption with steadily rising incomes.
- During this period, incomes did not rise, even though the economy consistently grew. Very real productivity gains during the late 1980s and 1990s were taken by others, fueling a massive increase in wealth and income inequality.

- The deregulation of consumer credit has led to the socialization of credit risk through the marketing of asset-backed securities. These debt instruments have made credit—and credit cards—more widely available and have fueled the spread of unconventional subprime lending schemes.
- Many (if not most) of these changes have been politically fueled by the marketing of an illusion—the idea that deregulated markets, federal tax cuts, and the gutting of public infrastructure will benefit everyone, including the middle class. The theoretical evidence supporting this claim was dubious, and the empirical evidence that exactly the opposite has happened is overwhelming. The federal government now exists as a vehicle for redistributing funds to the already prosperous, tax burdens have shifted toward the middle class, and costs for many of the goods that the middle class consumes have been rising. Yet in election after election, no candidate seems to point this out in a way that resonates with voters.
- This gutting of the middle class has led to serious declines in feelings of reciprocity and community; record numbers of personal bankruptcies; and a general "politics of displacement," in which people apparently get angry about virtually anything *except money and wealth*. The contradictions of American politics are now so pervasive that they are self-perpetuating: unfettered markets destroy jobs, families, and communities; politicians complain about cultural decline while expanding the purview of the unfettered markets that perpetuate it; yet another round of tax cuts and privatizations occurs, and still more complaints about cultural decline follow.

Our conclusion does not mince words: Our nation can do better than this. We can reconnect capital accumulation to middle class prosperity. We can acknowledge that most of us won't really benefit from a capital gains tax cut. We can value families and communities. We can acknowledge that cavernous inequality gaps are corrosive to the political and social order. And we can make better choices as consumers.

During much of the twentieth century, the American middle class served as the economic, cultural, and political bedrock of the United States. We, the authors, are products of the middle class, and we believe that future generations of Americans would benefit from the availability of the opportunities promised to this group. American capitalism owes the middle class these opportunities, and the American economy is more internationally competitive, productive, and just when the American middle class is treated fairly.

A Note Regarding Classroom Use

We have written this book primarily for use as a thematic or supplemental text in the undergraduate classroom. It is particularly well suited for courses in sociology, economics, political science, anthropology, and American Studies.

The book is written in accessible prose and technical academic discussions are held to a minimum. Data are presented in easy-to-read figures and graphs (as opposed to statistical tables), and extensive documentation provides resources for those interested in more detailed treatments. A few highlights:

1. **Wide range of topics.** We bring together a diverse set of issues to illustrate the interconnections between economics, politics, and civil society (e.g., macroeconomic theory; fiscal and monetary policy; productivity; consumer debt; subprime lending; rising economic inequality; trends in the cost of housing, health care, and higher education; feudal and contemporary economic arrangements; political discourse; the fraying of community bonds; the Great Recession; federal bailouts).

2. **Extensive use of figures and graphs.** We use figures and graphs throughout the book (including a few dozen in the appendix) to provide the evidence supporting our argument. This approach allows us to document our claims and provide guidance for readers interested in exploring these data and findings in greater detail without overwhelming readers with statistical tables and numbers. Using figures and graphs provides a quick and accessible way to present these data in a format accessible to non-experts, without sacrificing analytical rigor.

3. **Sociological analysis, and a primer on macroeconomics and finance.** Our argument is essentially a sociological one, and is developed by bringing together insights from various disciplines, especially political economic perspectives. Broadly, this approach demonstrates the importance of examining the intersection of politics and economics when analyzing the difficulties facing the American middle class. By doing so, we illuminate the sociological insight that lies at the heart of this analysis: our lives are shaped in profound ways by the economic, social, and political arrangements of our time.

4. **Pitched at a level appropriate for college students and interested general readers.** As much as possible, we employ non-technical language throughout the book and sidestep technical and arcane academic debates. At the same time, we provide useful resources (e.g., definitions) that can aid readers not familiar with terms related to personal finance, economic theory, and a variety of other topics. These concepts are relevant to readers trying to make sense of their own financial lives as well as students trying to learn about these subjects. Additionally, we present journalistic coverage of middle class families, and we also employ the literary device of composite profiles to help the reader understand the broad, macro-level trends and theories that we discuss. These characters (David and Monica, and Bill and Sheryl) appear throughout the book in order to illustrate how these broad forces can impact individuals and families. This approach is particularly effective in connecting personal troubles to public issues.

Acknowledgments

We would like to thank Steve Rutter for his input on and advocacy for our project, Margaret Moore for her expert production services, and our colleagues who provided valuable input on earlier drafts of our work, as well as the numerous audiences who have listened to and critiqued presentations of our work over the past six years. And a special thanks to our reviewers:

Sarah Swider	Wayne State University
Daniel Egan	University of Massachusetts, Lowell
Kathleen Fitzgerald	Loyola University, New Orleans
Kimberly Fox	Bridgewater State University
Rachel Dwyer	Ohio State University
Milan Zafirovski	University of North Texas
Beth Caniglia	Oklahoma State University
B. Mitchell Peck	University of Oklahoma
Graham Cassano	Oakland University
John Campbell	Dartmouth University
Lawrence E. Raffalovich	State University of New York, Albany
Eric Schutz	Rollins College

Finally, we would like to thank our families for their tireless support for our work and their toleration of tight deadlines and late nights.

CHAPTER 1

The Illusion of Middle Class Prosperity in the United States

I'm in debt up to my eyeballs. Please help me. . . .
—A smiling homeowner, riding a lawn tractor in front of a
white four-bedroom house, in a television commercial for
debt consolidation loans

Introduction

If we look back before the 2008 Great Recession and the record bankrupt-cies, layoffs, and foreclosures that came with it, and before Occupy Wall Street protestors pointed to growing differences between the haves and have-nots by proclaiming, "We are the 99%"—indeed, to nearly any time in the past four decades—we would find politicians and economic leaders telling us about the exceptional performance of the U.S. economy and the strength of the American middle class. For example, in 1997, the U.S. Council of Economic Advisers painted a relatively rosy picture of the state of the economy, claiming that a solid foundation had been laid for future growth, that unemployment was low, and that things were looking up. President Clinton summed up his first four years in office by pointing to low inflation and unemployment (5.4 percent), a reduction in poverty, and the highest rate of business investment since the 1960s.[1] Years later, President Bush's Council of Economic Advisers was simi-larly effusive about the recent performance of the American economy:

> In 2004, the U.S. economic recovery blossomed into a full-fledged expansion, with strong output growth and steady improvement in the

labor market. Real gross domestic product (GDP) grew by 4.4 percent in 2004 for the year as a whole. About 2.2 million new payroll jobs were created during 2004—the largest annual gain since 1999. . . . The U.S. economy is on a solid footing for sustained growth in the years to come.[2]

But for many members of the middle class all is not well. In fact, all has not been well for most of the past forty years.

The types of people that are having economic difficulties might surprise you. They are people pursuing the American dream—people who earned a college degree, bought a house and started a family, and worked long hours. It seemed that they were doing precisely what they were supposed to do in order to achieve and maintain a solidly middle class life. Jeff Einstein, for example, used to work at a digital media company, but after being laid off, he went to work in a Gap outlet making $10 an hour; it now takes him over two weeks to make what he used to make in a day. Jeff describes the ordeal as a "year-and-a-half long process of dehumanization."[3]

Likewise, Lou Casagrande, a Ph.D. chemist and technology consultant in Warren, New Jersey, had trouble paying the mortgage on his house when he lost his job in June 2001. While he and his wife could once afford their $2,700 monthly mortgage payment, they began delving into his retirement funds and into the money they'd saved to send their three children to college. Lou took a job as a substitute teacher in New Jersey and his wife moonlights at Starbucks to make ends meet.

To combat the financial squeeze, middle class Americans are resorting to unorthodox methods of borrowing and brokering their futures, digging even deeper into a pit of debt. Michael Knox, sixty years old and on disability, had run out of ideas for paying his credit card bills when a salesman contacted him and told him he could wipe out his $20,000 debt by taking out a new and bigger mortgage on his house. The broker sent him checks to pay off his creditors, but the payments on the new mortgage devoured 75 percent of his income. He quickly fell behind and the mortgage company moved to repossess his home. Tragically, this seems to have driven Knox, who had suffered for years from clinical depression, to commit suicide.[4]

The crisis affects both young and old members of the middle class. In 2004, James and Doris Stevenson of Espanola, New Mexico, seventy-one and seventy-seven, had twenty-nine years left on a mortgage they'd recently refinanced at a lower interest rate. They purchased the house six years prior by using two-thirds of James's retirement fund for the $35,000 down payment, and the two still work occasional jobs to pay off the remaining $75,000. The debt they have accrued is likely to last until the end of their lives.[5]

Why Study the Middle Class?

When we read the stories of Jeff, Lou, Michael, and the Stevensons, it is easy to write them off as individual accounts of bad luck. We feel bad for them, and we think about friends and family members who are struggling to keep their heads above water. We may even see ourselves in these stories. But we rarely stop to ask ourselves why it is that people who seem to be "playing by the rules" are working so hard just to get by. Why is it that despite all the talk about how prosperous past decades have been, and all our confidence that the United States is a global economic superpower, the middle class can't seem to get ahead?

A careful reading of the available data reveals that these stories are not simply isolated cases of misfortune, but part of a larger trend. They illustrate important but often-overlooked changes that have taken place during the past forty years. Since the early 1970s, the economic and social standing of America's middle class has been changing, often in undesirable ways.

The middle class of the United States—and, to a lesser extent, its Western European counterparts—is the standard by which economic opportunity and prosperity are judged. Large immigrant groups, from eastern and southern Europeans in the late nineteenth and early twentieth centuries to Hispanics and Southeast Asians in the late twentieth and early twenty-first, have come to the United States seeking economic opportunity. While many come hoping to "strike it rich," many more are drawn by the humble idea that the average labors of an average person mean more and are worth more in the United States than anywhere else. Their overwhelming economic perception is that people like them can "get ahead" in America, achieving simple goals: feeding themselves and their families; educating their children so they may lead better lives in this land of opportunity; and experiencing some of the luxuries that make work, saving, and sacrifice worthwhile.

We have written this book to examine critically the economic, political, and social forces shaping America's middle class. There are many definitions of the term "middle class." For our purposes, when we speak of the middle class we are referring to Americans who annually earn between $40,000 and $80,000, most of which comes from salaries and wages; who work as upper- or lower-level managers, professionals, or small business owners; and who graduated from, or at least attended, a four-year college. The median family income in the United States—the income that separates the top 50 percent of income earners from the bottom 50 percent—was $51,404 in February 2013, down 7.3 percent since the 2008 recession (see Chapter 2).[6]

Our book is not about the hopes, aspirations, dreams, or worldviews of the American middle class;[7] it is about the causes and consequences of their contemporary economic circumstances. Others have talked about social policy and the middle class,[8] the political orientations of the middle class,[9] and concerns about the changing communities of the middle class.[10] What we offer is a broad look at the changes in the economic standing of the middle class, and the social and political consequences of those changes over the past forty years.

Our basic argument is complex, but our conclusion is not. *Middle class prosperity in the late twentieth and early twenty-first centuries is an illusion.* When we look at the middle class below the surface, aggregate measures of economic vitality are hiding an ever-widening group of Americans who are struggling just to remain solvent. Worse still, and in contrast to the post-war economic boom of the 1950s and 1960s, there appears to be no institutionalized method for interpreting change, nor is there a new coherent set of "how-to" rules that describe how to get ahead. Almost all of the conventional rules no longer apply, and prosperity seems illusory or due to luck and being at the right place at the right time.

The Changing Rules of Middle Class Life

The rules of the middle class game used to be simple and stable—in fact, the stability of these rules helped *define* the American middle class. These rules were passed down from generation to generation and reinforced by popular culture. With the advent of television, families across the nation could see the American dream played out nightly, with shows like *Ozzie and Harriet* and *Leave It to Beaver* exemplifying middle class family life. To give us some standards for evaluating the changes taking place, let's review these rules:[11]

1. Find a good, steady job, and stick with it.
2. Be loyal and hardworking, and your company will reward you with pay raises and promotions. You can base your current decisions regarding debt and consumption on the promise of future compensation.
3. Get married and settle down. You will reap the rewards from peace of mind and investment in a community of like-minded fellow travelers.
4. Buy a house as soon as you can. Stay in it. Pay off the mortgage before you retire. Your house is your major financial asset and a sign that you are a responsible citizen who has "made it."
5. Save money for a rainy day. One day, the furnace will fail or your teenager will wreck the family car, and you will need to crack that nest egg. If you are lucky enough to avoid such calamities, you can retire with this money and use it to do the things you couldn't while you were working. Besides, no one will ever loan you money unless you prove you can save it and pay it back.
6. Look forward to retiring in your sixties. Your company will provide a pension that will fund this period of well-deserved rest, relaxation, and recreation.

7. Be proud of your hard work, and know that it will be rewarded. All types of work possess an inherent dignity that is worthy of respect. If your job lacks excitement, it still provides a decent living, and your sacrifices will be rewarded in the long run.

8. Provide your children with a good education. Education is vital for your children to get ahead in our society. If your kids can't get scholarships to an Ivy League school, they can still attend the local state university and receive a good education for a modest cost. Between the money you've saved for them, the summer jobs they work, and a financial contribution from your current earnings, your kids can pay for a good college education and good, steady jobs will follow for them.

For reasons that will become clearer, very few of these rules apply in the globalized, late-modern economic world of the current American middle class. The move from an economy centered on manufacturing to one centered on services, the globalization of markets, and the information age has altered the economic realities of middle class Americans. In this new post-industrial economic world there has been a shift "from a social world characterized by long-term, stable relationships to one characterized by short-term, temporary relationships."[12] The uncertainty surrounding short-term employment relationships leaves many middle class professionals filled with anxiety. Many members of the middle class intuitively sense this change, but can't put a finger on "what went wrong."[13]

Just ask Silvia Vides, a housekeeper in Los Angeles earning $11 an hour, who is struggling to pay the rent on her one-bedroom apartment and still have enough to eat. At the same time, the upper echelons of consumer spending—places like Saks Fifth Avenue, Neiman Marcus, and Nordstrom—report gangbuster business. "I'm surprised by how well we've sold high-priced fashion at this stage," says Pete Nordstrom, president of Nordstrom's full-line stores.[14]

The issues faced by Silvia are not the same issues faced by the patrons of Neiman Marcus and Nordstrom, yet they are inextricably linked by economic and political forces. Critically discussing these realities is made more difficult by the half measures and pseudo-solutions of political debate on the status of the middle class.

The empirical trends and practical economic lessons of the past forty years reveal painful economic realities. The general trends are not that complicated, and many average Americans who don't make a living thinking about these things could articulate the lessons drawn from these experiences. Taken together, these lessons form the "new rules" of middle class life:

1. *Good, steady jobs that last longer than a year or two are hard to come by.* Many jobs that appear to have long-term potential turn out not to.

2. *Companies do not reward employee loyalty, they reward* customer *loyalty.* There is no connection between working now and later rewards. At most, if you're lucky, your company will reward you with company stock or stock options, but the future value of these is beyond your control; moreover, critical vesting rules make it difficult to cash in at critical times (as top executives invariably do when they anticipate changes in the company fortunes).

3. *It is hard to obtain the economic security on which marriage and "settling down" are based.* Worse, two full-time workers' incomes are needed to support a lifestyle that one income used to buy.[15] Two jobs per family are necessary because at any time, one person might be out of a job. This economic uncertainty, the lack of coherent rules for what one should be doing, and larger sets of cultural changes drastically lessen the prospect that marriages will last.

4. *Buying a house is increasingly difficult.* Despite historically low interest rates, buying and keeping a house is very difficult in an economy where jobs don't last. Paying off a mortgage becomes an elusive dream. Increasingly, you borrow against the equity in the house to afford the consumer items that are the markers of a middle class life. Such borrowing acts as a buffer when you're between jobs.

5. *Saving for a rainy day—or any day, for that matter—is extremely difficult.* Your employer may contribute to a retirement package for you, but you won't work there long enough to accrue any money in the package. The package is only as good as the long-term viability of the company—a rather shaky prospect. So much of your money goes to meet current expenses that no money goes into a savings account or mutual fund for the future. You live from one paycheck to the next; a few missed paydays from bankruptcy.

6. *You may never be able to retire.* Coping with medical expenses as you age will be your major preoccupation. Medicare doesn't cover very much, and companies can't afford to provide healthcare benefits for their retirees. Supplemental insurance is expensive and eats up a substantial portion of the limited retirement benefits you receive.

7. *People who work hard and play by the rules are viewed as "suckers."* Modern television, movies, and music glorify glamorous lifestyles and unconventional, "get rich quick" ways of making money. Politicians ignore you or treat you as a "cow to milk";[16] big investors see you as a consumer who can be duped into borrowing money on easy credit to maintain the appearances of a middle class lifestyle.

8. *Your lifestyle itself is the subject of debunking by cultural elites.* Those who labor diligently at what they do find employers who pay too little, offload most of their risks and expenses onto employees and communities, demand too many working hours, don't follow or violate openly most

labor laws, and vote for political parties that glorify images of 1950s "traditional" lifestyles—lifestyles that this very economic system makes it all but impossible to emulate.[17] Employers move production to places where costs are low, offloading expenses for public infrastructure onto their employees, who must pay higher taxes, user fees, and private fees from their limited, non-growing, non-guaranteed paychecks. These same economic elites attempt to convince their employees that taxes are spent on "undeserving, lazy people" and that still lower taxes will benefit them. Yet tax cut after tax cut, the benefits never come.

9. *Your child's college education is paid for by student loans.* Your contribution involves moral support or money from your meager savings. The state you pay taxes to continues to cut support for the state institution your child attends while giving tax breaks to footloose investors. Because the earnings of those who don't go to college have fallen through the floor, everyone wants to go to college whether they are academically prepared or not, putting added strain on the higher education system. The degree your child earns might prevent downward mobility, but it doesn't provide upward mobility.

Some analysts don't see a problem with this almost complete reversal of the traditional rules; social change is, after all, social change. The American middle class has adapted to changes in the past—suburbia, automobiles, urbanization, and the sexual revolution, among others—and they will surely adapt to the new economy. Others have reasons to doubt such sanguine pronouncements, and they point to a variety of factors that are making middle class life in the United States more precarious.

Overview of Key Economic Trends and Outline of Chapters

Globalization and the rise of neoliberalism as a political ideology have a great deal to do with changes in middle class life.[18] *Neoliberalism* refers to the promotion of free markets, reduced trade barriers, and global movement of capital and labor to different parts of the world. This movement has produced a global "race to the bottom" in which investors search the world for the most favorable investment environments, disinvesting in operations and service delivery in first-world locations such as the United States, Western Europe, and Japan and moving operations to locations in the less-developed world where labor costs are lower and regulations are less burdensome. Neoliberalism incorporates a search for quick profits and the ability to deliver these in the short time frame that investors demand.

The American welfare state is also the least generous in the world. In place of extensive income assistance, universal healthcare, and a universal pension system, Americans face a privatized and byzantine system of health insurance, uncertain unemployment benefits, and a tottering Social Security system that doesn't provide much retirement security. Private pension systems, where they exist, are becoming less generous and are more dependent on the performance of specific companies at specific times. None of this is the lot of the average member of the middle class in any other industrialized nation in the world.[19]

Unions helped define the labor market during the middle class heydays of the 1950s and 1960s, negotiating contracts with employers in industries that were largely protected from global competition. The wages and benefits negotiated in unionized firms tended to set a pattern for wages and benefits in entire industries and economic sectors. The labor movement could negotiate these contracts because corporations had massive capital investments in specific places that could not be moved: manufacturing was labor intensive, and technology and the organization of work depended on a stable, competent, and happy workforce.[20]

Technology and the information age have altered the social organization of work. These changes include *flatter organizational hierarchies*, as new information technologies eliminate the need for middle layers of management; the growing use of *temporary workers* employed on an as-needed basis to perform specific jobs for the duration of single projects; the extensive use of *subcontracting and outsourcing* to external firms and/or suppliers for products and services once provided by permanent employees; *massive downsizing of the permanent workforce* as organizations need fewer management and support people and replace skilled workers with computer-skilled operators or unskilled machine tenders; a *post-unionized bargaining environment* in which unions have either no place or reduced power and no structural ability to gain a foothold for bargaining with employers; and *virtual organizations* that exist as a web of technologically driven interactions rather than as a distinctive, physical worksite located in a specific place.[21]

The pace of this change accelerated in the 1990s and 2000s, directly affecting the managerial and professional jobs the white-collar middle class relies on. No longer do layoffs, firings, job instability, ever-shifting earnings, and difficulty paying bills affect only blue-collar workers; these prospects have now "trickled up" into the middle class, where bedrock economic stability was once the norm.[22] As job instability grew, a new variable was added to the middle class economic equation: easily available consumer credit. Credit replaced earnings as the major source of middle class purchasing power.

The American middle class faces a set of stark choices that have been shaped by broad structural forces and by deliberate economic and political actions. In the pages to come we argue that a wide variety of factors have converged to produce this state of affairs and that the situation is worse than it appears on the surface. Stagnant incomes, rising taxes, the pocketing of productivity gains by the corporate elite, easily available credit, globalization, privatization, and labor market changes have altered what it means to be part of the American middle class.

Of course, it isn't simply the middle class that is having trouble. Across our country, hundreds of thousands of homeless men, women, and children live on the streets and in shelters. In 2003, over thirty-four million Americans lived below the official poverty line; by 2012, this number had grown to over forty-six million.[23] Families of migrant farm workers struggle to eke out a living, and women, primarily recent immigrants, work in sweatshop conditions in our cities. Fourth- and fifth-generation farmers are forced to take second jobs at Wal-Mart to avoid the slide into bankruptcy. Millions of children grow up in families locked in a vicious cycle of poverty, dead-end minimum wage jobs, and despair.[24] With so many Americans facing these stark realities, why focus on the middle class?

Our examination of the middle class is driven by two observations. First, by focusing only on the economic challenges facing the poor and the working class, observers often implicitly assume that the economic prosperity we read about in the paper and hear about on the news must be benefiting everyone else. Second, many observers assume that Americans who are struggling do so because they do not have the skills, motivation, and education to compete in a post-industrial economy. The college-educated professional is held up as the "poster child" of the new economy, and the middle class is said to be profiting from these economic shifts. But what if the very people who are thought to be gaining unprecedented wealth, freedom, and mobility are actually saddled with debt and locked into a system of work that provides little stability, few benefits, and no rewards?

To outline our argument: Chapter 2, "The Struggling Middle Class," provides case studies from the contemporary middle class, using composite scenarios created from the economic trends of the past forty years. This chapter also reviews the relationship between elites and workers in pre-industrial economic systems, not as a comprehensive overview of the history of agrarian class relationships but as a way of showing that we've seen this before. Chapter 3, "Macroeconomics and the Income/Credit Squeeze," compares the major macroeconomic theories that have shaped public policy in the twentieth and twenty-first centuries, and documents the stagnation of incomes for the middle class and the rise in available credit that occurred at precisely the same time.

Chapter 4, "Robbing the Productivity Train," examines trends in productivity in the 1980s to the present: worker productivity rose and earnings did not. Rather than being distributed to the average worker, these revenues financed executive compensation packages and investments in financial markets by the wealthy. We provide statistical simulations that illustrate that the compensation available through productivity gains, if it were paid in wages, would substantially offset the credit advanced to the middle class. To put it bluntly, the American middle class was loaned money that it could have received as earnings.

Chapter 5, "Where Did All That Credit Come From?," documents the rise of easily available consumer credit and the ways we use it. Starting in the 1980s, the deregulation of the banking industry and a shift in populations targeted by the banking and credit industry drastically changed the availability and implications of consumer credit. The widespread availability of personal credit cards (often at exorbitant interest rates), home equity loans, "no money down" car loans, and leases have changed the landscape of middle class finances. Investors and lenders have profited while the middle class has become trapped in a "work and spend" cycle that shows little sign of abating.

Chapter 6, "From Washington to Wall Street: Marketing the Illusion," argues that it isn't merely advertisers of shampoos, cars, and clothes that peddle a make-believe culture of glamour, riches, and prosperity. The economic struggles of the middle class have been effectively hidden from the public agenda through the promulgation of neoconservative ideology and supply-side economics. While politicians and lobbyists contend that these policies will benefit everyone, the "supply-side miracle" has never materialized for the middle class. Since the 1980s, a combination of tax cuts for the wealthy, deregulation, corporate tax avoidance, and an overall shifting of tax burdens onto earned income (and away from unearned income) have hurt the economic standing of middle class Americans. During the same period, the costs of maintaining a middle class lifestyle have continued to rise, and owning a home, buying a car, paying for college, obtaining healthcare, affording daycare, and retiring have become increasingly difficult.

Chapter 7, "The Great Recession of 2008–2009: The Illusion Exposed," examines the eighteen-month recession that officially ended in the summer of 2009—the longest economic recession since the Great Depression of the 1930s. We locate the causes of this massive economic downturn in the exuberant and speculative practices of an unregulated financial industry and the bursting of the housing bubble, and mortgage underwriting practices that disproportionately left low- and middle-income Americans saddled with unmanageable debt. The governmental response to these crises may well have prevented a catastrophic global finance meltdown, but to date it has done little to directly aid middle class homeowners and workers. The result is a middle class in 2013 that has even less wealth, less income, and less job security than in 2008, with no real light at the end of the tunnel.

Chapter 8, "The Consequences of Middle Class Meltdown," explores the consequences of the cycle of stagnant wages, rising debts, high taxes, and political disenfranchisement. The unemployment rate dipped to record lows in the 1990s, but wages barely moved. The debts acquired as a result of stagnant wages mean that no one is available to fight the current system of work, spending, and debt, so employers continue to pocket productivity gains and workers work harder and harder just to remain financially solvent. We identify four important consequences of middle class meltdown that are corroding the social order: the growing number of personal bankruptcies filed by middle class Americans, the cultural contradictions of American politics, the fraying of community ties, and the hardening of public discourse and development of a general politics of displacement.

Chapter 9, "What Can We Do? A Manifesto for the Middle Class," concludes the book by offering a multilevel recommendation to encourage active individual and collective responses to middle class meltdown.

For readers who generally view statistics and data with (a) fear and loathing, (b) anger, and/or (c) calloused indifference, we offer the following entreaty: We have done our best to compile a wide range of data from major governmental and academic sources in order to assess important trends during the past forty years. These data provide the empirical evidence for, among other things, our rather bold claim that the American middle class is in a state of meltdown. We present these data in graphs and figures because these are simple, yet accurate, visual representations of these data, and taken together help paint a picture of the plight of the American middle class. Our book can be navigated without paying close attention to the charts and graphs, and the basic points will still make sense. We provide extensive citations of our data sources and publications so that interested readers can readily find additional information and details by locating the original sources.

Clearly, in our efforts to bring together disparate literatures and evidence on a wide range of economic, social, and political topics in a non-technical book accessible to a general audience, we have had to sidestep many relevant academic and political debates and gloss over potentially important details and nuances in the data.[25] We acknowledge this limitation and believe that the trade-off is well worth it. This work is designed to contribute an emerging public debate on the status of the American middle class. No doubt there are sources that can provide individual accounts and stories of wealth, prosperity, and upward mobility during these last few decades, just as we have found individual accounts of downward mobility, rising debt, job instability, and economic despair. But this isn't a debate about who became individually wealthy and individually poor; it's about the continuing economic health of millions of people who were once the bedrock of a very prosperous developed economy.

One final note. It might be tempting to believe that the source of the crisis we discuss is a conspiracy hatched in a smoke-filled conference room on Wall Street, but we are not implying that a particular small group of people are completely responsible for the trends we discuss in this book. No particular set of elites sat down in the late 1970s and said, "By the year 2010, average Americans should be earning less than they are now, they should be working longer hours, and they should be mired in consumer credit that keeps them tied to the exploitative work system we've set up for them. It's a bonanza!" Some of these outcomes are clearly the product of deliberate political and economic decisions by people in power, but others are not.

While there is not conspiracy, there has been change. Jeff, Lou, Michael, the Stevensons, and others like them are clearly looking for answers. In these pages, we attempt to provide some.

Discussion Questions

- Why is it important to study the American middle class?
- What is the "American dream"? Do you think you will achieve it?
- Take a moment to list your three favorite TV shows. What do these shows teach us about social class and about being middle class?
- If you were to write your own set of rules for being successful, what would they be?
- How have globalization and changes in the organization of work affected the American middle class?

Notes

1. Council of Economic Advisers, *1997 Economic Report of the President,* (Washington, D.C.: U.S. Government Printing Office, 1997), 7, acccessed May 13, 2013, http://www.gpo.gov/fdsys/browse/collection.action?collectionCode=ERP
2. Council of Economic Advisers, *2005 Economic Report of the President,* (Washington, D.C.: U.S. Government Printing Office, 2005), 17, accessed May 13, 2013, http://www.gpo.gov/fdsys/browse/collection.action?collectionCode=ERP
3. Jonathan Mahler, "Commute to Nowhere," *New York Times,* Magazine, April 23, 2003, 46–47.
4. Michael Moss, "Erase Debt Now. (Lose Your House Later.)," *New York Times,* October 10, 2004, accessed June 2, 2005, http://www.nytimes.com/2004/10/10/business/yourmoney/10sub.html?ei=5090&en=e8573da3b340261b&ex=1255147200&adxnnl=1&partner=rssuserland&adxnnlx=1111486316-kF25AesAYNN02r7sUbMWKA
5. Jennifer Bayot, "As Bills Mount, Debts on Homes Rise for Elderly," *New York Times,* July 4, 2004, accessed August 2, 2005, http://www.nytimes.com/2004/07/04/business/04DEBT.html?ex=1246593600&en=ae19d269f6206c03&ei=5090&partner=rssuserland
6. Gordon Green and John Coder, "Household Income Trends: February 2013." Sentier Research, accessed May 22, 2013, http://www.sentierresearch.com/reports/Sentier_Household_Income_Trends_Report_February2013_03_25_13.pdf
7. For in-depth discussions of these issues, see, for example, Edmund L. Andrews *Busted: Life Inside the Great Mortgage Meltdown* (New York: W.W. Norton & Company, 2008); Barbara Ehrenreich, *Fear of Falling: The Inner Life of the Middle Class* (New York: Pantheon Books, 1989); Nan Mooney, *(Not) Keeping Up With Our Parents: The Decline of the Professional Middle Class* (Boston: Beacon Press, 2008); Katherine Newman, *Declining Fortunes: The Withering of the American Dream* (New York: Basic Books, 1993); Alan Wolfe, *One Nation, After All* (New York: Viking, 1998); and Arthur J. Vidich, ed., *The New Middle Classes: Life Styles, Status Claims and Political Orientations* (New York: New York University Press, 1995).
8. Jacob S. Hacker, *The Great Risk Shift: The New Economic Insecurity and the Decline of the American Dream* (New York: Oxford University Press, 2008); Jacob S. Hacker and Paul Pierson, *Winner-Take-All Politics: How Washington Made the Rich Richer and Turned Its Back on the Middle Class* (New York: Simon & Schuster, 2010); Robert Reich, *Aftershock: The Next Economy & America's*

Future (New York: Vintage Books, 2011) Theda Skocpol, *The Missing Middle: Working Families and the Future of American Social Policy* (New York: W.W. Norton, 2000).

9. See, for example, Steven Brint, *In the Age of Experts: The Changing Role of Professionals in Politics and Public Life* (Princeton, NJ: Princeton University Press, 1994); Thomas Byrne and Mary D. Edsall, *Chain Reaction: The Impact of Race, Rights, and Taxes on American Politics* (New York: W.W. Norton, 1992); and Jeff Manza and Clem Brooks, *Social Cleavages and Political Change: Voter Alignments and U.S. Party Coalitions* (Oxford, UK: Oxford University Press, 1999).

10. See, for example, Robert D. Putnam, *Bowling Alone: The Collapse and Revival of American Community* (New York: Simon and Schuster, 2000); Robert N. Bellah, Richard Madsen, William M. Sullivan, Ann Swidler, and Steven M. Tipton, *Habits of the Heart: Individualism and Commitment in American Life* (Berkeley: University of California Press, 1985); and Amitai Etzioni, *Next: The Road to the Good Society* (New York: Basic Books, 2001).

11. See Richard Sennett, *The Corrosion of Character: The Personal Consequences of Work in the New Capitalism* (New York: W.W. Norton, 1998), and Beth A. Rubin, *Shifts in the Social Contract: Understanding Change in American Society* (Thousand Oaks, CA: Pine Forge Press, 1996).

12. Rubin, *Shifts in the Social Contract*, 4.

13. Donald L. Barlett, and James B. Steele, *America: What Went Wrong?* (Kansas City, MO: Andrews McMeel, 1992), xii.

14. Eduardo Porter, "Hourly Pay in U.S. Not Keeping Pace with Price Rises," *New York Times*, July 18, 2004, accessed http://www.nytimes.com/2004/07/18/business/18WAGES.html?position=&ei=5090&en=d165cecaedae7891&ex=1247889600&adxnnl=1&partner=rssuserland&pagewanted=all&adxnnlx=1143932935-zq/RYqvnD0MfdJUT8Y5jcA

15. Elizabeth Warren and Amelia Warren Tyagi, *The Two-Income Trap: Why Middle Class Mothers and Fathers Are Going Broke* (New York: Basic Books, 2003), 7.

16. See Kevin Phillips, *The Politics of Rich and Poor: Wealth and the American Electorate in the Reagan Aftermath* (New York: Random House, 1990), 83, and *Boiling Point: Democrats, Republicans, and the Decline of Middle Class Prosperity* (New York: Random House, 1993), 103–29.

17. Anthony Giddens, *Beyond Left and Right: The Future of Radical Politics* (Palo Alto, CA: Stanford University Press, 1994), 9.

18. See, for example, Anthony Giddens, *The Third Way: The Renewal of Social Democracy* (Oxford, UK: Polity Press, 1998); Richard Harvey Brown, *Culture, Capitalism, and Democracy in America* (New Haven, CT: Yale University Press, 2005); Andrew E. G. Jonas, "In Search of Order: Traditional Business Reformism and the Crisis of Neoliberalism in Massachusetts," *Transactions of the Institute of British Geographers* 21 (1996): 617–34; Alejandro Portes, "Neoliberalism and the Sociology of Development," in *Population and Development Review* 23 (1996): 229–59; and Andreas Hasenclever, Peter Mayer, and Volker Rittberger, "Interests, Power, and Knowledge: The Study of International Regimes," in *Mershon International Review* 40 (1996): 177–228.

19. Skocpol, *The Missing Middle*, 22–58.

20. See, for example, David M. Gordon, Richard Edwards, and Michael Reich, *Segmented Work, Divided Workers: The Historical Transformation of Labor in the United States* (New York: Cambridge University Press, 1982); Richard Edwards, *Rights at Work: Employment Relations in the Post-Union Era* (Washington, D.C.: Brookings Institution, 1993); and Richard B. Freeman, ed., *Working under Different Rules* (New York: Russell Sage Foundation, 1994).

21. See, for example, Kevin T. Leicht and Mary L. Fennell, *Professional Work: A Sociological Approach* (Oxford, UK: Blackwell, 2001).

22. See, for example, Jeremy Rifkin, *The End of Work: The Decline of the Global Labor Force and the Dawn of the Post-Market Era* (New York: Putnam, 1995); Thomas S. Moore, *The Disposable Workforce: Worker Displacement and Employment Instability in America* (New York: Alden de Gruyter, 1996); William J. Baumol, Alan S. Blinder, and Edward N. Wolff,

Downsizing in America: Reality, Causes, and Consequences (New York: Russell Sage Foundation, 2003); and Martin Carnoy, *Sustaining the New Economy: Work, Family, and Community in the Information Age* (Cambridge, MA: Harvard University Press, 2000).

23. U.S. Census Bureau 2013. "Table 3: Poverty Status, by Age, Race and Hispanic Origin," *Historical Poverty Tables*, accessed on July 7, 2013, http://www.census.gov/hhes/www/poverty/data/historical/people.html

24. See Elijah Anderson, *Code of the Street* (New York: W.W. Norton, 1999); Jonathan Kozol, *Savage Inequalities: Children in America's Schools* (New York: Harper Perennial, 1992); and William Julius Wilson, *When Work Disappears: The World of the New Urban Poor* (New York: Knopf, 1996).

25. Perhaps the most significant of these simplifications is our decision to largely treat the "middle class" as a monolithic group rather than highlighting the many important ways that gender, race, ethnicity, and other dimensions influence lived experiences and life chances. Interested readers can explore the large sociological literature on these topics. Suggested sources include Annette Lareau, *Unequal Childhoods: Class, Race and Family Life* (Berkeley: University of California Press, 2011); Jose A. Cobas, and Joe R. Feagin, "Language Oppression and Resistance: The Case of Middle Class Latinos in the United States," *Ethnic and Racial Studies* 31 (2008): 390–410; Rachel L. Finn, "Situating Middle Class Identities: American College Women of South Asian Descent," *Gender, Place and Culture* 16 (2009): 279–98; Arlie Russell Hochschild and Anne Machun, *The Second Shift: Working Parents and the Revolution at Home* (New York: Avon, 1997); Leslie McCall, *Complex Inequality: Gender, Class and Race in the New Economy* (New York: Routledge, 2001); Rochelle Parks-Yancy, Nancy DiTomaso, and Corinne Post, "The Social Capital Resources of Gender and Class Groups," *Sociological Spectrum* 26 (2006): 85–113; Bart Landry and Krish Marsh, "The Evolution of the New Black Middle Class," *Annual Review of Sociology*, 3 (2011): 373–94; and Mary Pattillo-McCoy, *Black Picket Fences: Privilege and Peril among the Black Middle Class* (Chicago: University of Chicago Press, 1999).

CHAPTER 2

The Struggling Middle Class

*I'm a forty-five year old man. . . . I should be independent enough to pay my
own rent. I feel so grateful to my dad, who literally saved me from becoming
homeless. . . .*

—Steven Fields, a former systems administrator for
Electronic Data Systems in Dallas[1]

Most Americans identify themselves as members of the middle class, some-
times qualifying the designation by adding "upper middle" or "lower middle."
Nationally representative survey data from the General Social Survey show
that "at no time between 1972 and 1994 did more than 10 percent of the
American population classify themselves as *either* lower class or upper class."[2]
But is it true that the overwhelming majority of Americans are middle class?

That is a difficult question to answer because the term "middle class" means
different things to different people. For some, you are middle class if you make
more than minimum wage but less than Bill Gates, if you are an office manager
rather than a cashier at McDonald's, or if you have graduated from college
rather than dropped out of high school. There is also academic and popular disagreement on how to best identify the middle class. Most classification systems
rely on three criteria—income and wealth, occupational prestige, and educational level—that sociologists label *socioeconomic status* (SES). In this book,
we primarily identify the middle class based on SES characteristics, although
we consider cultural factors as well. In general, when we speak of the middle
class we are referring to those Americans who earn incomes approximately
between $40,000 and $80,000 annually;[3] who work as upper- and lower-level

managers, professionals, and small business owners; who graduated from or at least attended a four-year college; and whose primary source of wealth is homeownership. As we discuss in later chapters, there are different dimensions of economic well-being. *Income* refers to all forms of monetary compensation including earnings, rents, dividends, and gifts. Policy analysts occasionally speak of *unearned income*, generally referring to income from investments and other assets rather than earnings from a job. *Wealth* refers to economic assets that themselves generate income—stocks, mutual funds, and rental properties, for example—and economic assets that can be sold and turned into income through stock sales, sales of homes, and the like.

Another sociological approach to identifying classes focuses on culture, examining consumption patterns—i.e., how people spend their money and what they buy—and the beliefs people hold. Thorstein Veblen's *A Theory of the Leisure Class* and Pierre Bourdieu's *Distinction* represent important works in this tradition. From this perspective, the American middle class might be those families owning a house in the suburbs, driving an SUV, and believing in the importance of a college education.

Karl Marx (1818–1883), the father of modern class conflict theory, claimed that *analytically*, there are two classes—the owners of the means of production and the non-owners—while *descriptively*, there are many classes—for example, the lumpenproletariat, petite bourgeoisie, intelligentsia, capitalists, and workers. Max Weber (1864–1920) shared Marx's focus on the importance of ownership and non-ownership, but also claimed that it is important to differentiate between the types of productive assets possessed by owners and the types of labor performed by workers. These differences play a key role in determining the market activity of these groups, which in turn affects their opportunities and lifestyles.

More recently, neo-Weberians, such as sociologist Anthony Giddens (b. 1938), focus on how economic systems, institutions, individuals, and the state form a nexus of market capacities and life chances. Aage B. Sørensen describes the unearned portion of this nexus—the part that does not result from individual effort—as "rent."[4] Rents accrue to people based on whom they know (but not *what* they know), where they live, or their social background (SES or race, for example).[5] Charles Tilly perceptively describes how economic systems produce durable inequalities by allowing dominant groups to hoard opportunities for more income and prestige.[6] To understand the realities of the middle class, we must examine the configuration of these forces, looking at economic trends and conditions, financial institutions, corporate practices, and public policy.

To illustrate the plight of the middle class, let's visit two families. Unlike the examples in Chapter 1, our protagonists here are characters constructed from aggregate trends in our data on the middle class. These families represent the current dilemmas of middle class social and economic life, but are not in any sense "sob stories." They each have their own assets, liabilities, hopes, and dreams. They strive to "do the right thing," to engage their fellow travelers with honesty and compassion, and to play the economic game by the rules as they understand them. If we asked them to describe their lives to us, they would express gratitude for the opportunities they've had and the luck that has come their way. Yet something is wrong, as we will see.

Stories behind the Statistics: Trying Not to Drown in Debt

David and Monica Tread Water

David (thirty-six years old) and Monica (thirty-four) have been married for ten years. They have one child, two-year-old Jennifer, and live in suburban Tampa, Florida, having recently relocated from Minneapolis, Minnesota. David's company, Telemwhat Inc., relocated to Florida after a corporate merger because its corporate managers believed that the business climate was better in Florida than in Minnesota, and because the taxes in Florida are significantly lower. David received relocation assistance from the company, and sold their two-bedroom house in Minneapolis and purchased another in Tampa without great difficulty.

Because David agreed to relocate, he got to keep his job as an office manager, which pays $48,800 a year. Monica quit her job as a secretary in Minneapolis and took a similar job in Tampa for far less pay and no fringe benefits, "starting over" as the subordinate member of a small secretarial staff.

David has put in long hours in the hopes of getting ahead at Telemwhat. His job is considered steady by early twenty-first-century standards. He's received one raise—a 3 percent hike three years ago—in the five years he has worked for Telemwhat, and has received several cash bonuses when the company's quarterly profit numbers have looked good. He has purchased shares in the company's stock options plan with these bonuses, but the vesting period on employee shares is five years and the stock price fluctuates wildly. David says he "tries not to think about" which direction his shares are going or what they're worth.

David works about sixty hours a week, and Monica forty. Because of their busy schedules, Jennifer spends about forty hours each week in daycare, which costs the family $800 each month. Even with the flexible benefits package Telemwhat provides, David and Monica's daycare expenses eat up most of what Monica earns, less a few hundred dollars. Because they work at opposite ends of the city, David and Monica have purchased a second car (with no money down) that they make payments on each month, in addition to the minivan that they have two years left to pay off.

In addition to car payments, daycare, and mortgage payments, David and Monica have a substantial amount (over $10,000) of credit card debt. Each month they make minimum payments on their cards, which have interest rates of around thirteen percent, but these payments barely pay the interest. The mortgage on their house, purchased with a 5 percent down payment from the sale of their Minneapolis home, is large, and their payments stretch for a long time into the future before David and Monica will accumulate substantial home equity.

After making these monthly payments, David and Monica don't have much money left to do anything else. This void is filled by further credit card spending. The real estate taxes on their house are lower than they were in Minneapolis, but David wonders where his tax money goes. The ambulance, fire, and police service for his neighborhood is spotty; the highways are overcrowded; there seems to be no rhyme or reason to the development patterns of the city; almost no one he talks to sends their children to the public schools that his tax money pays for; and he pays a private company each month to pick up their trash and dispose of it. David dreams of retirement but can't foresee any way to finance it in his current circumstances. Both David and Monica would like to go back to school so they can find better jobs, but they cannot afford to risk their steady incomes and there is barely any time in their daily schedules for anything beyond work and the immediate needs of the family.

Bill and Sheryl Need a Snorkel

Bill and Sheryl, both forty-five years old, have been married for twenty years. They are the proud parents of two children, Dillon (twenty) and Clara (fifteen), one in college and another destined for college. Bill has worked most of his life as a computer software engineer, and Sheryl is a social worker for the county they live in near Cleveland, Ohio. They have a nice four-bedroom house in the suburbs. They have paid off two cars that look a little shabby and have a lot of miles, but Bill manages to keep them running with the help of local mechanics. Bill and Sheryl are active in their local Catholic parish and enjoy having roots in their community. By most middle class standards, Bill and Sheryl seem to have it made.

However, Bill and Sheryl's economic life is a shambles. Bill was laid off from the large engineering firm he worked for ten years ago—his job was eliminated in a leveraged buyout of corporate management by a takeover specialist—and since then he has not found steady employment, in spite of his considerable skills. He works on different consulting jobs around the area and maintains some semblance of an income this way, but his string of temporary positions provides no fringe benefits and the hours of work are not steady enough to provide a full-time wage approaching the $55,000 a year he used to earn. Worse, Bill gets the impression that the consulting business is reserved for young, eager workers with relatively new and portable skills. His ten years of work experience with his former engineering firm seem to be more a liability than an asset.

Sheryl's job as a social worker for the county at least provides benefits, including health insurance, making Bill and Sheryl relatively fortunate compared to the 40 percent of U.S. workers who have no employer-provided healthcare coverage. However, their state government has declared war on the poor, and the federal government's welfare reform provisions and state and local budget cuts make it harder for Sheryl to do her job. She hasn't received a pay raise in five years and there are signs that her entire unit might be eliminated as the county strives to consolidate its services and do more with less. Still, when Sheryl compares their lives to those of her clients, she thinks they are pretty lucky; "At least we're not sleeping under bridges," she tells the kids.

Bill and Sheryl have been cannibalizing their economic assets to keep their middle class lifestyle afloat. Bill cashed in his retirement plan from his former employer to provide cash to live on while he was looking for work. They started charging more on their credit cards, including groceries when the local supermarket started taking credit cards, and they now owe $15,000. They took out a second mortgage on their house when their son started college, and they've had a "home equity" line of credit for the past ten years. Between the home equity line of credit and their son's tuition bills at Ohio State, Bill and Sheryl have no equity in their house to call their own. The 2008 real estate crash in Cleveland lowered housing values further so that (technically) they owe more than their home is worth even though they've lived there for fifteen years.

Our Diagnosis

The people in these stories are just folks like you and me. Yet David, Monica, Bill, and Sheryl are part of a much larger group in the United States: the declining middle class. The combination of job losses, sketchy and unstable opportunities, consumer perceptions, corporate restructuring, and easy credit have produced an American middle class that is bordering on economic disaster. Bills are paid and appearances maintained by squandering savings and cannibalizing the future to maintain the present. The American economy moves toward a globalized, knowledge-intensive future, while the American people live in a cultural and consumption fantasyland built on the norms, values, and advice of a prior era. Old cultural ideologies die hard, especially when society is bombarded with media and political messages that suggest things are getting better and that you really can own the car or home of your dreams for no money down.

David, Monica, Bill, and Sheryl are trapped in a cycle of work, layoffs, debt, payments, and taxes that will never end. Regardless of the amount they earn at any given moment—and at times their earnings look pretty good—the instability of their job prospects contrasts sharply with their steadily mounting bills, diminished futures, rising debts, and middle class dreams.

Multiply these stories by several million and you discover that there is a large segment of the U.S. economy—the portion that stimulates aggregate demand and whose rising productivity once stimulated economic growth—that is so desperate just to pay their bills and keep their heads above water that they will work long, non-standard hours for poor pay, with no fringe benefits and no prospects for advancement. The reasons for this predicament involve globalization and the ability to move productive investment to different parts of the world electronically; the spread of neoliberal economic ideologies that promote free trade, low trade barriers, and reduced government regulations; the inability of the U.S. social safety net to provide insurance against the insecurities produced by the changing labor market and organization of work; national tax and spending policies that favor investors and those who are already well off at the expense of wage earners; and declining protections provided by a labor movement that has seen its ranks decline from 32 percent of the non-agricultural workforce in the 1960s to around 11 percent today.[7] As a result, the economic and political power of the American middle class has become increasingly limited, and in many ways represents a new form of indebtedness.

Three Examples of Indebtedness: Feudal Peasants, Southern Sharecroppers, and the Twenty-First-Century American Middle Class

We can tell a lot about society by examining how economic activity is organized. Since the late nineteenth century, American society has been defined by a particular form of capitalism. Capitalism is an economic system premised on private ownership of the means of production and the pursuit of profits. Within this system, those who do not own the means of production must sell their labor power in order to earn money—this is the familiar process of "getting a job." How much you get paid for a particular job depends on a variety of factors, including how many people are looking for work and are willing to take that type of job, the particular skills needed to perform the job, and whether employers need people in that position. Generally, workers with specialized skills and/or high levels of education in high-demand areas where there are few other potential workers (low supply) will get paid more. Sometimes employers may provide higher pay as an incentive to get people to take jobs that are dangerous or generally unappealing, but there are many jobs that are difficult, unappealing, and even dangerous that offer very little pay. In theory, workers are free to shop around to find the highest wages and best working conditions. This ability to "shop around" is a unique feature of capitalist economies and one that did not exist in agrarian economies prior to capitalism. Yet there are some disturbing similarities between the early twenty-first-century capitalism faced by the middle class and the agrarian economies of the Middle Ages, as we'll see.

Our Feudal Past

Most agrarian societies were built on two economic and political classes—a class of landlords who controlled the rights and access to vast tracts of land, and a class of peasants who worked the land in exchange for protection and control over small plots used to support their families. Other distinctive economic and political positions, such as priests, merchants, and craftsmen, took part in these societies, but the exchanges between landlords and peasants drove the economy, feeding the masses in good times, providing soldiers in wartime, and distributing rations in bad times.

The feudal system provided a measure of security in an uncertain world. The peasant received some protection from roving bands of thieves and marauding invaders, limited communal insurance in the event of crop failures and famine (frequent occurrences), and access to land to feed a family. The landlord received the proceeds from his vast tracts of land without having to work it himself; assurance that his property would be maintained; and access to surplus grain taxes, which he could use as barter for luxury goods produced in towns by craftsmen or brought from distant lands by merchants. He was also assured a regular army of conscripts to defend his property against intruders and to use in brokered alliances with other landlords.

While the peasants' lives have been idealized in theater and art, theirs was a hard lot.[8] As Gerhard Lenski describes the political philosophy of the feudal system, "The great majority of the political elite sought to use the energies of the peasant to the full, while depriving them of all but the basic necessities of life. The only real disagreement concerned the problem of how this might best be done. . . ."[9]

The absence of money meant that the stability of the agrarian system depended on a steady supply of laborers, and any force that interfered with the labor supply threatened the very existence of the system. In almost all agrarian societies, there were such forces. Famines, plagues, wars, and anything that reduced the size of the peasant population increased the bargaining power of the peasants that were left.[10] Opportunities in growing towns and rumors of better arrangements could induce peasants to leave rural landed estates and seek their fortunes elsewhere. Landlords tried to prevent such an exodus by imposing serfdom and indentured servitude.

Serfdom took an already exploitative situation and rendered it permanent. Serfs were peasants indentured to a landlord's lands. In principle, serfs could "buy" their freedom by paying huge sums of crop shares years into the future, but in practice, such individual emancipation almost never occurred. The feudal contract that bound serfs to the landlord's property often extended to their heirs, and usually to their heirs as well. The appearance of fixed time commitments was an illusion. In virtually no agrarian society on record were serfs emancipated because their feudal contracts with landlords ended;[11] instead, emancipation resulted when new elites rose up against landed elites to compete for the loyalty of the potential workforce that emancipated serfs represented.[12]

The material relationships between lords, vassals, peasants, and serfs were part of an extensive cultural system that identified social worth with inherited privilege. There is considerable debate over the effectiveness of landlords' psychological attempts to assert ideological control over average peasants,[13] but evidence suggests that whatever else produced social peace in feudal societies, happiness and acceptance of dominant ideologies were not at the top of the list.[14]

Along with the obvious and serious social inequalities of this system came elaborate ideologies on the virtues and divine favor of landlords and priests, who were "destined" to administer and control the system. On the other side of the coin were ideologies and cultural beliefs about the obvious unworthiness and inferiority of peasants and serfs. Attempts to change the functioning of the system outside the bounds of the existing corporate structure were viewed as assaults on the natural order of human life as conveyed and sanctioned by God.

The transition away from feudalism involved a series of economic changes and one big political change.[15] The move toward a capitalist global economy from global empires urged trade in the direction of exchange and away from conquest, tribute, and empire building. All these economic changes were fueled by the combined push of urban entrepreneurs and others with an interest in maximizing economic opportunities and separating political power from traditional concepts of fealty and landed proprietorship.

These economic changes coincided with the development of Enlightenment political philosophies in the fourteenth and fifteenth centuries. Enlightenment political philosophy, identified with Descartes, Montaigne, Locke, and Hume, advanced causes of human reason, freedom, and rationalism. Most Enlightenment thinkers were skeptical of traditional justifications of authority, especially those that tied the traditional social order to divine sanction. To Enlightenment thinkers, all truth claims were subject to evaluation by reason, and free inquiry and open intellectual development allowed people to reach the stations in life to which they were best suited. Enlightenment philosophy was often tied to the struggles of Protestantism and merchants against the Catholic Church and traditional nobles and landlords. Enlightenment philosophy inspired developments in France and Britain that hastened the decline of feudalism by providing an emerging urban merchant class with a political ideology to buttress the development of contemporary capitalism and urban labor markets.

Enlightenment philosophy also inspired the founding fathers of the United States and was the intellectual undercurrent for the American Revolution, the Declaration of Independence, and the Constitution. But this did not make the United States a bastion of enlightened practices. Freedom and equality developed slowly, and America had its own form of feudalism in the nineteenth-century tenant sharecropping system.

Feudalism in a Contemporary Context: Tenant Farming in the Deep South

In the United States, the experience closest to medieval feudalism was nineteenth- and early twentieth-century tenant farming in the former Confederate states after the Civil War. The Civil War left the states of the Deep South in an economic shambles. Plantation owners survived as landed elites, but had lost the African and African-descended slaves who performed the labor that maintained their economic position. The currency of the Confederacy, never worth much, was completely devalued. There was almost no banking system to speak of. The remnants of the plantation system included a mass of agricultural laborers with no access to land and a set of plantation owners with no workers and no money to pay them.

The practical solution to these problems was a system of tenant farming or *sharecropping*, providing many with access to labor and crops. For most rural laborers, both emancipated blacks and poor whites, it was the only practical way to gain access to food. Yet the transactions involved were extremely exploitative and not very different from those of medieval feudalism.[16]

In sharecropping, a landlord exchanged farm implements such as machinery, seed, and fertilizer to a group of tenants so the tenants could sustain themselves during the growing season. In return, the landlord received a percentage of the crop, due as payment to the landlord or merchant at the harvest. These *crop liens* were legal claims by landlords against current or future crops grown by tenant farmers. Landowners could file liens to seek payment of bills accrued during the crop season for tenants' clothing and subsistence. In many ways, both parties benefited from this economic arrangement:

1. Landlords didn't have any money to pay wages, so they advanced foodstuffs and dry goods in lieu of these, gaining laborers to work their land.
2. Tenant farmers generally owned no land and most were very poor and often illiterate. Gaining access to subsistence goods in exchange for growing a crop was thus a valuable arrangement.
3. The tenancy system dealt with the practical problem of the lag between the time of the harvest and the winter, when living expenses were incurred (similar to the cash flow problems many of us face in contemporary economic life).
4. In theory, at harvest a percentage of the crop would be handed over and the transaction—the exchange of labor for foodstuffs and dry goods— would be complete. The landlord would have farm produce, usually cotton, to sell; the laborer would have his or her family provided for. Not a bad arrangement.

But, like many things in life that look good on the surface, the devil was in the details. The foodstuffs and dry goods advanced to the tenant farmer were credited against the farmer's portion of the harvest rather than the landlord's. In effect, tenant farmers were buying subsistence on credit with their portions of the crop as payment. This system was open to abuse. Since the landlord was providing the subsistence goods to the tenant as an exchange, the tenant usually had no idea what the actual cost of the goods was in cash. The landlord could charge substantial markups on these goods in an attempt to gain access to all or most of the tenant's share of the crop. The landlord could set the cash price of the tenant's cotton at the price he would receive at harvest, when there was lots of cotton on the market and prices were low, and confiscate more of the tenant's cotton to pay the debts the landlord inflated. The landlord could then hold the cotton provided by the tenant farmer and sell it at some other time of year when the cotton price was higher, pay his own expenses, and pocket the difference.

Worse, the landlord could construct a pricing scheme for the dry goods he provided and the cotton turned over by the tenant so that the tenant's debts were not paid off at harvest time. At that point, the tenant was obligated to work for the landlord another year to pay off his debt. Crop liens were often legally enforceable between landlords so that tenants could not move from one landlord to another unless their debts were paid. If the tenant decided to move on, one of three things would happen:

1. local law enforcement officials could track him down and return him to the landlord, requiring him to work to pay off his debts;
2. the landlord could file a lien against any crops raised by the tenant on other landlords' properties, claiming rights of first claim on the labor of the indebted tenant; or
3. other landlords wouldn't hire the wandering tenant once they discovered that he owed debts to other landlords.

The combination of these outcomes made it almost impossible for the tenant to start anew.

The end result was a system of debt peonage in which tenants were tied to the landlord's land, perpetually in debt and perpetually "borrowing" subsistence goods to maintain their households in exchange for cotton crops whose value never managed to pay their bills.

The cultural and ideological underpinning of the sharecropping system was racial superiority and the "southern racial state."[17] Landlords were almost always white. Tenant farmers were not exclusively black, but whites from all economic circumstances identified with racial politics and the alleged inferiority of newly free African Americans. The elaborate racial etiquette—deference rituals, pecking orders, and "separate" accommodations—of interactions between the races reinforced the perceived cultural and biological superiority of whites, who were "burdened" with their role as overseers of the "childlike" free blacks whom they viewed as not fit to govern their own affairs. The entire criminal justice and legal system rested on the premise that white landowners were privileged elites to whom all others owed their allegiance. As we'll see, some of the racial divisiveness that helped to maintain this system returns in later political ideologies used to justify the policies of late twentieth-century elites.

Twenty-First-Century Middle Class Meltdown—The New Indentured Servitude?

Today, the average middle class worker is mired in falling wages, job instability, rising prices, increased work hours, higher taxes, and bigger debts. This combination of factors has produced a new indentured servant or (as we describe in our earlier work) a "post-industrial peasant"—someone who is so in debt that those to whom he or she owes money (and the employers and economic elites who provide the investment and consumption capital for the system) control his or her life. As detailed in Chapters 3 and 4, these elites are the same people who have absconded with productivity gains and paid themselves inflated salaries, benefits, and stock options. People in such economically precarious positions see few options other than working harder at jobs that provide relatively low wages, no benefits, and no security (see Exhibit 2.1).

Exhibit 2.1 Systems of Indebtedness: Feudal Peasants, Southern Sharecroppers, and the Twenty-First-Century American Middle Class

System characteristics	Feudal peasants	Southern sharecroppers	Twenty-First-Century middle class
Social Classes	Landlords and Serfs	Landlords and Sharecroppers	Capitalist Employers and Workers
Government	Landlord alliances	Planter-dominated democracy	Electoral-representative, capitalist-dominated democracy favoring the wealthy
Means of exchange	Land and labor services	Land and labor services	Money
Means of control by dominant classes	Direct coercion	Direct coercion and debt	Market discipline and credit
Type of expropriation	Direct taxation	Direct taxation	Taxation, long work hours, flat wages despite productivity gains
Terms of continued subordination	Control over land	Debt produced by crop liens	Debts from credit cards and financial manipulation

There are important parallels between agrarian systems and the contemporary situation of the American middle class. The most striking is the similarity between the system of debt peonage that emerged in agrarian systems and the system of work, wages, and debt facing the middle class over the past forty years. In agrarian systems, peasants and sharecroppers were indebted to specific landlords; in contemporary America, members of the middle class are indebted to bankers and financiers. In both cases, workers are locked into arrangements that force them to struggle continuously to make a living with little hope of breaking free from their subordinate positions.

The historical emergence of the middle class provides a context for understanding the importance of examining economic arrangements and social class. In Europe and the United States, the middle class began to form during the Industrial Revolution of the eighteenth and nineteenth centuries. In Europe, the economic expansion that resulted from industrialization, coupled with shifting political alliances, challenged aristocratic domination and fueled the emergence of a middle class. Unlike their European counterparts, the American middle class was never cleanly situated between an aristocracy and working class. During the late nineteenth and early twentieth centuries, the economic elite in America were often entrepreneurs and tycoons amassing vast fortunes during the course of a lifetime, not aristocrats born into wealth and privilege. For those who were able to avoid the factory floor and start out on their own, the incredible economic growth during this era provided unprecedented opportunities for creating new businesses and finding new markets. The result was an expanded middle class—one defined largely by the shopkeepers, small-business owners, and entrepreneurs who did not strike it rich but were able to make a decent living, and by the growing number of managers needed to oversee the daily operations of the new and expanding companies.

For all its warts, industrial capitalism (the development of market economies based on manufacturing in the wake of the Industrial Revolution) has increased the chances that average people can improve their lot. Some of this has to do with the basic structure of the system. The capitalist class is in constant competition for customers and against each other. This has changed in many ways the relationship between capitalists and those who work for them, especially when there are labor shortages. Factories and urbanism increased contact between groups of people, and especially members of the industrial working class. This led to unionization and myriad attempts to improve working conditions. The wide availability of money and an extensive banking system allowed capital investment, wages, and consumption to expand. Politics and economics were separated (at least in theory) so that political elites and economic elites were not the same people. Unlike the landlord in an agrarian society, a capitalist can, and often does, fail. Workers could improve their lot and "move up" into middle class positions.

And lest we forget, one major product of the industrial market economy was the creation of the middle class. No other set of economic arrangements has produced a middle class of the size and general prosperity of the American middle class and its European and Asian counterparts. As we stated in the introduction, the massive immigration of people into these parts of the world doesn't suggest to us that millions of people are greedy and want to make it big (which is not to say they wouldn't take those opportunities if they came up!) but that the economic contributions of "average people like me" are worth more here than they are back home. The aspirations of these migrants often are met. This in itself is a major achievement.

But there are also important differences between the post-industrial capitalism in the United States from the 1980s to the present and industrial capitalism. These differences have complicated the plight of the middle class. Work has reorganized, with downsizing, outsourcing, temporary work, and flat organizational hierarchies making it difficult for modern Americans to find steady jobs, establish careers, and build solid financial bases for middle class life. Increasingly, the globalized economy is changing the relationships between large corporations and cities as corporations attempt to stay competitive, moving from place to place looking for the most favorable investment conditions and demanding tax and infrastructure concessions from cities and government agencies.[18] The sheer scale of the post-industrial enterprise and the dispersal of functions to different parts of the world make it difficult to determine who is responsible for job creation and community welfare.[19]

Apart from the use of money and the sophistication of the exchanges involved, the economic position of the U.S. middle class looks much like that of the feudal peasant of the Middle Ages and the Southern sharecropper. While the specific means of control (how the dominant classes or elites maintain their privileged position), type of expropriation (how dominant classes or elites obtain funds needed to maintain the system), and terms of continued subordination (the condition that keeps the subordinate group under the control of the dominant classes or elites) are different in each system, the overall function is the same. So while it is true that members of the twenty-first-century American middle class are not tied to specific plots of land or specific lords, they *are* tied to a system that keeps them in a perpetual cycle of work and debt.[20]

Who are these people economically? The next chapter addresses their income and credit predicaments. As you'll see, it's not a pretty sight.

Discussion Questions

- What does it mean to be middle class?
- Does the story of David and Monica, or Bill and Sheryl, remind you of anyone that you know?
- In what ways is your daily life shaped by our economic system?
- What role did capitalism play in creating a large middle class?
- What role has it played in creating the "middle class meltdown"?

Notes

1. Jennie Green, "Leaning on Their Parents, Again," *New York Times*, July 20, 2003.
2. Alan Wolfe, *One Nation, After All* (New York: Viking, 1998), 1.
3. According to the U.S. Census Bureau (2012), the median family income in the United States in 2011 was $50,054. Carmen DeNavas-Walt, Bernadette D. Proctor, Jessica C. Smith "Income, Poverty and Health Insurance Coverage in the United States: 2011," *Current Population Reports,* accessed July 7, 2013, http://www.census.gov/prod/2012pubs/p60–243.pdf
4. Aage Sørensen, "Toward a Sounder Basis for Class Analysis," *American Journal of Sociology* 105 (2000): 1525.
5. See also Jonathon Kay, *Culture and Prosperity* (New York: Harper Business, 2004), 22–30.
6. Charles Tilly, *Durable Inequality* (Berkeley: University of California Press, 1998), 147–69.
7. See Beth A. Rubin, *Shifts in the Social Contract: Understanding Change in American Society* (Thousand Oaks, CA: Pine Forge Press, 1996), 9–13; U.S. Department of Commerce, Statistical Abstract of the United States, 2006, 436; and United States Department of Labor, Bureau of Labor Statistics "Table 1. Union Affiliation of Employed Wage and Salary Workers by Selected Characteristics," Various Years, accessed July 13, 2013, http://www.bls.gov/news.release/union2.t01.htm
8. Marc Bloc, *Feudal Society* (Chicago: University of Chicago Press, 1961), 250–51.
9. Gerhard E. Lenski, *Power & Privilege: A Theory of Social Stratification* (New York: McGraw-Hill, 1966), 270.
10. Jack A. Goldstone, *Revolution and Rebellion in the Early Modern World* (Berkeley: University of California Press, 1991). See also William H. McNeill, *Plagues and Peoples* (Garden City, NY: Anchor Press, 1976), 270.
11. Moore, Barrington, Jr., *Social Origins of Dictatorship and Democracy: Lord and Peasant in the Making of the Modern World* (Boston: Beacon Press, 1966), 451–83.
12. Richard Lachmann, *Capitalists in Spite of Themselves: Elite Conflict and Economic Transitions in Early Modern Europe* (Oxford, UK: Oxford University Press, 2000), 8–14.
13. Anthony Giddens, *The Nation-State and Violence* (Berkeley: University of California Press, 1987), 71–78.
14. For more on the ideology of such social inequality, see Max Weber, *Economy and Society: An Outline of Interpretive Sociology*, ed. Guenther Roth and Claus Wittich (New York: Bedminster Press, 1968).
15. For more detail, see Immanuel Wallerstein, "From Feudalism to Capitalism: Transition or Transitions?," *Social Forces* 55 (1976): 273–83.
16. Michael Schwartz, *Radical Protest and Social Structure: The Southern Farmers' Alliance and Cotton Tenancy, 1880–1890* (New York: Academic Press, 1976).
17. David R. James, "The Transformation of the Southern Racial State: Class and Race Determinants of Local State Structures," *American Sociological Review* 53 (1988): 191–208.
18. Manuel Castells, *The Rise of the Network Society* (Oxford, UK: Blackwell, 1996).
19. Manuel Castells, *The Power of Identity* (Oxford, UK: Blackwell, 1997).
20. See Juliet B. Schor, *The Overworked American: The Unexpected Decline of Leisure* (New York: Basic Books, 1992).

CHAPTER 3

Macroeconomics and the Income/Credit Squeeze

If we equate economic vigor with economic growth, the vigor of the United States since the mid-1970s has been striking. During this period, the annual growth rate (in terms of annual change in gross domestic product) has been consistently positive and strong.[1] The consumer economy depends on the purchasing power of the middle class to fuel economic growth, yet during the past few decades, middle class incomes have not risen. How is it that, despite the stagnant purchasing power of the middle class, the economy has continued to grow by leaps and bounds?

In this chapter we examine two characteristics of the middle class predicament: first, the stagnation of real incomes for most members of the middle class, and second, the expansion of easily available consumer credit. These trends are ominous symptoms of middle class decline, and they have been accompanied by other trends, including the drastically increased compensation of top executives and a new paradigm for stimulating consumer demand that is tied to destabilizing jobs and loaning domestic consumers money they could otherwise be paid.

To understand these trends, we must examine the workings of the consumer economy and theories about the relationship between consumer demand and aggregate economic health. These subjects are the purview of macroeconomics.

Market Economies and Purchasing Power: A Digression into Macroeconomic Theory

Macroeconomics is the study of the relationship between supply, demand, and income. The major issues macroeconomics addresses are the relationships between inflation, unemployment, wages, productivity, and (between business cycles) employment and growth. *Business cycles* are the periodic ups and downs that are an inevitable part of market economies. *Inflation* is the upward spiral of wages and prices. *Economic growth* refers to increases in economic output in the economy as a whole, usually measured as change in the gross domestic product. Like most of us, macroeconomists assume that less extreme business cycles, more employment, higher wages, relatively big productivity gains, and low inflation are desirable goals. Macroeconomics is policy oriented, designed to guide government policies on taxation, expenditure, interest rates, and money supply to either stimulate or slow down economic activity. In theory, the correct choice of macroeconomic policy—and, perhaps more important, the political will to pursue it—will promote economic stability and steady growth.

Most macroeconomists believe that government actions affect economic performance, though they differ on which government activities produce the effects and whether the effects are good or bad. All market economies depend on the same activities to distribute needed goods and services, as follows.

1. *Investment.* In private hands, investment drives the economy forward. Investors, entrepreneurs, venture capitalists, and average people saving for retirement or a rainy day see an opportunity to provide a good or service and invest in it. The ability to see such opportunities is the result of several signals, including personal experience, conversations, and monitoring the investments of others. All macroeconomics assumes that profits motivate investors to invest and that investment returns are a major force driving a prosperous market economy.
2. *Demand.* Consumers look at an array of goods and services that investors and their agents provide and "vote" with their money. The demand for different goods, relative to their supply, determines the price. In the absence of demand, markets collapse under the weight of their own unsold goods. Distortions of market signals lead to imbalances of supply and demand when consumers look for goods that aren't available and investors provide products no one wants to buy at prices that are too high.
3. *Credit and banking.* No market economy can function without credit and banking institutions, which act as intermediaries, providing money for investors and consumers to borrow. In more advanced credit and banking systems (like ours in the United States), investment banks may pool investors' money to engage in various market interventions, such as big

stock purchases, initial public offerings of stock by companies that are going public, and takeovers of firms that are underperforming.

Banks pool money from individual investors and loan it for investments and consumer purchases that they deem worthy. They charge interest on the money they lend (or in the case of investment banks, charge fees associated with the size of the investment pool they assemble). Prior to the Federal Reserve Act of 1913, banks issued bank notes directly, regulating the value of money in the economy. Now, in the United States and almost all other nations, a central bank (like the Federal Reserve Bank in the United States) does this.

But why is credit needed in the first place? Because there are inevitable gaps between when expenditures are needed and when money arrives to pay for them. For investors and firms, new plants and equipment cost millions of dollars, but the company rarely has millions of dollars lying around to make such investments all at once.[2] For consumers, the overall situation is similar. Most of us do not have $30,000 on hand to pay cash for cars or hundreds of thousands of dollars to pay for houses, and even if we had the cash, such purchases might not be the smartest ways to use our money. Instead, most of us borrow money to make such purchases. Credit institutions determine whether we're good credit risks by looking at our ability to pay off our loans in the future, using our employment record, record of paying past debts, and our current indebtedness as indicators. If they choose to loan money to us, they attach an interest rate, a fee they collect over time for borrowing their money.

To sum up, market economies work by offering credit, allowing investors to borrow money in anticipation of greater returns at some later date, and allowing consumers to purchase goods and services they could not afford because of cash flow problems separating when and how much income is earned and how much consumer goods cost in the here and now. So far so good.

Enter Macroeconomics

Macroeconomics as it is currently understood is a product of the Great Depression, which was precipitated by the stock market crash of October 1929. After the crash, unemployment rose to 25 percent of the labor force; investors lost billions of dollars of wealth, by some estimates over one-third of that available; and the economy was stagnant for most of the next ten years. Local conditions were often worse. In Pennsylvania in 1933, for example, only two-fifths of the working population had full-time work and over one million state residents were totally unemployed.[3]

The administration of Franklin D. Roosevelt (elected in 1932) promised to take on the Great Depression, claiming that astutely placed government intervention would fuel economic recovery. To stimulate aggregate demand, Roosevelt introduced his "New Deal," a series of government interventions such as the National Industrial Recovery Act, the Wagner-Connery Act, the Social Security Act, agricultural price supports, the Civilian Conservation Corps, and the Works Progress Administration. There is considerable debate about whether these policies worked; at the time Germany invaded Poland in 1939, one of the official starting points for World War II, unemployment in the United States was still at 15 percent.[4]

John Maynard Keynes (1883–1946) provided the rationale for government intervention in his book *The General Theory of Employment, Interest, and Money* (1936), which stated that the government has a responsibility to sustain the levels of aggregate demand necessary to promote full employment of productive capacity, and could adopt policy tools to promote economic growth, to lower inflation and unemployment, and to provide satisfactory levels of economic prosperity.[5] The central purpose of government policy was to close the "Okun gap," named after the economist Arthur M. Okun (1928–1980), between the potential and actual output that the aggregate economy could support. Without some attempt to close this gap, the aggregate economy would be stuck in a "liquidity trap" of insufficient economic activity to promote employment and satisfactory material prosperity. The implications of Keynesian economics, as this macroeconomic school came to be called, were that levels of economic output, inflation, and unemployment were political decisions rather than characteristics set by the "invisible hand" of markets. Keynesian economics drove much of the United States' macroeconomic policy from the 1930s through the 1960s.

The mechanism for altering economic output was to raise *aggregate demand*, the amount of goods and services that consumers and businesses wish to buy. The concrete policies resulting from Keynesian economics attempted to stimulate aggregate demand by putting money in people's pockets that they would spend almost immediately. Income maintenance programs like Social Security, targeted tax cuts (like the Kennedy-Johnson tax cut of 1964–1965),[6] public works spending, and investment to improve infrastructure and provide public works jobs were all major components of the Keynesian strategy. Raising aggregate demand would create new jobs and lower unemployment. The Depression-era assumption was that prices wouldn't rise because output was below capacity—the "maximum" output the economy could produce with a fixed set of capital stock. Such interventions in an otherwise *laissez-faire* economy must be understood in the context of the erosion of the political elite's confidence in markets from the 1920s through the 1960s.[7]

The recessions of the 1970s and "stagflation"—high inflation coupled with rising unemployment—led many economists and policymakers to question the further applicability of the Keynesian macroeconomic model.[8] This sparked a revival of and new developments in other theories of macroeconomics, each with its own policy implications. Something was clearly wrong—interest rates were high and rising, inflation was high and rising, unemployment was high and rising, and real purchasing power was declining. New classical, monetarist, and supply-side economics stepped in with their own assumptions and policy remedies for these serious problems.

The Revival of New Classical and Monetarist Economics

The core Keynesian assumptions concerning demand management are rejected in new classical economics, which is defined by the "policy ineffec-tiveness hypothesis"—the belief that the rational expectations of economic actors will lead them to negate whatever changes government intervention is intended to produce. This means that almost all forms of economic interven-tion have unintended consequences, and the intended consequences of any policy choice are not likely to come about.

Specifically, new classical economists believe that unemployment does not respond to government intervention at all; instead, it is affected only by its long-term trend. The rate of economic innovation also is not responsive to government policy to stimulate aggregate demand; instead, government fis-cal policy should be directed toward fighting inflation.[9] *Fiscal policy* refers to the expenditures of the government to provide goods and services, and the methods—such as taxes, bond sales, and borrowing—that governments use to finance these expenditures.

Monetarist economics, associated most notably with Milton Friedman (1912–2006), proposes that the money supply helps to explain unemploy-ment rate variations and inflation. In direct contrast to the Keynesian view that unemployment results from the gap between actual and potential output, monetarists claim that growth and contraction in the money supply determine inflation, and that restrictive fiscal policy (tight interest rates) without slowing expansion in the money supply won't reduce inflation. Unlike new classical economists, monetarists see a relationship between inflation and unemploy-ment: a decline in inflation will make unemployment rise. There is thus a social cost to fighting inflation: slow but steady monetary expansion should make the unemployment rate fall, even though it permanently raises the inflation rate.[10]

Returning to our central subject, middle class families could be either helped by fiscal policy decisions that attempt to close the gap between real and potential output or harmed by attempts to alter aggregate economic performance in ways that can't be controlled, contributing to inflation and the erosion of purchasing power. The debates between Keynesian, new clas-sical, and monetarist economics all boil down to the question of what costs are involved in fighting inflation. To new classical theorists, there is no cost because unemployment is not affected by anything the government does. To Keynesians and monetarists, policies that fight inflation would result in higher unemployment. Supply-side economics attempted to answer this question once and for all.

Supply-Side Economics and the Reagan Revolution

The 1980s brought a set of relatively obscure economic ideas for dealing with stagflation. Supply-side economics and its proponents claimed that the very interventions that Keynesian economics promoted—mechanisms for stimulating aggregate demand to smooth out the business cycle by shrinking the Okun gap—were behind the high-inflation and high-unemployment 1970s. These policies, and the cumulative effect of the federal government's activities in a wide range of areas, produced perverse incentives that made people work less, save less, and invest less. Inflation (directly) and high unemployment (indirectly) were caused by impediments the government erected that interfered with productivity growth in production inputs.

Since supply-side economists define the federal government as the locus of these perverse incentives, the logical conclusion supply-side economists reach is that the incentives that impede productivity growth should be removed. As the federal government removed disincentives to work, invest, and save, productivity and savings would increase, productivity would improve, inflation would be tamed, and unemployment would eventually decline.

One extension of supply-side economics was the "Laffer curve," named for Stanford economist Arthur Laffer. In 1974, Laffer was having dinner with Jude Wanniski, then associate editor of the *Wall Street Journal*; Donald Rumsfeld, chief of staff to President Ford (and later secretary of defense under George W. Bush); and Dick Cheney, then Rumsfeld's deputy (and later vice president). During the course of the evening he sketched out the now famous "Laffer curve" on a napkin.[11] In this variant of supply-side economics, the disincentives produced by the federal government were so great that federal government revenues were actually lower than they would be if these impediments were removed. The temporary deficits the federal government would have as a result of tax cuts and deregulation would be eliminated through the increased government revenues resulting from greater economic growth (see Appendix Exhibit 3.1). In another variant of supply-side economics, the removal of government disincentives was paired with substantial cuts in the federal budget. These cuts would allow the gap between government expenditures and revenues to close even faster as increased productivity drove economic growth.[12]

The policy tools advocated by supply-side economics differ considerably from those advocated by other macroeconomic perspectives. These policies include the deregulation of heavily regulated industries; the promotion of greater economic competition by lowering trade barriers; the repeal of special subsidies and tax loopholes for specific industries; across-the-board tax cuts, especially for corporations and those with higher marginal income tax rates (the wealthy); and cuts in government domestic spending in an attempt to remove disincentives to work, invest, and save. These policies became hugely influential during the presidency of Ronald Reagan in the 1980s, and

Exhibit 3.1 Industry Deregulation since the 1970s

Industry Deregulated	New Activities Allowed
Banking/Finance	Fewer restrictions on branch banking; eliminated limitations on interest rates, capital requirements, and loan restrictions
Airlines	Ended route restrictions and requirements; permitted competition on popular routes; ended mandatory service to smaller markets; created the "hub" airline system
Trucking	Increased fare competition; deregulated truck sizing and weighting
Telecommunications	Allowed competition for local and long-distance telephone service and cable television service
Electricity	Permitted competition for electrical generation in local markets; allowed grid sales of surplus electricity across regions; streamlined authorization for new power plants; eased some environmental restrictions

many, though not all, supply-side recommendations were implemented. The Reagan administration passed substantial cuts on corporate taxes and taxes geared toward high-income taxpayers, and continued the trend toward industry deregulation that had begun during the Carter administration. Subsequent administrations have also taken up the deregulation cause (see Exhibit 3.1).

The list below details how this theory was put into action. Note the differences between supply-side economics and other policies for stimulating economic change, and in particular how supply-side economics turns Keynesian economics on its head.

1. Government incentives are targeted toward those with the greatest "marginal propensity to invest"—people and corporations who would save and invest the money returned to them and respond to new incentives by investing in capital goods.
2. As this group responds to the new incentives, investment increases, inflation drops, unemployment drops, and tax revenues rise.
3. Inflation drops because productivity and productive capacity are rising faster than wages, and increased international competition keeps prices down.
4. Government revenues rise because increased economic activity brings new tax revenues into government coffers. The new incentives "pay for themselves."[13]

The domestic rise of supply-side economics dovetailed with the international spread of *neoliberalism*. Neoliberals believe that international trade and domestic economic activity are best governed by open and free markets, minimal government regulations, and maximum capital and labor movement. In addition, late-twentieth-century neoliberalism is identified with spreading markets to ever-broader sets of human activities, from healthcare to schools. Neoliberalism is an outgrowth of nineteenth-century liberalism, in which society, and by extension markets, should be allowed to develop through hands-off processes. Results from activities like market transactions are not to be interfered with, and the outcomes that these processes produce are assumed to be the best possible.

Neoliberalism has significant implications for middle class life in the United States. The most important dimensions of neoliberal thought involve the expansion of markets to new spheres of activity; an emphasis on contracts of short duration, including employment contracts; constant assessment and the continual production of performance information; the growth of the financial services sector and the expansion of financial exchanges divorced from the production of actual goods and services; and relentless outsourcing and supplier competition for goods and services (see Exhibit 3.2).

The drive for privatization and the downsizing of government that accompanied the Reagan administration in the United States and the Thatcher administration in Britain are examples of policies that result from neoliberalism. The actual tenets of neoliberalism, like those of Keynesian and supply-side economics, have never been fully implemented, but they still have some consequences for the middle class, including jobs of shorter duration with relentless pressure to work more hours, and more time for less pay and fewer benefits; a deregulated financial services sector with a considerable aftermarket for consumer and other forms of debt; and numerous ways for investors to make

Exhibit 3.2 Major Macroeconomic Schools, 1950–Present

Macroeconomic School	Reasons for Stagnation	Solution
Keynesian	Insufficient aggregate demand	Give money to those who will spend it
New classical economics	Policy ineffectiveness/ Unintended consequences of policy	Fight inflation; limited government
Monetarist economics	Inconsistent monetary policy using fiscal policy in place of monetary policy	Controlling money supply in a predictable way
Supply-side economics	Insufficient incentives to work, invest, and save	Tax cuts, deregulation, government spending cuts
Neoliberalism	Trade barriers, fiscal irresponsibility, regulations	Eliminate trade barriers, deregulate labor markets, and subject more societal and individual decisions to market forces

money that don't involve making anything, providing any service, or employing anyone.

These economic changes in the United States have made the pursuit of financial gain, without any accompanying economic or social obligation, a major component of the political landscape of the last forty years, so much so that even former Reagan administration officials have expressed misgivings about the system.[14] Where does this combination of supply-side economics and neoliberalism leave members of the middle class?

Public Policy, Purchasing Power, and the Middle Class

Only Keynesian and supply-side economics have received a "policy hearing" in the sense that they have shaped actual government policy; new classical economics and to a lesser extent monetarist economics have never been practically implemented. Generally the concepts of these theories are unpalatable to voters and politicians. Think about monetarism and new classical economics from the standpoint of a presidential candidate. How inspiring would it be for a candidate to say that he is going to change the way the federal government works by pegging the money supply to an automatic inflator that all economic actors can know in advance—and that's all he's going to do? This would be the monetarist prescription for macroeconomic change. How many candidates could run on the idea that the only thing the federal government should do is fight inflation, and that fighting inflation has no cost because "everyone will adjust"? In spite of the merits of these ideas—and there are some—these don't make for inspiring political messages.

Now think of a presidential candidate running with a real or implied Keynesian or supply-side economics policy position. The typical Keynesian candidate can say that she is interested in "getting America working again" and "maintaining the economic integrity of working Americans" during economic downturns. She can offer incentives from tax cuts, public works programs, and income maintenance programs (for example, unemployment insurance, job training, Social Security benefits, and interest deductions for incurring consumer debts) that appeal to voters who are down on their luck and who think that economic activity is "too slow." The typical candidate with a supply-side economic platform can claim that she's interested in "getting America to invest, save, and work," that she is "getting the government off people's backs," and that her array of tax cuts and deregulation activities will stimulate the economy and bring cheaper consumer goods for all. These are much more inspiring messages, regardless of their merit.[15]

To illustrate, in the 1980 presidential election, the middle class was not offered a choice between these four alternatives. Instead, they were offered a choice between Ronald Reagan's supply-side economics and Jimmy Carter's uncertain and tentative Keynesian economics. Supply-side economics seemed new and attractive; Keynesian economics seemed old and bumbling. When combined with the personalities involved—Reagan appeared decisive, while Carter appeared unsure and bumbling—and the high inflation and unemployment of the late 1970s, voters overwhelmingly chose the supply-side alternative.

While interpretations vary on what happened next, the statistics are not in dispute: the political and economic consequences of supply-side policies have been far reaching.

1. Since the 1980s, income inequality increased substantially, more so than during any other peacetime era in America's history.
2. The federal government ran record federal deficits, borrowing more money in the eight years of the Reagan administration than in the history of the U.S. federal government from 1776 to 1980.
3. Tax rates were lowered and tax cuts passed. Federal revenues did not rise fast enough to meet expenditures.
4. The administration had trouble finding domestic program spending cuts that would allow the budget to balance without appearing to be insensitive to the needs of the poor. (Most government spending does not go to help the poor anyway—see Exhibit 6.3 on page 97).
5. Public infrastructure, such as roads, airports, bridges, and dams, began to fall into disrepair as appropriations for their maintenance were trimmed or eliminated.
6. Individual state governments passed "supply-side tax packages" of their own in an attempt to match the federal government at reducing tax rates to increase revenues.[16] This shift in tax burdens hit the middle class especially hard (see Chapter 6).
7. The deregulation of industry included the financial sector—banks and investments—led to a rash of corporate takeover activity and other unproductive pursuits that were substitutes for saving and investment in actual business enterprise.[17]
8. This same deregulation ushered in the era of easy credit: cars and other consumer items could be purchased with "no money down"(see Chapter 5). Credit cards became much more widely available, and the debts accumulated started to grow as middle class consumers attempted to maintain their lifestyles.[18]
9. The economy never fully recovered until the first Bush administration, and then only tentatively. When Bill Clinton took office in 1992, supply-side economic policies were replaced by a focus on deficit reduction as a federal government priority. The administration of George W. Bush faced myriad difficulties, but passed a large tax cut anyway, and brought back record federal deficits—around $458 billion in 2008 as the recession began, $1.4 trillion in 2009 (current projections for 2014 sit at $744 billion).[19]

10. Tax cutting and business incentives stimulated new lobbying groups in Washington, all of whom look for special favors for their particular industry or product (see Chapter 6).[20]

11. The political claim that low taxes stimulate economic growth became entrenched in the American political landscape. State and local governments began to compete for footloose and mobile businesses seeking favorable tax treatment and the best economic deals to locate in specific places. The epidemic of tax cutting left state and local governments with reduced revenues, spawning further cuts in public services (see Chapter 6).

12. The view that investors and capitalists don't respond to incentives has been put to the test and found wanting. Not only do they respond to incentives, the incentives produce a new financial elite that does more to manipulate the system to its advantage.

13. Foreign competition has led to changes within American companies that have cost the economy hundreds of thousands of jobs.[21]

If we further develop the backstory of Bill (one of our examples from Chapter 2), we can see how the middle class became direct victims of the economic manipulations of supply-side economics and the deregulation that came with it. Bill had worked for his engineering firm since he graduated from college, and at the time he was laid off he had put in thirteen years. There were no outward signs that his firm was in financial trouble—there was plenty of work to do, orders and new business came in steadily, and the company had very little debt.

Unfortunately for Bill, these characteristics made his company a prime target to be taken over and dismantled. A group of corporate raiders organized a "hostile takeover" of Bill's firm, offering stockholders double the market price for their stock shares. The interest on the money the raiders borrowed to make this offer was tax deductible—another product of corporate tax reform and deregulation.[22] The offer was too good for the stockholders to refuse, and the corporate managers of Bill's firm, who themselves owned substantial company stock, also would benefit from lucrative severance packages, or "golden parachutes," if they were fired by the new owners. A *golden parachute* is a clause in the employment contract of an executive-level employee, specifying large benefits in the event the company is acquired or the executive is fired or laid off. These benefits can come in the form of cash, stock options, or both.

Bill's company changed hands. Instead of keeping the company intact and attempting to improve its performance, the new owners, a small group of investment bankers and wealthy stockholders, started selling off and closing entire segments of the firm. The manufacturing wing of Bill's firm was sold to an overseas investment consortium. All but a few employees of the engineering wing were let go. "The company can outsource engineering services on the open market," explained the new CEO.

This giant sell-off immediately brought in millions of dollars to the new investors. It cost Bill's company several hundred jobs and its local community hundreds of thousands of dollars in future tax revenues. The small group of investors took their new "downsized" firm and began selling their shares on the open market. Wall Street loved it: the shares sold for their original asking price and more, netting the set of corporate raiders still more profits for a few months' work.

Of course, there is the problem of what happened to Bill. He not only lost his job with good pay and fringe benefits, he went to work as an independent contractor with an income that shifts wildly, no fringe benefits, and no steady employment. There are millions of people like Bill. So how did the economy keep growing and profits keep rising? Perhaps the biggest revelation of this era—amidst rising inequality, financial manipulations, and job insecurity—was that the purchasing power of the middle class was a public good, something that was good for everyone but that nobody had any incentive to help contribute to. This is the root of the "income/credit squeeze," to which we turn next.

The Income/Credit Squeeze

The Deflated Income Balloon

One major problem facing the middle class is the decline of real income and purchasing power (see Exhibit 3.3).

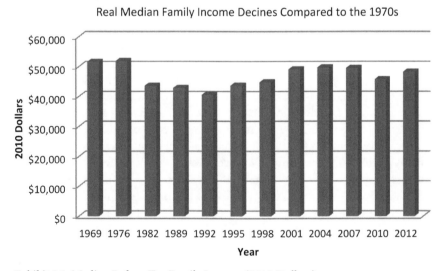

Exhibit 3.3 Median Before-Tax Family Income (2010 Dollars)

Source: Federal Reserve Bulletin, various years

By any measure we use, the real earnings of individuals and the real income of families (in 2010 dollars adjusted for inflation) have undergone a period of stagnation at the middle. Median before-tax family income—the figure that separates the top half of the income distribution from the bottom half— dropped from a high of $52,000 in 1976 to $41,000 in 1992. Median income has inched upward again but it has never reached the real purchasing power families had in 1976 ($48,324 in 2012). This evidence suggests that family income for those at the middle of income distribution has not recovered from relatively high levels in the late 1960s and early 1970s, and the 2010–2012 figure reflects the lingering effects of the 2008 recession (see Chapter 7).

We can see a similar trend in the average (mean) real hourly earnings of production workers, all non-supervisory, non-agricultural, non-self-employed workers in the economy (Appendix Exhibit 3.2). Here the dip is less extreme, but the overall lack of growth is obvious—average real hourly production worker earnings dropped from $20.30 an hour in 1970 to $19.50 in 1990 (a drop of 9 percent) and has never really returned to its former level (mean real hourly production worker earnings in 2010 were $19.84). Median weekly real earnings for wage and salary workers (including managers and adminis- trators in addition to non-supervisory workers) dropped as well, from $747 per week in 1979 to a low of just over $705 per week in 1992, and recently inched back up toward $752 weekly in 2012 (approximately $37,600 yearly if the median salaried worker takes two weeks' vacation each year).[23] But stag- nation has been accompanied by quite serious income growth for the top 20 percent of all income earners—those at the median moved from making 42 percent of the incomes of those in the top quartile in 1970 to just 28 percent in 2010 (Appendix Exhibit 3.3).

Regardless of who is included in the calculation—individuals, families, wage and salary workers, non-supervisory workers, or hourly workers—the trends in real earnings and income at the middle of these distributions sug- gest that median income and earnings were between $8,000 and $10,000 less at their lowest than they were during the late 1960s and early 1970s. All these figures started to trend upward again the mid- to late 1990s. These are differ- ences in the real purchasing power of earnings and income accruing to people at or near the middle of earnings and income distributions. Because these are median figures, no one could argue that earnings and income have grown such that most people aren't middle class anymore. Instead, these figures reflect the movement of the middle of the distribution of income and earnings over the past thirty years.

Stagnant Incomes for the Middle, Rising Incomes for the Top

The stagnant income and earnings at the middle of the distribution mask long-term changes and sharp increases in income inequality (see Exhibit 3.5).

What's the difference between a mean and a median, and why should we care?

The *mean* is the arithmetic average of a set of numbers. When discussing income and wealth, the mean is calculated by adding up individual income and wealth and dividing by the number of people. Let's say we have an economy with five workers in it, with earnings of $10,000, $20,000, $30,000, $40,000, and $70,000. To calculate the mean, we add all these values together:

$$\$10,000 + \$20,000 + \$30,000 + \$40,000 + \$70,000 = 170,000$$

And then divide the sum by 5, the number of wage earners in our economy:

$$\$170,000 \div 5 = \$34,000$$

Means are useful calculations, providing the basis for most other advanced statistics by taking into account all values that appear in a population or sample.

The *median* is the middle set of numbers, the numbers that divide the top half of the distribution from the bottom half. The median is less sensitive to extreme scores than the mean is and is a better measure of central tendency when the distribution is highly skewed (i.e., different from a normal distribution curve). The median of our distribution of five earnings is simply the number in the middle, in this case $30,000. If the distribution contains an even number of cases, then the median is the mean of the two middle numbers.

Your authors' discussions of income, earnings, and wealth favor medians over means because medians are less sensitive to the skewed distributions associated with each of these topics. The mean is much higher than the median because the wealthy and affluent have remarkably greater resources than the middle class or the poor.

Here's a simple example of how the implications of mean and median calculations are dramatically different. You are sitting in a Starbucks coffee shop with four of your friends. The wealth and assets controlled by all five of you are distributed as follows:

You:	$10,000
Friend 1:	$30,000
Friend 2:	$50,000
Friend 3:	$60,000
Friend 4:	$100,000

The mean distribution of wealth and assets in this Starbucks is $50,000, and the median is $50,000. In this case the mean and the median are equal, so the impression you get from either figure is the same. The distribution of wealth and assets in this example is much more even than the distribution in most market economies.

Now suppose Bill Gates walks into the Starbucks. In 2013, the value of his estimated net wealth and assets was $67 billion. What happens to our distribution? To put it mildly, the mean changes drastically, but the median barely moves. First, let's add Gates's wealth distribution and recalculate the median:

You:	$10,000
Friend 1:	$30,000
Friend 2:	$50,000
Friend 3:	$60,000
Friend 4:	$100,000
Bill Gates:	$67 billion

$$(\$50,000 \div \$60,000) \div 2 = \$55,000$$

The median moves from $50,000 to $55,000. We've added $67 billion dollars to our Starbucks economy, but the typical person in our Starbucks economy is worth only $55,000. But look at what happens to the mean calculation:

You:	$10,000
Friend 1:	$30,000
Friend 2:	$50,000
Friend 3:	$60,000
Friend 4:	$100,000
Bill Gates:	$67 billion

$$\text{Sum} = \$67,000,250,000 \div 6 = \$1,116,670,833$$

The mean wealth and assets controlled by everybody in the room is now about $1.1 *billion*.

Does the mean or the median more accurately describe the distribution of wealth and earnings for the typical person at this Starbucks? You and your four friends are much closer to the median's $55,000 than the mean's $1.1 billion—in fact you are nowhere even close to the mean!

Granted, wealth and asset inequality in a real economy is not distributed this extremely, but the extreme values at the top of the distribution in most market economies make the median represent the status of middle class people much more effectively than the mean.

Exhibit 3.4 The Mean and the Median; or, What Happens When Bill Gates Walks into a Starbucks?

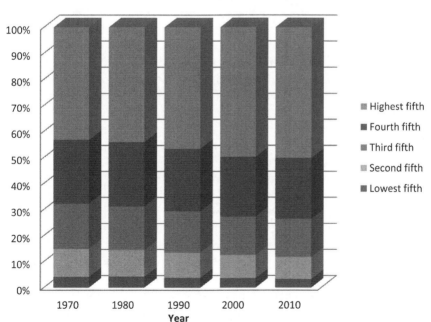

Exhibit 3.5 Share of Aggregate Household Income Received by Each Fifth of All Households, 1970–2010

Source: U.S. Census Bureau, Current Population Survey, Annual Social and Economic Supplements

A standard way to assess the relative equality or inequality in an income distribution is to divide it into parts representing equal shares of the population. Dividing the population into fifths is one popular way of dividing up these distributions. To make statements about inequality, researchers look at the percentage of all income that is awarded to each fifth of the population from the top to the bottom. In the case of "perfect equality," each fifth of the population (20 percent) would get 20 percent of the total income.

Since total equality is an elusive goal most societies never approach, it is useful to compare income distributions over time within the same society or across societies. This way we can judge whether inequality is trending upward or downward over time or whether the income distribution is more or less equal in, for example, Sweden and the United States.

Income inequality has risen substantially in the United States since 1970. The top 20 percent of all families went from receiving 43.3 percent of the income in 1970 to receiving 50 percent of all family income in 2010. More interesting from our perspective is the change in the relative size of the middle fifth of the family income distribution (those families that made between $41,000 and $62,500 in 2001), whose relative share of the family income distribution has dropped from 17.4 percent to 14.6 percent over the past thirty years. In fact, the shares for all families in the bottom four-fifths of the income distribution have declined relative to the top, suggesting that there has been a strong movement of income in the direction of the nation's richer families.[24]

Another way to look at this trend is to plot the ratio of the middle fifth of the family income distribution to the top two-fifths and to look at the real difference between mean and median family income (see Appendix Exhibits 3.3 and 3.4). The mean is simply the arithmetical average, calculating the sum of all household incomes and dividing by the number of households. Unlike the median, which splits the distribution of households exactly in half, the mean takes into account the actual dollars households take in.

The evidence clearly shows that family incomes have ballooned for the upper classes and stagnated for the middle class, the group right in the middle of the family income distribution. The ratio of the middle fifth of family income to the top fifth drops from 42 percent to 28 percent from 1970 to 2010.[25] The difference between real mean and median family income increases from under $10,000 in 1969 to almost $34,000 in 2007, and currently sits at $33,000.[26] "The fact of the matter is, income trends have favored people at the top of the income distribution," says Gary Burtless, Senior Fellow at the Brookings Institution in Washington. "There is no data source that disagrees with the simple statement. In fact, the better the data, the more that the skew appears."[27]

The preponderance of evidence suggests that middle class purchasing power has eroded as income and earnings have either stalled or declined.

Income inequality across households has increased and the relative standing of those we label "middle class" has eroded as well.

What Was Happening at the Top? The Captains of Industry Cash In

Yet another phenomenon is eroding the relative standing of the middle class, involving the rapid rise in the compensation accruing to corporate chief executive officers (CEOs). In 1970 and 1980, the top CEOs as listed by *BusinessWeek* made between $1.7 million and $3.5 million (in 2002 dollars)—big salaries, to be sure, but not ridiculously high. Since then, compensation packages for U.S. CEOs have spiraled upward at a staggering pace. In 1990, the CEO at the bottom of the *BusinessWeek* list made $8.1 million, and Michael Eisner, the president and CEO of Walt Disney Studios, was paid $39.9 million (in 2002 dollars); by 2012, total compensation packages topped out at about $75 million in 2002 dollars and bottomed at around $10 million.[28]

In short, CEO salaries in the United States, already the highest in the world, moved further away from our economic competitors in Western Europe and Asia since the 1980s, while compensation for average workers stagnated or fell. To reveal how enormous the gap is between the salaries of average, middle class workers and those of CEOs, compare mean CEO pay to average annual production worker pay (see Exhibit 3.6).

Ratios that started at about 35 to 1 in 1970 (with top CEOs making roughly thirty-five times what the average worker makes) had mushroomed to nearly 323 to 1 by 2002, and stood at 354 to 1 in 2012, the highest pay gap in the

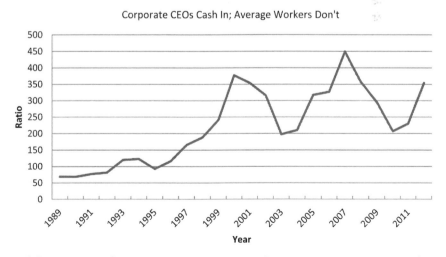

Exhibit 3.6 Ratio of Average Top CEO Compensation to Average Non-Farm Worker Pay, 1989–2012 (2011 dollars)

Source: Forbes CEO Compensation; U.S. Census Bureau, Statistical Abstract of the United States

world.[29] Clearly, the economic landscape for the average worker has shifted and his or her relative economic standing has slipped.

Lower Wages and Job Instability

There is no denying that these trends exist, but their causes have been widely disputed.[30] The simplest explanation points to globalization and the changing role of international competition in increasing skill-based rewards and technological change.[31] Others point to the massive reorganization of the workplace and the enormous drive to cut employee costs to increase profit margins.[32] Is there any evidence for these explanations?

As skill-biased compensation goes, it is hard to see how a CEO in 2012 can make $92 million when in 1970 he or she would have made $400,000. It's even more difficult to see how that difference can be justified in real dollars. But if corporate executives are supposed to maximize profits and shareholder value, then plenty of evidence shows that they did just that, especially since 1980. Stock market returns were historically as high from 1980 to 2000 as they were at any time during the post–World War II period, and the Dow Jones Average passed 15,000 in 2013. This can also be seen by looking at the change in the size of the Standard and Poor's Stock Index and the Dow Jones Industrial Average. Indeed, it wasn't until the onset of the 2001 and 2008 recessions that these stock market indices turned away from historic highs and unprecedented returns (see Exhibits 4.6 and 4.7).[33] Did all this translate into a good corporate bottom line? Definitely. In the 1990s, corporate profits rose to record levels, dropped a bit during the 2001 and 2008 recessions, and have again returned to record levels as of 2013. These trends left most CEOs compensated with stock options in great economic shape compared to their average employee.

What happened to this average employee's job? Trends in mass layoffs are difficult to detect; in fact, the U.S. government didn't start tracking what it terms "mass layoff events" until 1996. But plenty of anecdotal evidence shows that job instability increased during the 1990s, and that middle class workers were buffeted by the changes produced by globalization (see Appendix Exhibit 3.5).[34] The instability is not only in jobs for individuals, it's in incomes for families that rise and fall more quickly than in prior generations. As Jacob Hacker writes, "[O]ver the past generation the economic *instability* of American families has actually risen faster than economic *inequality*—the growing gap between rich and poor that is often taken as the defining feature of the contemporary U.S. economy."[35]

U.S. balance of payments figures (the difference in the value of what we import compared to what we export) began to look uglier as cheap imports that competed against American-made goods flooded the consumer market (Appendix Exhibit 3.6). The dollar stayed strong, but now partially because foreign investors invested heavily in U.S. government debt to pay for our budget deficit.[36]

Our picture so far is of economic stagnation and instability among the middle class, and growing economic prosperity among the relatively wealthy and the captains of American business. Yet the consumer economy continued to go full steam ahead. How was this possible? What was fueling all that consumption?

Consumer Credit!

Even though their incomes and earnings stagnated and their CEOs left them in the economic dust, members of the middle class enhanced their purchasing power. They did this by increasing their working hours, reducing their savings, and increasing their debt load.

American workers are supplementing their incomes by working more hours themselves and by bringing a second wage earner, usually a spouse, into the family (see Exhibit 3.7 and Appendix Exhibit 3.7).

From 1970 to 1997, the average for-pay hours per week worked by all married couples rose from 52.5 to 62.8. During this same period, the percentage of families in which both husband and wife worked for pay rose from 35.9 percent to 59.5 percent.[37] In addition, the number of married couples working more than 100 hours a week (like David and Monica from Chapter 2) has increased dramatically (See Appendix Exhibits 3.7 and 3.8). Considering the lack of movement in average and median earnings among the middle class over the past three decades, these trends suggest that workers work more hours just to keep their heads above water.

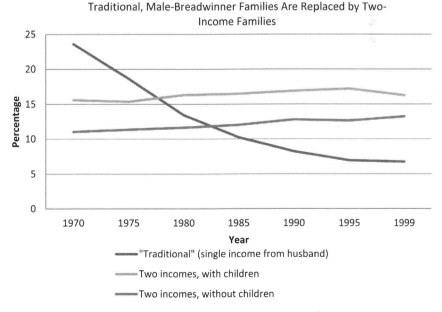

Exhibit 3.7 contents:

Traditional, Male-Breadwinner Families Are Replaced by Two-Income Families

Legend:
- "Traditional" (single income from husband)
- Two incomes, with children
- Two incomes, without children

Exhibit 3.7 Percentage of "Traditional" and Two-Income Families, 1970–1999

Source: U.S. Census Bureau, Current Population Survey, Annual Social and Economic Supplements

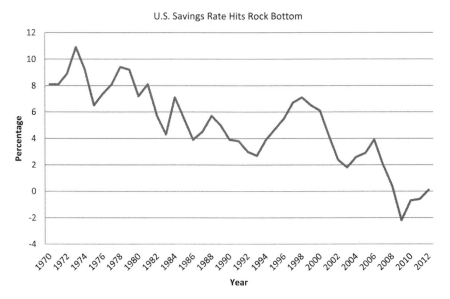

Exhibit 3.8 U.S. Net Savings as a Percentage of Gross National Income

Source: U.S. Bureau of Economic Analysis, National Income and Product Accounts

Workers also have stopped saving money and started living from paycheck to paycheck, leaving them little or no buffer against the whims of misfortune (see Exhibits 3.8, 3.9, and 3.10).[38]

Not only has real average credit card debt per household risen from just over $4,000 in 1990 to $9,000 in 2003—a change in real dollars of $5,029

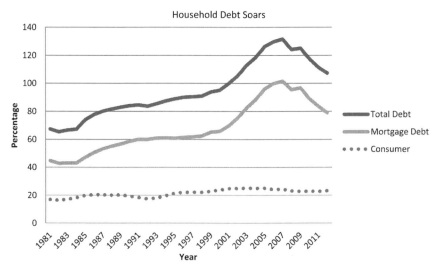

Exhibit 3.9 Household Debt as a Percentage of Disposable Income, 1981–2011

Source: Federal Reserve Flow of Funds Accounts

(in 2002 dollars)[39]—but college students are also plunging into the credit hole (see Appendix Exhibit 3.9).

The average student credit card debt has risen from $1,222 to $3,100 from 1998 to 2008 and the percentage of students with balances between $3,000 and $7,000 has risen to 21 percent of the college student population.[40] Students graduating from college in 2011 had on average $26,600 in student loans.[41] The post-industrial economy demands a well-educated workforce, and a college degree has increasingly become the admission ticket to the middle class. But when graduates rack up consumer debt from school loans during their time in college, they enter the labor force already in precarious financial situations.

If we add home mortgages to this equation, household debt as a percentage of personal income has risen steadily since 1980 as well. The costs of homes and credit cards have risen while average incomes have not (see Chapters 5 and 6), so Americans are borrowing more money and a greater percentage of their income and earnings to pay for the goods and services that a middle class lifestyle demands. The debt-to-income ratio has risen in recent years because debt has gone up and incomes have remained stagnant (see Exhibit 3.10).

Real average incomes have not kept pace with consumption spending. But that's not the whole story. Because it isn't measured in dollars, the ratio of debt to income isn't sensitive to inflation, which means that the amount of debt the average consumer in the American economy is carrying is much larger than it was twenty years ago.

Credit and debt in the United States far outstrip the incomes of average people. Compared to their counterparts of a generation ago, members of the

Exhibit 3.10 Household Debt as Percentage of Personal Income: Average Earnings of Production Workers (2011 Dollars)

Source: Federal Reserve Flow of Funds Accounts; Bureau of Labor Statistics

modern middle class are in greater debt, are earning less money, and are working more hours at less stable jobs.

Discussion Questions

- What can be done to close the gap between CEO and average worker pay?
- How can economic growth benefit the middle class?
- Which do you think is more important, increasing overall economic growth or ensuring that workers receive a livable wage?
- How have politics shaped our economic policies?

Notes

1. Bureau of Economic Analysis data show that during this four-decade period, the annual growth rate was negative only during the following years: 1974, 1975, 1980, 1982, 1991, 2008, and 2009, accessed July 7, 2013, www.bea.gov/national/xls/gdpchg.xls
2. Even if they had this money, this is not always the wisest thing to do with it. In investment banking, investors may have only the stock and anticipated returns on the stock to show for their money. In this case, the "loan" to the company is akin to buying part of the company and betting that your investment will pay off in terms of greater value for the stock or dividends paid on the stock from the profits accruing to the investment.
3. David M. Kennedy, *Freedom from Fear: The American People in Depression and War, 1929–1945* (Oxford, UK: Oxford University Press, 1999), 166.
4. Frederick S. Weaver, *Economic Literacy: Basic Economics with an Attitude* (Lanham, MD: Rowman & Littlefield, 2002), 105.
5. John Maynard Keynes, *The General Theory of Employment, Interest, and Money* (1936, repr. New York: Harcourt Brace Jovanovich, 1964).
6. For more on this tax cut, see Martin F. J. Prachowny, *The Kennedy-Johnson Tax Cut: A Revisionist History* (Cheltenham, UK: Edward Elgar Publishing, 2000).
7. Weaver, *Economic Literacy*, 105.
8. For one thing, if wages responded to government intervention directly, then many Keynesian assumptions about closing the "output gap" without increasing inflation were problematic. See Jerome L. Stein, *Monetarist, Keynesian and New Classical Economics* (Oxford, UK: Blackwell, 1982), 1–10.
9. See Stein, *Monetarist, Keynesian and New Classical Economics*, 85–104.
10. Explaining persistent inflation in the face of high unemployment—the "stagflation" of the late 1970s—proved as difficult for monetarists as it was for Keynesians. Monetarists could only suggest that slowing the growth in money supply would directly increase unemployment but that inflation remained high because of past rates of monetary expansion and inertia caused by inflationary expectations.
11. Arthur B. Laffer, "The Laffer Curve: Past, Present, and Future," *The Heritage Foundation Backgrounder* 1765 (2004).
12. We will avoid the question of whether the purpose of supply-side economics was to shrink the actual size of government by undermining the ability of government to fund itself. See, for example, David Stockman, *The Triumph of Politics: How the Reagan Revolution Failed* (New York: Harper and Row, 1986), 44–76, and Paul Krugman, *Peddling Prosperity: Economic Sense and Nonsense in the Age of Diminished Expectations* (New York: W.W. Norton, 1994), 151–169.
13. This assumes that the prior tax rate was on the "dysfunctional" side of the Laffer curve. Because taxes in the United States are among the lowest in the industrialized world, this

strikes most economists as a dubious claim. Differences between supply-side economics weren't simply with the Keynesians. Unlike classical economists, supply-side economists believe that economic actors respond to government incentives, and that fighting inflation will result in higher unemployment—in short, supply-side economics disregards the policy ineffectiveness hypothesis. And supply-side economics differed from monetarist economics as well. The money supply wasn't tightened during the Reagan years; instead, interest rates were increased to reduce incentives to borrow. Supply-side economics regulated money supply through interest rates, much as Keynesians did, and keeping a tight rein on the money supply was not part of the program.

14. See David Stockman, *The Great Deformation: The Corruption of Capitalism in America* (New York: Perseus Book Group, 2013). Stockman was the director of the Office of Management and Budget during the Reagan administration. See also Paul Craig Roberts, *The Failure of Laissez-Faire Capitalism* (Atlanta, GA: Clarity Press, 2013). Roberts was a former assistant secretary of the Treasury under the Reagan administration.

15. It's not as if each of these macroeconomic theories has nothing to offer the middle class. Monetarists offer steady prices, steady wages, and slow but steady economic growth—nothing flashy, but very predictable. New classical economics offers low inflation. Keynesian economics offers to increase purchasing power, and the demand-multiplier effects from this should keep you employed and productive as long as potential output is above actual output. Keynesians also offer a hedge against hard times with a series of income maintenance programs that will help you if you get laid off or sick, or otherwise lose your job. Supply-side economics offers tax cuts, lower prices through deregulation, and productivity gains that, in theory, translate into higher wages.

16. See Kevin Phillips, *The Politics of Rich and Poor: Wealth and the American Electorate in the Reagan Aftermath* (New York: Random House, 1990), 84, and *Boiling Point: Democrats, Republicans, and the Decline of Middle Class Prosperity* (New York: Random House, 1993), 114–122.

17. Paul Krugman, *The Great Unraveling: Losing Our Way in the New Century* (New York: W.W. Norton, 2003), 27–51, 101–124.

18. See Juliet B. Schor, *The Overworked American: The Unexpected Decline of Leisure* (New York: Basic Books, 1992) and *The Overspent American: Upscaling, Downshifting, and the New Consumer* (New York: Basic Books, 1998); Teresa A. Sullivan, Elizabeth Warren, and Jay L. Westbrook, *As We Forgive Our Debtors: Bankruptcy and Consumer Credit in America* (Washington, D.C.: BeardBooks, 1999) and *The Fragile Middle Class: Americans in Debt* (New Haven, CT: Yale University Press, 2000); Robert D. Manning, *Credit Card Nation: The Consequences of America's Addiction to Credit* (New York: Basic Books, 2000); and Elizabeth Warren and Amelia Warren Tyagi, *The Two-Income Trap: Why Middle Class Mothers and Fathers Are Going Broke* (New York: Basic Books, 2003).

19. "The Budget and Economic Outlook: Fiscal Years 2007 to 2016" (Congressional Budget Office, 2006), accessed July 13, 2013, http://www.cbo.gov/publication/17601. See also http://www.usgovernmentdebt.us/federal_deficit

20. See David Cay Johnston, *Perfectly Legal: The Covert Campaign to Rig Our Tax System to Benefit the Super Rich—And Cheat Everybody Else* (New York: Portfolio Hardcover, 2003), 1–70; Kevin Phillips, *Arrogant Capital* (Boston: Back Bay Books, 1995), 29–66; and Brian Reidl, "Ten Common Myths about Taxes, Spending, and Budget Deficits," *The Heritage Foundation Backgrounder*, June 13, 2003.

21. The New York Times Company, *The Downsizing of America* (New York: Three Rivers Press, 1996).

22. Donald L. Barlett, and James B. Steele, *America: What Went Wrong?* (Kansas City, MO: Andrews McMeel, 1992), v–xii.

23. United States Department of Labor. Bureau of Labor Statistics, "Median Usual Weekly Earnings in Current Dollars, Wage and Salary Workers, Second Quartile," converted to 2011 dollars, accessed July 7, 2013, www.bls.gov/data

24. United States Department of Commerce. U.S. Census Bureau, "Table H-2. Share of Aggregate Income Received by Each Fifth and Top 5 Percent of Households, All Races: 1967 to 2010," accessed July 13, 2013, http://www.census.gov/hhes/www/income/data/historical/household/

25. Ibid.

26. See Robert B. Avery, Gregory E. Ellihausen, Glenn B. Canner, and Thomas A. Gustafson, "Survey of Consumer Finances, 1983," *Federal Reserve Bulletin*, September 1984; Arthur Kennickell and Janice Shack-Marquez, "Changes in Family Finances from 1983 to 1989: Evidence from the Survey of Consumer Finances," *Federal Reserve Bulletin*, January 1992; and Ana M. Aizcorbe, Arthur B. Kennickell, and Kevin B. Moore, "Recent Changes in U.S. Family Finances: Evidence from the 1998 and 2001 Survey of Consumer Finances," *Federal Reserve Bulletin*, January 2003.

27. David Leonhardt, "Time to Slay the Inequality Myth? Not So Fast," *New York Times*, January 25, 2004.

28. *Forbes*, "Two Decades of CEO PAY," accessed July 23, 2013, http://www.forbes.com/lists/2012/12/ceo-compensation-12-historical-pay-chart.html

29. Ibid.; U.S. Census Bureau, *Statistical Abstract of the United States, 2012* (Washington, D.C.: U.S. Government Printing Office, 2013).

30. For arguments on the cause of these trends, see Krugman, *The Great Unraveling*, 376–378; Joseph E. Stiglitz, *The Roaring Nineties* (New York: W.W. Norton, 2003), 180–202; David M. Gordon, *Fat and Mean: The Corporate Squeeze of Working Americans and the Myth of Managerial Downsizing* (New York: Martin Kessler Books, 1996), 15–33; and James K. Galbraith, *Created Unequal: The Crisis in American Pay* (New York: Free Press, 1998), 3–65.

31. Michael Mandel, *The High-Risk Society: Peril and Promise in the New Economy* (New York: Times Business, 1996).

32. These include Gordon, *Fat and Mean*, 61–94, and Kevin T. Leicht and Mary L. Fennell, *Professional Work: A Sociological Approach* (Oxford, UK: Blackwell, 2001), 96–112.

33. U.S. Census Bureau, *Statistical Abstract of the United States, 2002* (Washington, D.C.: U.S. Government Printing Office, 2003).

34. For example, see the New York Times Company, *The Downsizing of America*; NOW with Bill Moyers, "Changing Face of Unemployment," August, 29, 2003, accessed www.pbs.org./now/politics/unemployment.html; Manuel Castells, *The Rise of the Network Society* (Oxford, UK: Blackwell, 1996), 243–308; and Martin Carnoy, *Sustaining the New Economy: Work, Family, and Community in the Information Age* (Cambridge, MA: Harvard University Press, 2000), 56–105.

35. Jacob Hacker, *The Great Risk Shift: The New Economic Insecurity and the Decline of the American Dream* (Oxford University Press, 2008), 2.

36. United States Department of Commerce. U.S. Census Bureau, Foreign Trade Division, 2003. "FT900: U.S. International Trade in Goods and Services," accessed June 23, 2013, www.census.gov/foreign-trade/www/press.html

37. Jerry A. Jacobs and Kathleen Gerson, "Overworked Individuals or Overworked Families? Explaining Trends in Work, Leisure, and Family Time," *Work and Occupations* 28 (2001): 40–63.

38. Elizabeth Warren and Amelia Warren Tyagi, *The Two-Income Trap*.

39. CardWeb.com, Inc., accessed cardweb.com/

40. Marie O'Malley, "Educating Undergraduates on Using Credit Cards," Nellie Mae, 2004, accessed www.nelliemae.com

41. The Institute for College Access & Success, 2012, *Student Debt and the Class of 2011*, accessed June 23, 2013, http://projectonstudentdebt.org/files/pub/classof2011.pdf

CHAPTER 4

Robbing the Productivity Train

GOOD NEWS: YOU'RE FIRED
—July 2005 *Newsweek* headline for a report on a $113 million payout
to Phil Purcell, ex-CEO of Morgan Stanley, fired for poor performance[1]

So far, we've examined the plight of some typical middle class families and the increasingly problematic relationship between income and credit since the 1980s. In this chapter, we'll look at changes in productivity among American workers and ask where productivity gains went. But first, we need to discuss how productivity is measured.

What Is Productivity?

Productivity is an imprecise concept that yields considerable disagreement among economists, sociologists, and policy analysts. In general terms, productivity is the relative rate at which inputs into a production system turn into outputs. In a market economy, productivity is very important—increases in productivity increase aggregate wealth and income in the economy as a whole. Such increases make wage hikes, extensive fringe benefits, longer vacations, and shorter working hours possible without reducing the overall efficiency of the economy. More to the point, flat or declining productivity renders all competitions over economic output zero-sum, as gains by workers equal losses by employers and vice versa. Those gains that accrue to workers in the form of higher wages are "taken" directly from foregone profits for capitalists or reinvestment capital to keep cutting-edge technologies in place that (in theory) increase productivity. Regular, steady productivity gains ease negotiations between managers and workers: since the pie is getting bigger, everyone can have a slice.

Productivity in economics reflects a technical relationship between outputs and inputs in a production system or process. Appendix Exhibit 4.1 summarizes some of the more technical issues associated with different measures of productivity, the overall goal of which is to show how efficiently inputs are turned into outputs. The more efficiently raw materials, machinery, utilities, and labor are turned into a product or service and sold, the higher productivity is. Productivity is not strictly associated with increased output or work effort—in fact, some very labor-intensive processes are not very productive (mining for iron ore, for example), and some processes that seem to require little effort are very productive (booking a discount hotel reservation online, for example).

Analyses from the National Bureau of Economic Research[2] suggest that productivity measures are wildly inaccurate and tend to underestimate productivity gains in the economy. Different measures of productivity result in different economic outlooks, with real implications for determining whether the economy is growing and how quickly. In particular, the "difference in growth rates" method used by the Bureau of Labor Statistics (growth in outputs minus the growth in inputs) drastically underestimates productivity growth. In particular, this method fails to take into account changes in technology and the organization of work that occurs when new, more advanced inputs are used. Workers tend to get "excess credit" if productivity rises and "excess blame" if productivity falls. The BLS methodology is the most widely used and quoted, which renders its impressions important for policymakers and business analysts attempting to chart the strength of the economy.

There is no easy way to measure productivity, and the decision of which measure to use is not just an esoteric dispute between academic economists. Measures of productivity are viewed as indicators of the overall health of the economy.[3] If indices suggest that productivity isn't growing, the standard political response by the right (in the United States, at least) is to recommend policies that favor capital investment and profits at the expense of wages and employee welfare. From the supply-side perspective, this makes sense: improving inputs will increase productivity and future productivity gains can be more widely distributed. Other indicators that suggest that productivity is improving, or even lagging behind wages, could be used as a justification for providing average workers with better pay and benefits packages without necessarily harming investment capital or the investment environment.

Fred Block and Gene Burns show that there are quite serious differences in the conclusions one would reach from slight differences in the calculation of productivity.[4] For example, the critical differences come between 1973 and

1979, an era widely recognized as the source of the U.S. crisis in productivity (see Appendix Exhibits 4.2–4.5). Productivity growth before 1973 was between 2 and 3 percent—below the growth rates of the 1960s, but still not bad. But from 1973 to 1979, productivity levels fell to 1 percent, constituting a productivity crisis. Business and political leaders cited the crisis as a symptom of an overregulated, overburdened economy with wages and government spending that were too high, and government regulations that were too burdensome.

But these simple measurements are complicated by other changes that affect productivity, almost all for the better and some in drastic ways. These include technological innovations (replacing an old, antiquated, expensive technology with a relatively cheap, new, and efficient one), economies of scale (lower production costs for big producers), improvements in management techniques and the organization of work (teamwork, quality circles, continuous quality improvement, and workplace changes designed to harness the creativity of the workforce), and improvements to the efficiency and productivity of the labor force. These factors make measuring productivity an inexact science.

Do increases in productivity cost workers their jobs? This debate has raged for many years. The Luddites of the English Industrial Revolution, for example, destroyed weaving machines, believing that technological improvements led to unemployment and massive social dislocation. Some policy analysts claim that the current "jobless recovery" in the United States is a product of increased productivity. Plants and offices that use labor efficiently don't necessarily need to hire more workers as demand for products grows and orders increase. This is especially true if, as we said in Chapter 3, there is unused existing capacity or "slack" in the economy.

Still, productivity increases are supposed to improve the economy, producing profits for investors and companies at the same time that they generate wages and benefits for employees and tax revenues for governments to provide public goods.

Profits and Reinvestment: The Other Activities That Productivity Gains Support

In a market economy, productivity gains can be and are used for a variety of purposes, not all of which are for the best. For prosperity to be maintained in a market economy, the gains must be reinvested in the enterprises they came from. Without this reinvestment, output starts to grind to a halt as machines wear out, computers and other electronic devices become obsolete, and the technologies that make a modern economy work fall into disrepair. Such setbacks reduce workplace productivity and reduce the gains that can go to other activities such as profits, consumption, and wages.

Reinvestment maintains the momentum of productivity increases. Since the 1930s, many governments have maintained good investment environments, following certain guidelines. These guidelines have recently been reinforced as state socialist economies have begun to move slowly toward becoming market economies. Specifically, economies need a sound banking system, sound currency, fiscally responsible government spending, consistently collected and preferably low taxes, and social stability.

Unfortunately, reinvestment also produces worker displacement. Some of this displacement is probably inevitable, and it is impossible to tell how many workers have been technologically displaced rather than laid off for other reasons. But as we saw with Bill's company in Chapter 2, and as we'll see below, the activities responsible for the huge job losses of the past forty years had little to do with productive reinvestment.

What Did Corporate America Do with Profits and Productivity Gains?

Instead of investing in new technologies to spawn further productivity gains, corporate managers overpaid themselves, doled out cash to investors, consumed luxury items, and engaged in corporate takeovers and mergers and acquisitions (see Exhibit 4.1). Whether or not these activities contribute to the overall productive capacity of the American economy is, to say the least, an open question.

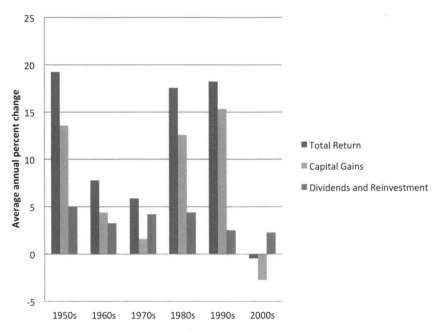

Exhibit 4.1 Investment Returns on the Stock Market by Decade, 1950–2010

Source: U.S. Census Bureau, Statistical Abstract of the United States

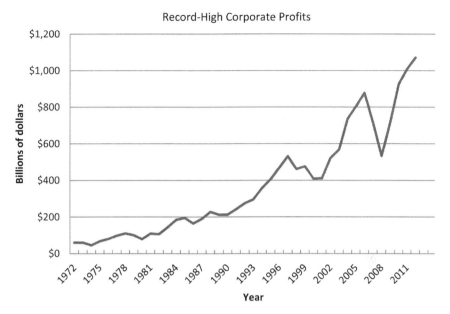

Exhibit 4.2 Corporate Profits

Source: U.S. Bureau of Economic Analysis

Corporate profits during the 1990s peaked above $500 billion in 1997, and with the exception of the 2001 and 2008 recessions, have continued to rise to record levels (see Exhibit 4.2). The Standard and Poor's (S&P) index and the Dow Jones Industrial Average, the standard indices of stock market performance, increased over 1,000 percent during the 1990s, and stocks did better during the 1990s than at any time since World War II (see Appendix Exhibits 4.6 and 4.7).

By any standard, these are tremendous changes in the wealth and profit available for redistribution, consumption, or investment. But the rate of dividend payment and reinvestment, never high in the first place, *declined* through the 1980s and afterwards. Isn't this where the funds come from to invest in new technologies? And what about those record-high corporate profits?

So Some People Got Rich! Doesn't Everyone Own Stock These Days?

Without question, the overall level of activity in the U.S. stock market has risen dramatically. But how have these gains been distributed? The answer is clear: not very equitably.

Only 22 percent of all U.S. households have direct stock holdings[5] (also see Appendix Exhibit 4.8), and the overwhelming majority of stocks are owned by

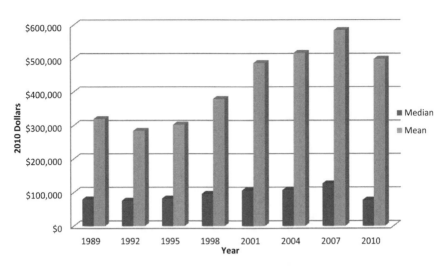

The Middle Class Left in the Dust

Exhibit 4.3 Median and Mean Family Net Worth, 1989–2010

Source: Federal Reserve Board, Survey of Consumer Finances

an extremely small percentage of wealthy people. In 2010, the bottom 95 percent of stockowners *combined* owned just 33 percent of total stock value.[6] This is not the only measure of wealth, nor is it the one most Americans rely on, so let's look at broader indicators of wealth and its distribution.

A more complete story is told by looking at changes in family net worth, the total value of the wealth held by different classes of wealth holders (see Exhibit 4.3).

Family net worth is calculated by adding up the value of assets owned by members of the household (e.g., home, vehicles, investments, checking and savings accounts) and subtracting all liabilities (e.g., mortgages, car loans, credit card and other debts). In spite of the spectacular gains in the U.S. stock market since the 1970s, median net worth for all Americans barely moved. However, mean family net worth (the average value of all the assets a family has minus its liabilities) increased substantially, to almost $600,000 prior to the 2008 recession. Since these changes are in real dollars, they represent improvements in the wealth profile of Americans. But since the median doesn't move, the numbers suggest big wealth gains among those who already possess wealth and not much movement near the middle of the wealth distribution. More ominously, median net worth *declined* almost 40 percent between 2007 (before the recession) and 2010. The wealthy lost money as well but the effects on those near the median were much more devastating.

These suspicions are borne out further by an examination of distributions of net worth across wealth and income distribution. The growth in wealth displayed by the change in median family net worth is overwhelmingly concentrated at the top of the income and wealth distributions. The median family net worth in the top quintile of the family income distribution almost doubles during the stock market boom of the late 1990s, rising from around $500,000 per household to $850,000 per household (see Appendix Exhibit 4.9), and then rises to stratospheric levels after that, reaching $1.5 million by 2007. There are more modest changes in the next two quintiles of the earnings distribution, as median net worth rises from $114,000 to $216,000 for those in the second-highest quintile and from $71,000 to $92,000 for the middle quintile (the people we define as "middle class" for our purposes). But almost all of these modest gains in the second and third quintile were completely wiped out during the recession—those in the second quintile from the top lost almost half of their net worth between 2007 and 2010 (moving from $216,000 to $129,000 on average), and those in the middle quintile lost almost a third (from $92,000 to $66,000).

The rise of wealth inequality in the 1990s and afterward is even more apparent when we examine the distribution of wealth by quartiles (see Appendix Exhibit 4.10). Here the changes are much more stark and inequality much more apparent. Specifically, the bottom quartile of the wealth distribution essentially controls no wealth at all. After that, wealth does grow at all quintiles of the wealth distribution, but it grows disproportionately at the top: the median wealth holder in the top tenth of the distribution was worth over $2.5 million by 2007, and was still worth $2.3 million in 2010 after the recession.[7]

One consumer manifestation of changes in wealth and income has been a boom in luxury retail sales. During the 1990s, the sales index among luxury retailers doubled, as affluent consumers rushed to spend their new gains on the latest luxury goods from Tiffany's, Gucci, Saks, and Waterford. The rise in consumption from these luxury retailers was a sign that relatively wealthy Americans were reaping the consumption benefits of their newfound income and wealth.[8]

Corporate Takeovers as a Competitive Strategy

Merger and acquisition activity (sometimes referred to as "M&A") is the act of buying, selling, and merging existing businesses through stock and equity exchanges. Business owners and stockholders engage in such activity to merge companies that profit from combining operations, while investors do so to direct management practices. Merger and acquisition activity almost always changes the value of stock shares as investors buy up publicly held stock in an attempt to take over or merge with an existing company.

Merger and acquisition activity is part of an advanced, globalized market economy, but it becomes problematic as corporate officers (CEOs, CFOs, and other executives) are awarded stock options. If stock options allow executives to purchase company shares at a predetermined price and merger and acquisition activity drives up that price, executives have a built-in incentive to see their company's stock become the target for merger and acquisition activity; they can sell their stock option shares when the price is at its peak and pocket (in many cases) millions of dollars without changing the underlying productive standing of their company at all. The existence of stock option compensation packages along with merger and acquisition activity is one reason for the massive rise in CEO salaries documented in Chapter 3.

Aside from luxury goods, much of the enormous capital raised during the 1990s expansion went toward merger and acquisition activity and corporate takeovers. The value, size, and amount of merger and acquisition activity in the United States and in cross-border transactions increased substantially during the 1990s and afterward, as did the number of bank mergers and acquisitions (see Exhibit 4.4).[9] The deregulation of financial services is largely responsible for these changes.

Favorable tax policies played a huge role in the increase of mergers and acquisitions of the 1980s and 1990s. Federal tax laws allow corporations to write off all the debt they assume as a result of merger and acquisition activity.[10] Thus, there are incentives for corporations to engage in takeover activity to hide cash surpluses, lower tax bills, and potentially make money from selling off the pieces of acquired companies for more than the acquired corporation cost in the first place.

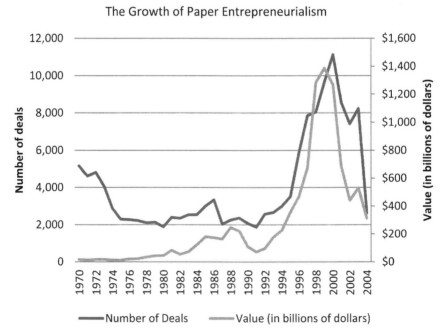

Exhibit 4.4 Merger and Acquisition Activity, 1970–2004

Source: MergerStat Free Reports, 2004

Debate rages on the merits of corporate merger and acquisition activity, but several patterns resulting from it are clear:

1. To engage in merger and acquisition activity, corporations often take on massive debts they can't pay. This creates enormous pressure to "squeeze" average employees—through pay cuts, slashing benefits, or adding work hours—to find new sources of cash.[11]
2. Companies are rarely acquired and kept intact; instead, they are sold off, either in whole or in part. For the average worker, layoffs often result from this practice.
3. Many of these transactions allow companies to pay little or no income tax.[12] In fact, the corporate debt assembled through merger and acquisition activity is tax deductible!

By the year 2000, the Dow had risen past 10,000, and some observers confidently claimed it would keep on soaring (as of this writing, the Dow is near 15,000).[13] Investors, particularly in technology stocks, were getting richer by the minute. To many observers it seemed that happy days were here again. But just as the "housing bubble" had done in the 1980s, the "tech bubble" eventually burst, leaving high-skilled workers jobless and with worthless stock options. The stock market continued to climb, but a series of corporate scandals and large bankruptcies were just around the corner. Though several of these took place during President George W. Bush's first administration, the seeds had been planted during the Clinton administration, which backed the continued deregulation of electricity, telecommunications, and finance.[14] The deregulation of these industries encouraged a range of corporate activities designed to boost stock prices and create added wealth for investors. Unfortunately, many of these practices turned out to be smoke and mirrors, artificially inflating profits and stock prices,[15] and eventually leading to the collapse of several gigantic corporations. On December 2, 2001, Enron filed the biggest Chapter 11 bankruptcy in U.S. history; at the time of filing, the company reported $62 billion in assets. Enron held its ignominious title only until the next summer, however, when WorldCom filed for bankruptcy with assets totaling $100 billion. In 2008, Lehman Brothers filed for bankruptcy with a staggering $639 billion in assets.[16]

These cases expose common problems resulting from the payment of executives in stock options and the obsession of Wall Street traders with ever-growing and immediate profit margins. In a deregulated financial environment, it was possible for these executives to represent their companies as making money hand over fist, when in fact profits and performance were either more down to earth or, in the case of Enron, nonexistent. With each public announcement of the latest achievement in corporate performance, the price of the company's stock went up and top executives could sell their shares, making millions in immediate profits. The transactions were so fast and so complex that most investors had no idea what was happening. It was only after outsiders began questioning accounting statements that the extent of the fraud in each case was exposed. In the meantime, investors lost millions, tens of thousands of workers lost jobs, and many employees lost their entire retirement funds (see Chapter 6).[17]

There have been a few cases where executives have been held legally accountable for these activities. L. Dennis Kozlowski and Mark H. Swartz, both top executives at Tyco International, were convicted in the summer of 2005 of looting the company of over $150 million and were sentenced to eight to twenty-five years in a New York State prison. These sentences were preceded by the conviction and sentencing of Bernard J. Ebbers of WorldCom to twenty-five years in prison and John J. Rigas of Adelphia Communications to fifteen years in prison for financial frauds that allowed them to pocket millions of dollars in compensation. Kenneth L. Lay and Jeffrey K. Skilling, former executives at Enron, were convicted in May 2006 of multiple counts of securities fraud and conspiracy. Currently, Jeffrey Cohen of SAC Capital is facing charges of insider trading by the Justice Department, the latest in a long line of financial improprieties to emerge in the wake of the 2008 recession.[18]

As Joseph Stiglitz, winner of the Nobel Prize in economics and chairman of President Clinton's Council of Economic Advisers, points out, Enron and WorldCom were products of deregulation. Enron's growth was fueled by deregulation of the energy industry, and WorldCom's by deregulation of telecommunications. Both businesses benefited from and adapted to financial industry deregulation, which provided incentives for mergers and other techniques to maximize short-term profits.[19] Deregulation also set the stage for questionable, deceptive, and outright fraudulent accounting practices. Many referred to these practices as "aggressive accounting," but as Jim Hightower writes, "That's the same as saying that robbing 7-Elevens is 'aggressive consumerism.'"[20]

Clearly, the productivity gains of recent decades went to those with considerable income and wealth, or were used by corporations to engage in activities designed to bolster their immediate bottom line. They were not used to improve the lot of average workers, who received no increase in their average paychecks.

What If Wages Were Indexed to Productivity?

What would the distribution of earnings for average workers look like if some of those productivity gains had been distributed to them rather than spent on these other activities? There are complications involved in answering this question. For one thing, workers could be rewarded for increased productivity in several ways, including working fewer hours and taking increased leisure time. (Evidence indicates that this has not happened: Americans now work more hours than anyone else in the industrialized world except for South Koreans).[21]

Another complication is that, rather than increasing the compensation of the workers that produce productivity gains, businesses could choose to hire more workers at existing wage rates, thus distributing productivity over a larger group of workers. Indeed, in the 1990s the United States saw an impressive trend in job growth.[22] However, if the number of available jobs grew rapidly and the workforce did not grow at the same pace, then there should have been pressure for upward wage movement even if productivity stayed the same—more employers would have chased relatively fewer workers. Since productivity was growing, this should have eased pressure on hiring, as fewer workers could do the work that more workers did before.

Because of these complications, judging the distribution of productivity gains to average workers accurately is difficult.[23] To do so, we'll make a series of assumptions and then see how earnings would change if those assumptions hold.

Radically oriented economists and social scientists would argue that wages should rise in direct proportion to productivity. This is not the same as saying that all productivity gains should be redistributed completely to workers; instead, workers' earnings should rise as productivity does, in equal proportion. We'll call this the *100 percent solution*.

Others would argue that most if not all productivity gains are necessary to keep up with technological changes and to remain competitive. Under this assumption, the costs of no wage gains should be compensated for by increased investment in new equipment and the organization of work—investments that would yield more employment and higher wages later on. Since those who produced the productivity gains should receive something for their trouble, we'll give them a quarter of the productivity boost as wages. We'll call this scenario the *25 percent solution*.

Still others would argue that productivity gains are equally the product of labor and capital, and should be split accordingly. Since both investors and workers make sacrifices during bad times (though this is not a safe assumption, given the events of the last twenty years), they should both be rewarded in good times. We'll call this the *50 percent solution*.

Before we present the results of the simulations, a reminder of the real hourly earnings changes for average workers: For manufacturing and non-farm business workers in non-supervisory positions, real hourly wages declined for most of the 1980s and 1990s, and started to rise again in the late 1990s. Hourly earnings in non-farm business never again came close to their real value in 1970 regardless of when we look. Manufacturing hourly earnings come close to returning to their 1970 levels in real dollars. It is

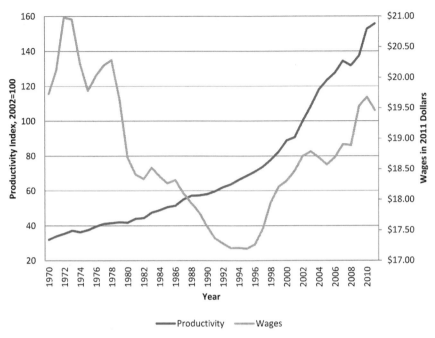

Exhibit 4.5 Non-Farm Business Wages and Productivity Index

Source: Bureau of Labor Statistics

also clear that real wages have declined as productivity has increased (see Exhibit 4.5).

For non-farm business wages we can go all the way back to 1970. In both manufacturing and non-farm work, real hourly wages decline as productivity rises, indicating that there are considerable revenues and profits to redistribute, as we've suggested. The result of our simulation is presented in Exhibit 4.6.

By any standard we use, from the 25 percent solution to the 100 percent solution, the lot of average workers would be much improved were they allowed to share in at least some of the productivity gains they've helped produce. The changes would be in real dollars accounting for inflation, representing boosts in standard of living and purchasing power. Even using the most modest proposal, the 25 percent solution, the average non-farm private business worker would have netted a $2.21 per hour percent raise in 2011, or an additional $4,420 per year. Granted, this takes into account continuous raises tied to productivity from 1990 to the present, but an extra $4,420 is enough to make payments on a new car or to take on significantly less credit card debt (see Chapter 5).

The sustained purchasing power of the middle class is the engine the drives economic growth. During the past forty years, the American economy has grown dramatically—despite slowdowns, downturns, and periodic

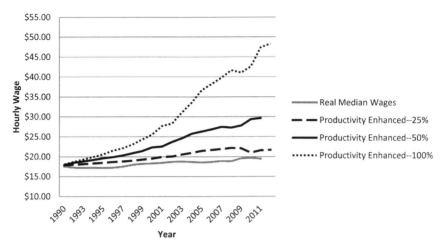

Exhibit 4.6 Real Hourly Wages for Non-Farm Business Workers plus Productivity-Enhanced Wages in 2011 Dollars

Source: Bureau of Labor Statistics

recessions—as the middle class continued to spend, albeit often with borrowed money. Sometimes, as when companies invest profits in financial markets by purchasing asset-backed securities, the money that could have been given to workers as increased compensation provides the financial backing for lending institutions to extend credit. This is direct evidence supporting our contention that the middle class has been *loaned money that it could have been paid*! Of course, it is often not technically the "same" money, and there is strong evidence that companies use enhanced productivity and profits to finance executive compensation packages rather than raises for average workers. Workers appear to be relying on consumer credit to provide income that they may not have needed if their wages were higher.

The average worker could accomplish much with such gains in purchasing power. The average worker with employer-provided health insurance now pays almost $330 per month,[24] and $800 a month would allow workers whose employers don't provide insurance to afford healthcare of their own. Putting some of this money in savings and retirement accounts would mean the difference between retiring comfortably and retiring on Social Security. Saving this money would provide workers' children with college educations, especially if savings accrued over a number of years in interest-bearing accounts.

The results of our calculations may seem large, but if we extend this logic, the average worker is owed even more money than we've suggested. Productivity-enhanced wages are cumulative and accrue for each year that the median real wage is below the productivity-enhanced wage, and each year that workers are not paid the productivity-enhanced wage, the workers lose the productivity-enhanced wage for that year and all raises based on the enhanced wage for the years after that. The cumulative effect over the twelve-year stretch from 1990 to 2011 in even the most conservative scenario would be almost $80,000 real 2011 dollars. This is the difference between paying for a new car in cash and leasing it using diminished earnings, giving children substantial boosts toward college funds, enhancing health insurance, saving for retirement, or simply having a nice vacation.

Even the 100 percent calculation, which raises real earnings in proportion to productivity growth, assumes that the division of proceeds among employers, investors, and workers was equitable to begin with. We took for granted the prevailing split among workers, profits, and reinvestment that existed in 1990. If we question this relationship between employers and workers, wage and benefit gains are greater still.

But of course, the distribution of productivity gains over the past forty years has not come close to any of these solutions. Without these gains to benefit them, middle class Americans rely instead on substantial credit. But where did all this credit come from? That's the subject of our next chapter.

Discussion Questions

- Why is productivity such an important concept?
- What factors are responsible for the increased productivity of the American workforce?
- In what ways does the middle class benefit from this increased productivity?
- In an ideal world, what percentage of productivity gains do you think workers should receive? Why?

Notes

1. Charles Gasparino, "Good News: You're Fired," *Newsweek*, July 25, 2005.
2. William Nordhaus, "Alternative Methods for Measuring Productivity Growth," Working Paper 8095, National Bureau of Economic Research (2001), 1–20.
3. See, for example, Fred Block and Gene Burns, "Productivity as a Social Problem: The Uses and Misuses of Social Indicators," *American Sociological Review* 51 (1986): 767–80; Fred Block, *Postindustrial Possibilities: A Critique of Economic Discourse* (Berkeley: University of California Press, 1990); and Erik Olin Wright, "Working-Class Power, Capitalist-Class Interests, and Class Compromise," *American Journal of Sociology* 105 (2000): 957–1002.
4. Block and Burns, "Productivity as a Social Problem."
5. Lawrence Mishel, Josh Bivens, Elise Gould, and Heidi Shierholz, *The State of Working America*, An Economic Policy Institute Book, 12th ed. (Ithaca, NY: ILR Press, 2012), 392.
6. Ibid., 387.
7. Board of Governors of the Federal Reserve System, *Federal Reserve Bulletin*, Volume 98(2) (2012), accessed http://www.federalreserve.gov/pubs/bulletin/2012/PDF/scf12.pdf
8. Yacine A t-Shalia, Jonathan Parker, and Motohiro Yogo, "Luxury Goods and the Equity Premium," *Journal of Finance* 59 (2004): 2186–2222.
9. Financial Advisors, , *Mergers and Acquisitions Review, 2011*. Thomson Reuters, accessed June 23, 2013, http://dmi.thomsonreuters.com/Content/Files/4Q11_MA_Financial_Advisory_Review.pdf#page=4

10. Donald L. Barlett and James B. Steele, *America: What Went Wrong?* (Kansas City, MO: Andrews McMeel, 1992), v–xii.
11. See David M. Gordon, *Fat and Mean: The Corporate Squeeze of Working Americans and the Myth of Managerial Downsizing* (New York: Martin Kessler Books, 1996), and Barlett and Steele, *America: What Went Wrong?*, v–xii.
12. Barlett and Steele, *America: What Went Wrong?*, v–vxii.
13. See, for example, James K. Glassman and Kevin A. Hassett, *Dow 36,000: The New Strategy for Profiting from the Coming Rise in the Stock Market* (New York: Crown Business, 1999).
14. Joseph E. Stiglitz, *The Roaring Nineties* (New York: W.W. Norton, 2003), 241–68.
15. See David Cay Johnston, *Perfectly Legal: The Covert Campaign to Rig Our Tax System to Benefit the Super Rich—And Cheat Everybody Else* (New York: Portfolio Hardcover, 2003), 215–28, and Stiglitz, *The Roaring Nineties*, 115–39.
16. Reuters, "Lehman Brothers Bankruptcy: Bank Wins Approval to End Largest Bankruptcy in U.S. History," *Huffington Post*, December 6, 2011, accessed June 7, 2013, http://www.huffingtonpost.com/2011/12/06/lehman-brothers-bankruptcy_n_1131925.html
17. Bethany McLean and Peter Ekland, *The Smartest Guys in the Room: The Amazing Rise and Scandalous Fall of Enron* (New York: Fortune, 2003).
18. Ben Protess and Peter Lattman, "In Case against SAC Capital, A Show of Force," Dealb%k, *New York Times*. July 24, 2013, accessed July 27, 2013, http://dealbook.nytimes.com/2013/07/24/indictment-of-fund-is-a-rare-and-bold-move/?emc=eta1&_r=0
19. Stiglitz, *The Roaring Nineties*.
20. Jim Hightower, *Thieves in High Places: They've Stolen Our Country—And It's Time to Take It Back* (New York: Penguin Group, 2003), 56.
21. Susan E. Fleck, "International Comparisons of Hours Worked: An Assessment of the Statistics," *Monthly Labor Review* (May 2009): 31.
22. United States Department of Labor, Bureau of Labor Statistics, Business Employment Dynamics, Various Years, accessed July 7, 2013, http://www.bls.gov/bdm/
23. Some economists would argue that productivity gains should be paid to marginal workers, not average workers. See Michael Mandel, *The High-Risk Society: Peril and Promise in the New Economy* (New York: Times Business, 1996), 23–74.
24. United States Department of Commerce, U.S. Census Bureau, *Statistical Abstract of the United States, 2004–2005*, accessed June 2, 2013, http://www.census.gov/prod/www/statistical_abstract.html, ; Kaiser Family Foundation, "Average Family Premium per Enrolled Employee for Employer-Based Health Insurance," accessed June 2, 2013, http://kff.org/other/state-indicator/family-coverage/

CHAPTER 5

Where Did All That Credit Come From?

For two months now, federal banking regulators have signaled their discomfort about the explosive rise in risky mortgage loans. . . . The impact so far? Almost nil.

—*New York Times*, July 15, 2005[1]

We can show that productivity has reached its highest levels since the 1960s, but tracing where these gains have gone is tricky. Evidence suggests that much of these gains have been siphoned off by corporate executives in big pay packages and investors and speculators looking for deals, jeopardizing the middle class. Incomes and earnings have stagnated and wage inequality has risen, and only since 2008–2009 have American consumers stopped buying products and services at unprecedented rates as consumer confidence declined.[2] To understand how this paradox happened, we must examine the rapidly expanding pool of credit provided by the financial services industry. Basic changes in this industry have allowed for the rapid expansion of credit of all kinds, miring the middle class in ever-expanding debt.

The deregulation of the banking industry during the 1980s set the stage for the transformation of the consumer credit landscape. Limits on the maximum interest rates that lenders could charge were lifted, constraints on securities dealings were removed, and interstate branch banking was allowed. These changes led to a dramatic rise in the types of credit available to consumers and the profitability of lending. The number of credit card users and the levels of debt carried on credit cards have skyrocketed since the 1980s. Home equity loans, leased vehicles, car title loans, pawnshops, and rent-to-own stores

The banking and financial services industry uses various terms to describe different types of credit instruments and the relationships between what you borrow and what you pay, and their resulting profit or loss. Some of these terms describe unscrupulous and questionable practices that consumers should be on the lookout for. The list below covers most of the terms that are used in this chapter.

Annual percentage rate (APR)—an interest rate designed to measure the true cost of loans, including fees and pre-paid interest. Lenders are required to disclose the annual percentage rates on loans as part of Federal Truth in Lending laws.

Asset-backed securities—bonds that represent pools of loans of similar types, duration, and interest rates. Individual lenders such as banks and financial-services companies recover cash quickly by selling their loans to asset-backed securities packagers. Home equity loans and credit cards accounted for 46 percent of the asset-backed securities market in 2004.

Bank spread—the difference between the interest rate a bank charges borrowers and the interest rate they pay to depositors, or the interest rate they pay on the money they borrow.

Car-title loans—loans extended with car titles used as collateral. Interest rates on car-title loans are usually much higher than rates on conventional loans and credit cards. To qualify, the loan applicant must own a car.

Close-end lease—a fixed-rate lease (usually for cars) in which the leaser agrees to fixed-lease payments representing the depreciation of the car over the duration of the lease. If the vehicle depreciates more than the amount covered by the lease, the car dealership is responsible for the loss. In an open-end lease, the person leasing the car is responsible for the loss.

Credit-card rate—the interest rate that credit card issuers charge users on their balances.

Equity stripping—depleting the borrower's equity (ownership) in property through deceptive loan practices, refinancing, and fee packing. Through equity stripping practices, the borrower's equity is transferred to the lender.

Federal Deposit Insurance Corporation (FDIC)—an independent U.S. federal executive agency that insures individual bank deposits up to $250,000. The FDIC was created in 1933 to avoid the economic consequences of bank failures during the Great Depression, when banks could not return money deposited in them. The FDIC is managed by a five-member board of directors, appointed by the president with the consent of the Senate. Deposits are covered in banks, the Federal Reserve system, and some state banks.

Federal Reserve rate—the interest rate the Federal Reserve Bank charges banks for "overnight" borrowing from the Federal Reserve Bank. This particular number receives a lot of press because it reflects the Federal Reserve Bank's estimate of how the economy is working overall. Increases in Federal Reserve rates usually signal that the Federal Reserve (or "Fed") thinks the economy needs to slow down because inflation is threatening. Decreases in Federal Reserve rates are designed to stimulate borrowing and more economic activity.

Federal Savings and Loan Insurance Corporation (FSLIC)—formerly a government corporation under the direction of the former Federal Home Loan Bank Board, the FSLIC insured deposits at savings institutions. Congress authorized the FSLIC in the National Housing Act of 1934, and it was abolished under the Financial Institutions Reform, Recovery, and Enforcement Act of 1989. Its deposit insurance function was assumed by a new insurance fund, the Savings Association Insurance Fund (SAIF), administered by the Federal Deposit Insurance Corporation (FDIC).

Fee packing—attaching excessive fees and ancillary products onto loans in an attempt to increase the lenders' profit.

Home equity credit—credit offered to a borrower based on the amount of equity the borrower has in his or her house (the portion of the house the borrower owns or has paid off, usually reflecting the principal of the mortgage plus any appreciation or increase in value of the property).

Loan flipping—the repeated refinancing of existing loans so that lenders can earn more fees.

Loan-to-value (LTV) ratio—a value determined by dividing the total amount of the loan by the appraised value of the property. For lenders, high LTV ratios represent more risky loans than low LTV ratios. Loans for more money than an appraised property is worth (for example, a "125 percent mortgage") have loan-to-value ratios greater than 1.

Prime rate—interest rates charged by banks and financial service lenders to their most credit-worthy customers.

Self-banking—refers to people who do not have checking or savings accounts at banks or savings and loan institutions.

Subprime loans—loans offered at an interest rate above the prime lending rate to people who do not qualify for prime-rate loans.

Exhibit 5.1 A Primer on Banking and Finance Terms

have become popular ways for middle class Americans to access credit and fall further into debt. Investors have fueled the lending industry by purchasing asset-backed securities that help lenders spread the risk of lending and further maximize profits. Middle class Americans are trapped in a work-and-spend cycle that has only recently slowed down.

The Evolution of Consumer Credit

Prostitution may be the world's oldest profession, but in ubiquity and longevity, the practice of extending credit surely comes in a close second. Since biblical times, lenders have played an important role in the expansion of commerce and nations. Columbus never would have "sailed the ocean blue" if not for funds provided by Queen Isabella and the Spanish government. Early American pioneers never could have survived harsh prairie life if not for general stores extending personal credit lines to be repaid after the harvest, allowing struggling farmers to purchase seed, tools, and other supplies. In growing cities across the country during the first half of the twentieth century, installment plans allowed cash-poor urban dwellers to fill their homes with furniture as they pursued the American dream.

Throughout World War II, many businesses offered payment cards and/ or installment plans to customers as a way to encourage and facilitate the purchase of their products. Credit cards that could be used at a wide range of unaffiliated businesses were practically nonexistent; not until the Diners Club International Card was issued in 1950, followed by American Express and Carte Blanche in 1958, did this practice take off on a large scale.[3] These early forms of "plastic" were charge cards, requiring payment of bills upon receipt, rather than credit cards. The creation of credit card giants like Visa and MasterCard in the mid-1960s revolutionized the credit industry. Their cards could be used at a variety of establishments and the balances did not have to be paid each month but could instead be rolled over to the next payment cycle.[4]

As Robert Manning points out, in post-industrial society the economic balance of power has shifted from industry to banking: "General Electric's GE Capital (consumer credit) division generates higher profits than its core manufacturing division."[5] The policy changes of the deregulation of the banking industry during the 1980s led to increased interstate banking, the consolidation of the financial industry, and a dramatic increase in the maximum interest rates and fees that lenders could charge. Lenders scrambled to capitalize on this favorable financial environment by issuing more credit cards and expanding the pool of potential borrowers by developing other forms of lending. These other forms include personal credit cards, home equity loans, "no money down" car loans and leases, rent-to-own plans, title loans, check cashing, and other "fringe banking" practices. To understand why Americans now have so many different ways to borrow money, we must examine how the banking industry has changed over the last century.

The Deregulation of the Banking Industry: A Sleepy Industry Wakes Up

Until the 1980s, the banking industry was guided and regulated by Depression-era laws that limited the types of loans banks could issue, the reserves that banks were required to have on hand to cover their deposits and loans, the interest rates they could charge, and their ability to open branch banks. This legislation also produced the Federal Deposit Insurance Corporation (FDIC) for banks, and the Federal Savings and Loan Insurance Corporation for savings and loan businesses.

The 1978 Supreme Court decision in *Marquette National Bank of Minneapolis v. First Omaha Service Corp.*, which ruled that lenders could charge the highest interest rate allowed in their state regardless of a lower rate limitation in the customer's state of residence,[6] had a profound impact on consumer lending and usury laws. The practical effect of the *Marquette* decision was to force states to relax their usury laws or risk losing banking business as banks moved to states with higher rate ceilings. This judicial decision, coupled with the legislative changes to the banking industry discussed below, set the stage for the current state of the industry: "The average 18 percent rate that consumers have been paying on credit cards would have landed the credit company executives in the penitentiary twenty years ago. Today it lands the same executives in flattering profile stories in *Forbes* and *BusinessWeek*."[7]

The formal deregulation of the banking industry led to three important changes: maximum interest rates on bank deposits were eliminated, constraints on securities dealing were removed, and interstate branch banking blossomed.[8] The 1956 Bank Holding Company Act prohibited out-of-state holding companies from operating in several states unless both states involved explicitly allowed it. Interstate banking was effectively prohibited from the mid-1950s until 1980.[9] From the 1960s until the late 1990s, the number of bank branches, including supermarket branches—i.e., branches that provide a reduced set of banking products—grew dramatically.[10]

Since the 1980s there has been steady consolidation of the banking industry. We can see this trend in the growing number of mergers and the amount of assets acquired in these acquisitions. In 1980, a total of 190 acquisitions took place, with a value of about $10 billion; in 1990, there were 366, valued at approximately $45 billion; in 1998, 518, valued at nearly $630 billion; and in 2009, there were 1800, valued at $500 billion.[11] Mergers between banks, brokerages, and investment banks—for example, the $21 billion merger of Morgan Stanley and Dean Witter Discover in 1997—further consolidated the financial industry.[12] The majority of bank mergers represented attempts to break into new geographic markets by extending the markets served (see Appendix Exhibit 5.1).[13]

Savings and loan (S&L) associations were also affected by this deregulation, leading to a debacle in the late 1980s that cost taxpayers dearly.[14] At the start of the decade, federally chartered S&Ls had to keep almost all their loans in relatively stable and safe home mortgages. Changes to federal law in 1982 reduced restrictions on how S&Ls invested; for example, they could now invest completely in commercial real estate ventures—a much riskier form of investment than home mortgages.[15]

S&Ls gambled with their federally guaranteed deposits as they tried to cash in on the changes. As a result, thousands of S&Ls became insolvent and the industry collapsed. The federal government bailed out these failing S&Ls—with taxpayers footing the bill, at an estimated total cost of $300–$500 billion.[16] Post-S&L crash legislation—for example, the Gramm-Leach-Bliley Act of 2000[17]—opened the door for further industry consolidation by allowing banking, securities, and insurance activities to be housed together.

Deregulation has also further split first-tier ("traditional") and second-tier ("fringe") banking. As first-tier banks across the country left inner cities to pursue the higher debt ceilings offered in other states, they were quickly replaced by a variety of companies seeking to fill the void and to profit while doing so. These second-tier financial companies, such as check cashing and payday loan services, pawnshops, and rent-to-own companies, appeal to customers who do not have access to traditional banks either because traditional banks have left the area or because of previous credit problems. This type of lending is very profitable: "Consumer-finance companies earn profits that make most businesses jealous. They routinely produce returns on assets that are three to four times what banks produce."[18]

Traditional banks have not completely forgotten the growing population of "self-banked" households, those without bank accounts: many first-tier banks provide fringe banks with the funds they need to operate. Some banks profit from reselling subprime loans through subsidiaries, while others earn profits by providing lines of credit to payday loan and check cashing centers.[19]

In addition to expanding the availability and types of credit, banking deregulation has also contributed to fraudulent and abusive lending practices. Federal Reserve Board Governor Edward Gramlich states, "The growth in numbers and types of subprime credit has been accompanied by disturbing reports of abusive mortgage practices. . . . Many incidents of fraud and abuse have been reported and in certain sections of large cities, mortgage foreclosures are rising to worrisome heights."[20] These practices include loan flipping (the repeated refinancing of existing loans to generate more fees to be paid by the borrower), fee packing (placing additional fees into a mortgage without the borrower's knowledge or understanding), and equity stripping (extending credit when the borrower does not have the ability to repay, then foreclosing on the home when the borrower can't keep up with payments).[21]

In *Merchants of Misery*, Michael Hudson describes the deceptive practices some predatory lenders use. Wilma Jean Henderson, mother of seven children and stepchildren, borrowed $2,000 from Associates Financial Services to fix her car. During the deal, "the loan officer flipped through the papers so that only the signature portion of the document showed, and some of the numbers on one document had not been filled in until after she signed it. She didn't read anything, she said, because 'I trusted him—to do right.'" She later learned that in addition to the $2,000 loan, she owed another $1,200 for three kinds of credit insurance and an auto club membership—"add-ons" that she knew nothing about.[22]

It doesn't take such fraudulent lending practices to trap borrowers in the vicious cycle of debt. Most borrowers are eager to apply for credit that can help them stay afloat.

A Credit Card for Everybody

Credit cards have become status symbols. If you want to show the world that you've made it, whip out your Platinum Visa; if you want to show your commitment to the environment, use your Sierra Club MasterCard the next time you buy a cup of organic, shade-grown, fair-trade coffee. Though credit cards were originally intended for those with high incomes, since the 1980s their issuers have dramatically expanded the market by targeting different groups and offering different products. Marketers first went after the middle class, and then the working class, including many of the blue- and white-collar workers who lost their jobs as a result of the trends discussed in Chapters 3 and 4. When these markets proved highly profitable, the industry shifted its attention to the poor, the elderly, and most recently, students. Robert Manning observes, "Ironically, it is easier for college students to obtain a credit card while in school than after they graduate and begin an entry-level job."[23] He warns that "we're going to see students routinely with $5,000 and $10,000 in credit card debt, which is subsidized by their ability to rotate into federally subsidized student loans, who are going to be entering a job market maxed out before they begin looking for a job."[24]

Credit card–issuing banks aggressively market to college students. As soon as students step onto campus to begin their academic career, they are often met by companies offering "freebies" with brand logos and "great deals" on credit cards. The low teaser rates, the free tchotchkes, and the lure of financial ease encourage students to get their cards quickly and to use them right away. Universities play an important role in setting up their students for future indebtedness by signing lucrative contracts with credit card–issuing banks that grant access to students.[25] The aggressive marketing of credit cards to students is problematic in part because of the very low levels of financial literacy among students and youth.[26] Mandell's study of American twelfth graders reveals that students who use credit cards have no more "financial literacy" about them than those who don't use them.[27]

Some companies have even turned their attention to children. In 2004, Sanrio announced the introduction of a "Hello Kitty"–brand debit card. Ads for the card on their Web site bubbled, "Freedom! You can use the Hello Kitty Debit MasterCard to shop 'til you drop!" The senior vice president of licensing for Sanrio, Bruce Giuliano, stated, "We think our target group will be from ten to fourteen, although it could certainly go younger."[28]

As a result of this aggressive marketing, the American youth is being socialized to live on debt, developing spending behaviors disconnected from financial realities. As discussed in Chapter 3, many graduates leave college already in a financial quagmire, with large credit card debts and student loan payments. Their financial difficulties can be made even worse as they struggle to find a job: employers can and often do look at credit scores during the hiring process. By "emphasizing financial independence and social indulgence, banks enabled cardholders to maintain the image of middle class respectability and the material accoutrements of economic success even as they struggled simply to stay afloat."[29]

We can see the dramatic rise of the credit card industry by examining the percentage of U.S. families using general-purpose credit cards. In 1970, about half of all families used these cards, but by 2001 usage had jumped by 50 percent to approximately three-quarters of all families. In 2001, 60 percent

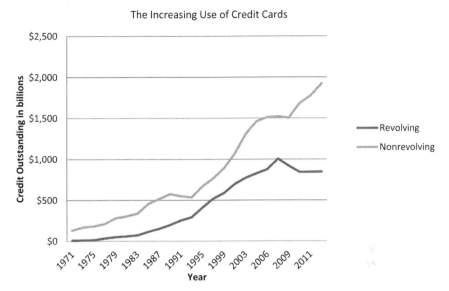

Exhibit 5.2 Consumer Credit Outstanding, 1971–2011, in Billions of Dollars

Source: Federal Reserve Statistical Release

of credit card users with incomes between $25,000 and $49,999 were carrying a balance (see Exhibit 5.3 and Appendix Exhibits 5.2 and 5.3). Average debt per household started to decline in the mid- to late 2000s, mainly because credit card companies wrote off delinquent credit card debt, not because people started to pay back their loans.

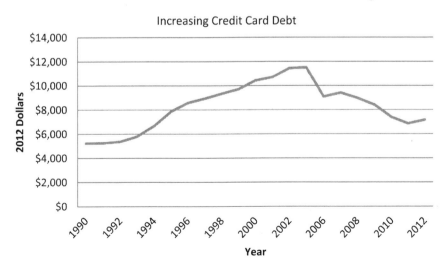

Exhibit 5.3 Average U.S. Credit Card Debt per Household (2012 Dollars)

Source: Nerdwallet.com

The credit card industry distinguishes between two types of credit card users: revolvers and convenience users. Revolvers carry debt from one month to the next, while convenience users pay off the outstanding debt at the end of each billing cycle. In 2012, 72 percent of Americans had credit cards; approximately 39 percent of these users were revolvers and the rest were convenience users. The numbers in 2007 were almost the reverse, with 72 percent of households carrying a balance as revolvers.[30] Convenience users are derided as "deadbeats" by some in the industry because they do not produce the revenues that revolvers do;[31] by paying their balances each month, these customers avoid paying interest or fees on their purchases. In essence, convenience users receive an interest-free loan from the card issuer for up to four weeks, the length of the billing cycle. Even so, credit card companies profit from convenience users because merchants pay issuing companies a fee based on a percentage of every purchase made with their cards. If all credit card users were convenience users the industry would not be nearly as profitable, and it is unlikely that we would have seen the dramatic rise in the number of credit cards issued in the past decades.

Lenders profit from revolvers through climbing interest rates and fees. For example, a borrower who pays only the minimum payment each month (usually either 2 percent or $10, whichever is higher) on a $4,000 credit card loan at 21 percent APR will pay about $5,592 in interest alone. At this rate, this $4,000 loan will cost $9,952 and take ten years to repay. But paying more than the minimum payment due, or even paying off the full debt each month, does not guarantee protection from increased rates or fees, for the following reason:

> A provision now built into most card agreements allows the companies to reset anyone's interest rate based on the size and status of other debts. And improvements in information technology and a change in federal law have spurred card companies in the last couple of years to check their customers' data regularly, not only when they review applications or notice missed payments.[32]

For decades now, credit card firms have argued that high fees and interest rates are necessary to cover losses due to fraud. This excuse is not valid, however, and examination of the losses due to fraud at Visa and MasterCard in the early 1990s, for example, revealed that a simple "surcharge of $2 or $3 per card per year would have paid for the cost of fraud to those companies. . . . Nevertheless, fraud offers the credit card industry a convenient excuse for high fees and interest rates."[33]

Another reason the credit card industry has become so profitable can be seen by looking at the "spread" (see Exhibit 5.4). Four key figures affect industry profits: the credit card's rate (the interest rate charged by lenders on credit card loans), the Federal Reserve rate (the interest rate charged by banks to other banks that need overnight loans), the prime rate (the base rate banks use in

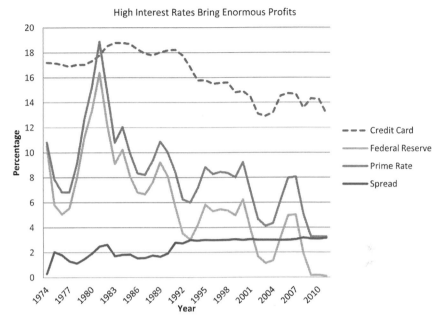

Exhibit 5.4 Average Annual Rates of Credit and Bank Spread, 1974–2011

Source: Federal Reserve Board

pricing commercial loans to their customers), and the bank spread (the difference between the rate banks charge to credit card borrowers and the rate they pay to borrow money from other banks to cover their needs). As Exhibit 5.4 shows, the prime rate closely follows the pattern of the Federal Reserve rate; this is because the prime rate is based on the Federal Reserve rate. Both these rates reached their peaks in the early 1980s, dropped dramatically through the mid-1990s, and then rose slightly after that. While the Fed and prime rate dropped, the credit card rate began this period around 18 percent (close to the prime rate) and has remained around 15 percent, so bank spread and profits from credit cards have remained very high.

The profitability of the credit card industry, the volume of credit extended, and the sheer number of credit cards available all point to the proliferation of credit card usage over the past decades. The ease of credit card use can also create a "temptation to imprudence": people buy more and more because of the ease of the transactions. Ritzer writes, "Consider the introduction of credit cards into fast-food restaurants. The use of credit cards leads to more sales and transactions that are 60 percent to 100 percent larger than cash transactions."[34]

In 2009, the Credit Card Accountability, Responsibility and Disclosures Act (referred to as the CARD Act) was signed into law. President Obama stated that the law is designed to bring "fairness, transparency, and accountability" to the credit card industry.[35] Additionally, a new federal agency was created, the Consumer Financial Protection Bureau (CFPB), charged with administering and monitoring the new law.

Other Sources of Ready Money: Home Equity—Betting the House?

Remember Bill and Sheryl, whom we first met in Chapter 2? Like millions of middle class Americans, they are caught in a web of financial precariousness and debt. Having already acquired $15,000 in revolving credit card debt, they took out a second mortgage to help cover their son's college tuition. Let's look at how this type of credit works and what it means for Bill and Sheryl's financial future.

There are two types of home equity credit. The first type, a closed-end loan (traditionally called a "home improvement" loan or second mortgage), provides borrowers with a fixed amount of money to perform improvements or repairs to their homes (although the money can be put toward a variety of uses—for example, buying a car, paying college tuition, or consolidating debt). These loans are repaid in installments over a three- to five-year period. The second type, the home equity line of credit, is similar to credit cards: consumers receive a credit limit based on the value of their homes. Home equity lines of credit can be tapped at any time during the designated life of the credit line, and can be paid back in part or in full at any time.[36]

Between 1996 and 1998, more than four million households shifted approximately $26 billion from credit card debt to home equity loans. Households use home equity loans for a wide range of purposes, the most common being debt consolidation, followed by home improvements, automobile financing, and education.[37] In 1997, almost 50 percent of home equity lines of credit borrowers used these funds to pay off other debts, while over 60 percent of traditional home equity borrowers did so.[38] Home equity loans represented 30 percent of the asset-backed securities market in 1997 and had a total value of $64 billion for that year;[39] the total value of outstanding home equity lines of credit continued to grow, reaching $450 billion by 2004 (see Exhibit 5.5).

Bill and Sheryl chose a home equity loan for a few different reasons. For one, there are tax benefits to this type of loan. The ability to deduct interest payments was once available for both mortgages and non–real estate consumer loans, but the Tax Reform Act of 1986 phased out tax deductions for non–real estate consumer loans, leaving this benefit in place for home equity credit lines. Home equity lines of credit are appealing also because their interest rates are considerably lower than those of credit cards, even at subprime home equity lenders.[40] And by the mid-1990s, lenders began to market home equity credit lines aggressively, dramatically increasing the ease of obtaining a loan, and in some cases extending credit beyond the value of the borrower's home, sometimes up to 200 percent above the value.[41] These characteristics—flexibility,

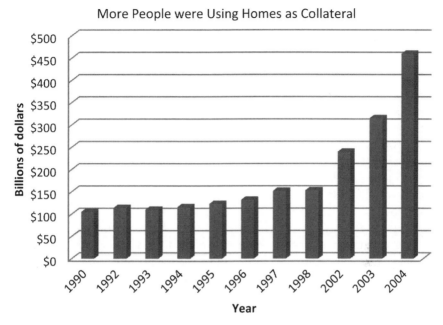

Exhibit 5.5 Home Equity Lines of Credit Outstanding, 1990–2004

Source: U.S. Census Bureau, Statistical Abstract of the United States; FDIC Statistics

tax breaks, lower interest rates, ease, and high loan-to-value ratio—make home equity loans extremely attractive.

Offering home equity loans is attractive to lenders because of the low delinquency and foreclosure rate.[42] Financially strapped Americans often have to decide which creditors get paid and which don't, and home equity and home mortgage payments get paid most frequently: collection managers report that home equity and home mortgage payments are most frequently paid on time, followed by auto loans, installment loans, retail credit, and bank credit cards. One reason for this may be that mortgage lenders do not have the same flexibility as other lenders when it comes to payment options; requirements set by the secondary market on this type of asset-backed security stipulates that they cannot even accept partial payments.[43]

However, if homeowners' overall debt becomes overwhelming, mortgages and second mortgages may lead to personal bankruptcy:

Homeownership is one of the most visible signs of participation in the middle class. Families in bankruptcy often want desperately to hold on to their homes, and their bankruptcy filings may be an attempt to clear out other debts so they can pour their often shrinking incomes into their mortgage payments. For many, hanging on to their home is no longer a matter of economic rationality; it has become a struggle to save an important part of their lives, one that a financial adviser might tell them to let go.[44]

The threat of bankruptcy may become even more common as certain types of home mortgages become more popular. In June 2005, Federal Reserve Chairman Alan Greenspan told Congress of his concern over the "dramatic increase in the prevalence of interest-only loans, as well as the introduction of other relatively exotic forms of adjustable-rate mortgages." Interest-only loans accounted for "at least 40 percent of purchase loans over $360,000 in areas with fast-rising home prices, like San Diego, Washington, Seattle, Reno, Atlanta and much of Northern California."[45] All of these places were in prime areas where housing prices collapsed during the 2008–2009 recession (see Chapter 7). These loans allow people to buy more expensive houses than they perhaps should because payments are much lower than those of more traditional mortgages. However, the payments may eventually jump, and unless the borrowers' incomes have done so as well, they may default on their loans and lose their houses.

Auto Leasing—Renting the Car

Over 85 percent of the U.S. population owns one or more vehicles,[46] and for most Americans owning a car is an economic and cultural necessity. New vehicles come with dazzling features marketed to the "responsible middle class family." Since the early 1990s, leasing instead of buying has become an increasingly popular way to get "that new car smell" (Exhibit 5.6). Leasing a vehicle basically finances the use of the vehicle instead of the purchase, offering customers a new vehicle every two or three years with no major repair risks. The most common type of vehicle lease is the closed-end lease.[47] Up-front costs when leasing may include the first month's payment, a refundable security deposit, capitalized cost reduction (basically a down payment), taxes, registration, and other fees, plus additional charges such as "gap insurance." The lease is for a set period of time and the cost is based on the anticipated depreciation of the vehicle, calculated by assigning a limit (generally about 10,000 to 12,000 miles a year) to the miles driven during the period of the lease, with any overage penalized an additional 12 to 25 cents per mile.

A closed-end lease allows the buyer to walk away at the end of the contract after returning the vehicle and paying any final costs, or to re-lease or buy the vehicle. While monthly lease payments are almost always lower than vehicle loan payments on the same vehicle, in the long run leasing is considerably more expensive. To buy a car and continue to drive it after the loan is paid off is always less expensive than leasing: the longer an owner drives a paid-off car, the more he or she saves.

As Exhibit 5.6 illustrates, despite its greater expense, more and more Americans—especially in the middle class—turned to leasing. After rising in

Despite the Higher Cost, Leasing is Increasingly Popular

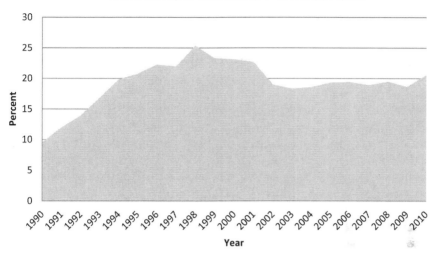

Exhibit 5.6 New Passenger Car Leases as a Percentage of All Passenger Car Sales, 1990–2010

Source: U.S. Department of Transportation, Bureau of Transportation Statistics

the early 1990s, the percentage of new car leases has stayed around 20 percent of all car sales. This increase was across all income brackets. For example, in 1989, there were too few households with annual incomes more than $25,000 but less than $50,000 that leased vehicles to even be counted. By 1995, 3.4 percent of these households were leasing, and by 1998, this percentage had grown to 5 percent. Households with annual incomes between $50,000 and $99,999 demonstrate a similar increase. In 1989, slightly over 6 percent of these households leased vehicles; by 1998, 9.5 percent did (Appendix Exhibit 5.4), but the numbers declined after the recession so that by 2012, only 6 percent of these American households were leasing vehicles.[48]

Pawnshops Go Middle Class

Bill and Sheryl's finances have gotten worse, and they have tapped out their credit card and home equity lines of credit. Their credit rating is shot and they need cash quickly to pay for an unexpected trip to the emergency room. What are their options?

One option is a trip to the pawnshop. The number of pawnshops nearly tripled since the start of banking deregulation in the 1980s. In 1985 there were 4,849 pawnshops in the United States; by the late 1990s the number had grown to approximately 14,000 and has stayed at or near that level since then. A drive through any major city reveals that this growth has taken place both in poor urban neighborhoods and the suburbs alike. Suburban strip malls and inner-city blocks are dotted with the red, white, and blue awnings of Cash America and other pawnshops.

Pawnshops used to be known as dark and dangerous, but now many are clean and well-lit. Still, their basic premise remains: they provide short-term loans based on collateral provided by the customer. Collateral can be guitars and other musical instruments, jewelry, stereo equipment, guns, leather jackets, watches, power tools—just about anything that has value.

All Bill and Sheryl need to do is to take something of value—for example, the guitar Sheryl bought Bill for his thirty-fifth birthday—to the pawnshop, and walk out with a cash loan, generally 25–30 percent of the item's appraised value, without having to go through a credit check or waiting to get approved by a loan officer. A typical loan is for 120 days, after which Bill and Sheryl can repay the loan in full (plus interest) and get the guitar back. If they do not have that much money, they can just pay the interest due and receive a "new" loan. If they default on the loan by not paying at least the interest due after 120 days, the pawnshop keeps the guitar and resells it to cover the original loan plus some profit. If this happens, Bill and Sheryl lose the guitar, but no further damage has been done to their credit rating and there are no additional fees or penalties.

Taking Your Pay before You Earn It: Check Cashing, Payday Loans, and Title Loans

Another outgrowth of banking deregulation is the propagation of check-cashing outlets (CCOs). In 2012, nearly 28 percent of Americans conducted some or all of their financial transactions outside of conventional banks, and as members of the "self-banked" population, they relied on check-cashing outlets to turn paychecks into cash.[49] Check-cashing outlets typically charge between 1 and 3.25 percent to cash government, payroll, and bank checks. Some also provide "payday loans," which are short-term loans generally between $100 and $300 given for a fixed fee payable to the lender that represents the finance charge, often ranging from 300 percent to 1,000 percent APR.[50]

Bill and Sheryl have pawned the possessions they can easily do without, but they still need another $100 in cash. To get a payday loan, Sheryl brings in some personal documents—a driver's license, checking account information, paycheck stubs, and a recent utility bill—and if her minimal requirements are met, she then writes a check for $115 (the amount of the loan plus the fee charged by the lender, in this case 391 percent APR) to the lender, who agrees to hold the check until her next payday. The good news is that Sheryl now has $100 cash in her pocket; the bad news is that at the end of the two weeks, if she cannot pay off the loan plus interest, she will have to pay another $15 in fees to roll over the loan. Assuming she is able to pay off the loan by the next due date, she has already paid $30 in fees for this $100 loan. This cycle is very difficult to break:

Once a consumer falls into the debt trap, lenders will use various methods of ensuring repayment. Most lenders threaten to cash the check that secures the loan. Since these borrowers may not have sufficient money in their account, the check will bounce, cause overdraft fees, and prevent them from using their checking account to pay other bills. Lenders also report borrowers to check reporting agencies, thus effectively barring them from writing checks at local stores.[51]

The number of payday lenders has exploded. There were fewer than 500 in the early 1990s, but there were approximately 12,000 in 2002 and over 20,000 in 2010.[52] The payday loan industry is extremely profitable; the Federal Reserve estimates that payday loan fee revenues were close to $2 billion in 2010.[53] In 2010, there were an estimated 180 million payday loans in the United States with a gross dollar volume of $29.[54]

A typical payday loan customer makes eleven transactions a year.[55] Who uses payday loans? The answer might surprise you. In 2004, the Community Financial Services Association of America, a trade group of the payday loan industry, released customer profile data revealing that 52 percent of payday loan users have incomes between $25,000 and $50,000, while an additional 25 percent have incomes greater than $50,000. The majority of payday loan users are married couples with children. Forty-two percent own their own homes and 94 percent have at least a high school diploma.[56] Watchdog groups such as the Consumers Union warn borrowers "to avoid payday lenders at all costs":[57]

Payday lenders claim they are the only option for debt-strapped consumers. **But borrowing more money at triple-digit interest rates is never the right solution for people in debt.** Instead, payday loans make problems worse. . . . In fact, because most consumers believe they could be prosecuted for passing a bad check, the payday loan suddenly becomes their priority debt. Thus, the original debt problems that brought them to the lender often cannot be resolved.[58]

Bob and Sheryl need still more money, now to cover the cost of some necessary home repairs, so they put up the title to their car as collateral. As with a payday loan, Bob and Sheryl sign over the title of their vehicle to the lender. If at the end of the loan term they are unable to repay the loan or pay minimum financing fees, the car is confiscated. Companies like FastCash and Fast Title Loan, which offer car title loans, now dot the United States, particularly in the South. Title loans are legal in twenty-five states, and are thriving in twelve.[59] These loans can be particularly dangerous for financially precarious households, because when the cars are confiscated to penalize for late payments, the household's source of transportation is gone, making transportation to work difficult or impossible.

Rent-to-Own or Rent-to-Drown?

Yet another way financially strapped Americans can maintain a middle class lifestyle is through rent-to-own stores. According to the Association for Progressive Rental Organizations, a national trade association devoted to the rental-purchase industry, the $5.7 billion rent-to-own industry, with over 5,500 businesses, serves approximately 2.8 million customers a year.[60] The rent-to-own industry began in the 1960s and differs from traditional retail credit sales. Customers rent items such as furniture, appliances, computers, or jewelry without credit checks or interest charges and retain the right to return the merchandise at any time. Customers can also purchase the merchandise at any time during the rental agreement (which is typically for either one week or one month). Renters pay as they go and credit is not extended, so customers do not acquire debt by engaging in rent-to-own agreements.

However, the costs of this tactic are extremely high: renters who rent to own a new stereo will pay approximately 3.5 times more for the stereo than if they bought it all at once from a chain retailer like Best Buy. A $300 television at Best Buy will cost over $1,000 through rent-to-own.[61]

According to industry statistics, 92 percent of rent-to-own customers have at least a high school diploma, and almost 69 percent of renters have annual household incomes between $24,000 and $49,999.[62] The average store has over 600 items for rent at any one time and has annual revenue of nearly $500,000. The average income per unit per month is approximately $65.[63]

The meteoric rise of the rent-to-own industry leader, Rent-A-Center (RAC), highlights the growing industry. From 1993 until 2000, RAC went from controlling 27 stores to over 2,000 in all fifty states, Washington, D.C. and Puerto Rico.[64] Annual RAC (traded as RCII) stock prices during this period increased each year. The company reported net earnings of $44 million in 2012.[65] As Robert Manning points out, these companies are "growing so large and so quickly that major manufacturers are eagerly courting them to forge strategic alliances. In spring 2000, for example, Gateway negotiated an exclusive rental-supply agreement with Rent-Way and its 1,100 stores for low-cost Internet-equipped computers."[66]

And to Spread the Risk, Investors Buy Asset-Backed Securities

At the start of this chapter we discussed how bank deregulation has affected the lending practices of both "traditional" and "fringe" banking. An important component of these changing practices has been the development of new ways for lenders to spread risk and thus be able to lend more and more. Credit securitization refers to a complex process of packaging, underwriting, and selling loans and other receivables as securities.[67] These securities are referred to as asset-backed securities (ABS), a general term that encompasses conventional home mortgages (i.e., mortgage-backed securities) and credit card loans (i.e., credit card asset-backed securities). In 2007, the ABS market was comprised of $6.6 trillion in tradable securities (see Appendix Exhibit 5.5). Approximately 70 percent of this market was mortgage-backed securities issued primarily by government-sponsored secondary market lenders such as Fannie Mae, Ginnie Mae, and Freddie Mac. The remaining 30 percent of the securitized asset market was backed by assets including home equity loans, vehicle loans, and credit cards. Credit card ABS comprise approximately $400 billion of this market.[68]

While the process of securitizing conventional mortgages has been around since the 1960s, it was not until the mid-1980s that credit card loans began to be bundled and sold. Banc One Corporation initiated the first issue of a credit card asset-backed security, a $50 million "Certificates for Amortizing Revolving Debts (CARDS)" issue that laid the foundation for subsequent securitizations.[69] Since its introduction, this process has become the primary way for the credit card industry to provide unsecured loans to consumers.[70] This process allows credit card issuers to spread the risk of lending you money, thereby making it more attractive to do so.

The basic process of securitizing credit card loans works as follows. A card issuer—let's call them BigBank—provides credit card loans to fifty customers, each of whom maintains a card balance of $1,000. BigBank then may decide to securitize these customers' receivables by placing them into a $50,000 "package." This package is then sold to a trust created for the exclusive purpose of purchasing loans from BigBank. Once the package is in the trust, securities (i.e., bonds) are created that are backed by the $50,000 and are sold to investors who then receive the payments that the customers are making on those loans. The price at which the security is traded is determined by the characteristics of the receivables that are pledged.

In 1989, the amount of consumer credit outstanding, as measured by pools of revolving securitized assets, was less than $18 billion. By 2003, it was nearly $400 billion, and on the brink of the 2008 recession it was $450 billion.[71] This market collapsed during the 2008–2009 recession as investors lost confidence in the ability of debt holders to pay off their debts (see Chapter 7). The majority of credit card asset-backed securities are purchased by institutional investors (Manning 2003 testimony). As Robert Manning (2003) suggests, this practice can lead to perverse results. For example, when institutional investors such as pension funds purchase credit card asset-backed securities, they are basically attempting to finance workers' future retirement by profiting on workers' current consumer debt.

Are Credit Cards and Pawnshops Substitutes for Getting Paid?

American consumers are offered ever-diversifying ways to borrow money against their future earnings. The percentage growth in mortgage and consumer credit debt has been impressive. The annual percentage growth in home mortgage debt ranged between 5 and 15 percent from 1980 to 2003 and only

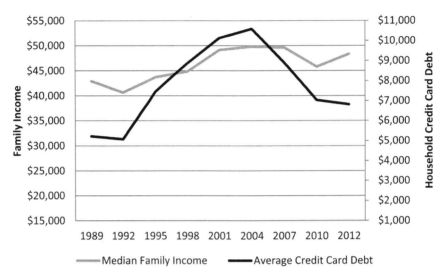

Exhibit 5.7 Median Before-Tax Family Income and Average Credit Card Debt per Household (2010 Dollars)

Source: Federal Reserve Bulletin; Nerdwallet.com

declined with the onset of the 2008 recession. The annual growth in consumer debt was between 5 and 18 percent in all but six years during this period (Appendix Exhibit 5.6). At the same time that real consumer purchasing power stagnates, the savings rate declines, and wages and incomes go flat for most Americans, all this credit suddenly becomes available to keep the consumer economy afloat (see Exhibit 5.7).

We are not suggesting that this state of affairs is a part of a master plan devised by corporate America or politicians in Washington, D.C. Nor did thousands of business owners simultaneously sit down one day and say, "Hey, I've got an idea—let's stop increasing the wages for our workers and then tell our banking buddies to make it easier for them to borrow money to buy things. That way, they'll never even notice the missing wages. Brilliant!" Instead, the confluence of the circumstances we've described over the past thirty-five years has led to the American middle class being given more and more credit in order to keep spending, thus maintaining the illusion of economic prosperity.

Some authors, such as John de Graaf and his coauthors in *Affluenza: The All-Consuming Epidemic* and Juliet Schor in *The Overspent American: Upscaling, Downshifting, and the New Consumer*, argue that the rampant consumerism of American culture is to blame for this outcome. Americans are in debt, they argue, because they can't stop buying things that they really don't need. But this problem is not caused simply by individual weakness or frivolity. Marketers and companies spend billions of dollars to *create* demand for products. The perpetual bombardment of glitz and glamour provided by television and the increasing commercialization of every aspect of our daily lives produce tremendous pressures to consume.[72] As Alan Wolfe writes, this is why "so many of the middle class Americans to whom we talked think that wearing school uniforms is a good idea—anything that detracts from the pressure of peers to buy more things would be welcome." Discussing these pressures, Denise Lott of Rancho Barnardo, California, said, "The values are so skewed. I think that it is very difficult to combat that. You know how kids are. They want what other kids have. They want expensive sneakers and jackets. They have to have these things."[73]

Rich Moroni, a onetime debt collector who switched careers to become a credit counselor, articulates how individual choices interact with structural issues to create problematic consumer spending:

> The bottom line for most people is they just simply don't think about what kind of money they make and what kind of lifestyle they're living. . . . And then add merchandisers and advertisers to that, and it's a formula for disaster for a lot of people.[74]

Other authors argue that the main culprit in the rise of consumer debt is not frivolous purchases but increased housing costs.[75] Regardless of what the American middle class is buying, the key to keeping the economy afloat is their spending. Workers who are in debt work more hours as they fall into the cycle of "work and spend."[76] This cycle is unnecessary and detrimental to the future of the American middle class. Most of the workplace changes that would enable the middle class to benefit from the productivity gains they've produced are in the hands of investors and financial elites.

Yet practical changes could help workers break out of this destructive work-and-spend cycle. In theory, we have several choices, each of which should have the same level of economic utility. Workers can work shorter hours as productivity rises without sacrificing their own welfare; they could take longer vacations, have more leisure time, take care of infants and sick relatives, travel, plant gardens, join civic clubs of various kinds, become more politically active, exercise, or get more sleep.[77]

The cycle of work and spend may be fanned by consumer tastes, but it is fueled by an economic system that will indenture its consumers, loaning money, stripping assets and income in interest payments and new loans, and issuing payday loans so that hard-earned paychecks are "spoken for" by the time they arrive. The system does everything it can to avoid simply paying people more money.

Discussion Questions

- What lessons have you learned from your family and friends about managing money?
- Which do you think is better, a credit card or a debit card?

- What are the benefits of having access to consumer credit? For you? For society?
- What are the drawbacks/dangers of having access to consumer credit? For you? For society?

Notes

1. Edmund L. Andrews, "A Hands-Off Policy on Mortgage Loans," *New York Times*, July 15, 2005, accessed May 13, 2013 http://www.nytimes.com/2005/07/15/business/15mortgage.html
2. Federal Reserve Bank of St. Louis, Economic Research, FRED Data, accessed May 13, 2013, http://research.stlouisfed.org/fred2/series/UMCSENT/
3. George Ritzer, *Expressing America: A Critique of the Global Credit Card Society* (Thousand Oaks, CA: Pine Forge Press, 1995), 36.
4. David S. Evans and Richard Schmalensee, *Paying with Plastic: The Digital Revolution in Buying and Borrowing* (Cambridge, MA: MIT Press, 1999), 61–77.
5. Robert D. Manning, *Credit Card Nation: The Consequences of America's Addiction to Credit* (New York: Basic Books, 2000), 4.
6. Diane Ellis, "The Effect of Consumer Interest Rate Deregulation on Credit Card Volumes, Charge-Offs, and the Personal Bankruptcy Rate" *FDIC Bank Trends* (March 1998), accessed http://www.fdic.gov/bank/analytical/bank/bt_9805.html
7. Teresa A. Sullivan, Elizabeth Warren, and Jay L. Westbrook, *The Fragile Middle Class: Americans in Debt* (New Haven, CT: Yale University Press, 2000), 18.
8. Bernard Shull and Gerald A. Hanweck, *Bank Mergers in a Deregulated Environment: Promise and Peril* (Westport, CT: Quorum Books, 2001).
9. Evans and Schmalensee, *Paying with Plastic*.
10. Gary Dymski, *The Bank Merger Wave: The Economic Causes and Social Consequences of Financial Consolidation* (Armonk, NY: M.E. Sharpe, 1999).
11. Stephen A. Rhoades, "Bank Mergers and Banking Structure in the United States, 1990–1998," Federal Reserve Staff Study 174 (2000); The Institute of Mergers, Acquisitions and Alliances (IMAA), accessed http://www.imaa-institute.org/statistics-mergers-acquisitions.html#M&A_Ind_Banks
12. Evans and Schmalensee, *Paying with Plastic*, 45.
13. Dymski, *The Bank Merger Wave*, 51.
14. See Kevin Phillips, *The Politics of Rich and Poor: Wealth and the American Electorate in the Reagan Aftermath* (New York: Random House, 1990), and Shull and Hanweck, *Bank Mergers in a Deregulated Environment*.
15. Phillips, *The Politics of Rich and Poor*, 97.
16. Ibid., 87.
17. For more on the Gramm-Leach-Bliley Act, see Federal Trade Commission reports available at the Bureau of Consumer Protection Business Center website, accessed June 14, 2013, http://business.ftc.gov/privacy-and-security/gramm-leach-bliley-act
18. Michael Hudson, *Merchants of Misery: How Corporate America Profits from Poverty* (Monroe, ME: Common Courage Press, 1996), 29.
19. Manning, *Credit Card Nation*, 225.
20. Federal Reserve Board, "Remarks by Governor Edward M. Gramlich at the Texas Association of Bank Counsel 27th Annual Meeting," October 9, 2003, accessed http://www.federalreserve.gov/BOARDDOCS/Speeches/2003/20031009/
21. Jerry Anthony, "Home Burdens: The High Costs of Home Ownership," in *Broke: How Debt Bankrupts the Middle Class*, ed. Katherine Porter (Palo Alto, CA: Stanford University Press, 2012), 65–84; Marianne Culhane, "No Forwarding Address: Losing Homes in Bankruptcy," in *Broke: How Debt Bankrupts the Middle Class*, 119–135.
22. Hudson, *Merchants of Misery*, 3.

23. Manning, *Credit Card Nation*, 5.
24. Robert D. Manning, prepared statement for hearing on "Giving Consumers Credit: How Is the Credit Card Industry Treating Its Customers?" (Subcommittee on Financial Institutions and Consumer Credit, U.S. House of Representatives, Washington, D.C., November 1, 2001, 3), accessed http://www.creditcardnation.com/pdfs/110101rm.pdf
25. See Manning, *Credit Card Nation*, and prepared statement for hearing on "The Role of FCRA in the Credit Granting Process" (Subcommittee on Financial Institutions and Consumer Credit, U.S. House of Representatives, Washington, D.C., June 12, 2003), accessed http://www.creditcardnation.com/pdfs/061203rm.pdf
26. See Lewis Mandell, "Our Vulnerable Youth: The Financial Literacy of American 12th Graders—A Failure by Any Measurement," *Credit Union Magazine*, January 1999; Manning, "The Role of FCRA in the Credit Granting Process"; Manning, prepared statement for hearing on "Current Legal and Regulatory Requirements and Industry Practices for Card Issuers with Respect to Consumer Disclosures and Marketing Efforts" (U.S. Senate Committee on Banking, Housing, and Urban Affairs, May 17, 2005), accessed http://banking.senate.gov/_files/manning.pdf
27. Mandell, "Our Vulnerable Youth."
28. Caroline E. Mayer, "Girls Go from Hello Kitty to Hello Debit Card: Brand's Power Tapped to Reach Youth," *Washington Post*, October 3, 2004, http://www.washingtonpost.com/wp-dyn/articles/A2959–2004Oct2.html
29. Ibid., 22–23.
30. http://www.creditcards.com/credit-card-news/credit-card-industry-facts-personal-debt-statistics-1276.php
31. Manning, *Credit Card Nation*, and "Current Legal and Regulatory Requirements," 3.
32. Jennifer Bayot, "Surprise Jumps in Credit Rates Bring Scrutiny," *New York Times*, May 29, 2003.
33. Ritzer, *Expressing America*, 85.
34. Ibid., 60.
35. http://www.consumerfinance.gov/credit-cards/credit-card-act/feb2011-factsheet/
36. Richard F. DeMong and John H. Lindgren, Jr., "How Lenders Are Marketing Home Equity Products," *Journal of Retail Banking Services* XXI, 1 (1999): 31–37.
37. Linda Punch, "The Home Equity Threat," *Credit Card Management* (1998), 113.
38. U.S. Census Bureau, *Statistical Abstract of the United States, 2000* (Washington, D.C., Government Printing Office, 2001), 517, accessed http://www.census.gov/prod/2001pubs/statab/sec16.pdf
39. Thomas Financial Inc., "Introduction and Summary," *Mortgage-Backed Securities Letter* 13 (December 1998), 1.
40. Punch, "The Home Equity Threat," 116.
41. Ibid.
42. DeMong and Lindgren, "How Lenders Are Marketing Home Equity Products."
43. Joanne Cleaver, "Moving up to the Top of the Pile," *Credit Card Management* 16, 2 (2003): 48–51.
44. Sullivan, Warren, and Westbrook, *The Fragile Middle Class*, 21–22.
45. David Leonhardt and Motoko Rich, "The Trillion-Dollar Bet," *New York Times,* Real Estate Section, June 16, 2005.
46. Ana Aizcorbe and Martha Starr-McCluer, "Vehicle Ownership, Vehicle Acquisition and the Growth of Auto Leasing: Evidence from Consumer Surveys," Federal Reserve Board of Governors, 1996,. accessed www.federalreserve.gov/PUBS/feds/1996/199635/199635pap.pdf
47. Federal Reserve Board, "Vehicle Leasing: Quick Consumer Guide," May 2013, accessed May 12, 2013, http://www.federalreserve.gov/pubs/leasing/
48. Hedges & Company. http://hedgescompany.com/auto-mailing-lists-and-marketing
49. *Forbes,* "Who Needs Banks? The Number of Americans without Bank Accounts Rises," September 17, 2012, accessed http://www.forbes.com/sites/halahtouryalai/2012/09/17/who-needs-banks-number-of-americans-without-bank-accounts-rises/

50. See Federal Deposit Insurance Corporation, "Payday Lending" (2003), accessed http://www.fdic.gov/regulations/safety/payday/; and the Consumers Union, "Payday Lenders Burden Working Families and the U.S. Armed Forces" (2003), accessed http://www.consumersunion.org/pdf/payday-703.pdf#search='Payday%20Lenders%20Burden%20Working%20Families%20'

51. Consumers Union, "Payday Lenders Burden Working Families."

52. Community Financial Services Association of America, "Payday Advance Industry Overview" (2004), accessed http://www.cfsa.net/govrelat/PaydayAdvanceIndustryOverview; National People's Action, "Profiting from Poverty," January 2012, accessed http://npa-us.org/files/profiting_from_poverty_npa_payday_loan_report_jan_2012_0.pdf

53. Cited in Manning, *Credit Card Nation*, 205; National People's Action, "Profiting from Poverty."

54. Federal Deposit Insurance Corporation, "Payday Lending" (2003), accessed http://www.fdic.gov/regulations/safety/payday/; National People's Action, "Profiting from Poverty."

55. Consumers Union, "Payday Lenders Burden Working Families."

56. Community Financial Services Association of America, "Payday Advance Industry Overview."

57. Consumers Union, "Payday Lenders Burden Working Families."

58. Consumers Union, "Fact Sheet on Payday Loans" (2004), accessed http://www.consumersunion.org/finance/paydayfact.htm

59. Manning, *Credit Card Nation*, 205–6.

60. The Association of Progressive Rental Organizations, "Industry Overview," accessed March 21, 2006, http://www.rtohq.org/About_rent-to-own/Industry_overview/index.aspx#industry

61. Manning, *Credit Card Nation*, 215.

62. The Association of Progressive Rental Organizations, "Industry Overview"; cf. the discussion of results from the FTC study of rent-to-own business in Manning, *Credit Card Nation*, 210.

63. The Association of Progressive Rental Organizations, "Industry Overview."

64. Manning, *Credit Card Nation*, 210.

65. Rent-A-Center, "Company Fact Sheet" (2004), accessed http://www6.rentacenter.com/site/page/pg4425.html. The Rent-A-Center NASDAQ listing is available at Yahoo Finance.

66. Manning, *Credit Card Nation*, 208.

67. James A. Rosenthal and Juan M. Ocampo, *Securitization of Credit: Inside the New Technology of Finance* (New York: Wiley, 1988).

68. Mark Furletti, discussion paper, "An Overview of Credit Card Asset-Backed Securities" (Payment Cards Center, Federal Reserve Bank of Philadelphia, 2002), accessed http://www.phil.frb.org/pcc/workshops/workshop11.pdf

69. Rosenthal and Ocampo, *Securitization of Credit*, 120.

70. Furletti, "An Overview of Credit Card Asset-Backed Securities."

71. Ibid.

72. See George Ritzer, *Explorations in the Sociology of Consumption: Fast Food, Credit Cards, and Casinos* (Thousand Oaks, CA: Sage Publications, 2001) and *The Globalization of Nothing* (Thousand Oaks, CA: Pine Forge Press, 2004).

73. Alan Wolfe, *One Nation, After All* (New York: Viking 1998), 118.

74. Juliet B. Schor, *The Overspent American: Upscaling, Downshifting, and the New Consumer* (New York: Basic Books, 1998), 73.

75. Elizabeth Warren and Amelia Warren Tyagi, *The Two-Income Trap: Why Middle Class Mothers and Fathers Are Going Broke* (New York: Basic Books, 2003).

76. Juliet B. Schor, *The Overspent American*, 73.

77. For more on civic activity, see Robert D. Putnam, *Bowling Alone: The Collapse and Revival of American Community* (New York: Simon and Schuster, 2000).

CHAPTER 6

From Washington to Wall Street
Marketing the Illusion

Nothing is more important in the face of a war than cutting taxes.
—House Majority Leader Tom DeLay, March 12, 2003

We're an empire now, and when we act, we create our own reality. And while you're studying that reality—judiciously, as you will—we'll act again, creating other new realities, which you can study too, and that's how things will sort out. We're history's actors . . . and you, all of you, will be left to just study what we do.

—Karl Rove, 2001

The private sector is not solely to blame for the economic distress of the middle class. The public sector persists in marketing the misleading illusion that American prosperity is tied to the affluence of the wealthy, and that government policies that improve the economic prospects of the wealthy will trickle down to the middle class. Neoconservative politics and supply-side economics, manifested through a combination of tax cuts, deregulation, corporate tax avoidance, and a shift of tax burdens onto earned income and away from unearned income, have fundamentally shaped the economic realities of the middle class. The increased presence of corporate lobbyists in Washington has contributed to policies that benefit investors by emphasizing short-term economic growth. But the "supply-side miracle" has yet to materialize for the middle class; instead of improving the state of those indentured to big banks and financial houses, government has only added to their plight.

The Neoconservative Persuasion

The reelection of George W. Bush in 2004 marked an important victory for neoconservatives. During his first term, Bush pushed through a major tax cut ostensibly to help the middle class that primarily benefited the wealthy, sought greater deregulation in multiple arenas, froze or cut funding for many government social programs, and dramatically increased spending on homeland security and defense. This combination of economic, social, and foreign policy reflects the neoconservative outlook of the administration.

Economist and op-ed writer Paul Krugman and other critics challenged that the Bush administration, with intellectual and rhetorical guidance from think tanks like the Heritage Foundation, were engaging in a "starve the beast" strategy that sought to "slash government programs that help the poor and middle class, and use that savings to cut taxes for the rich."[1]

Neoconservatives refuted this characterization; neoconservatism is, William Kristol has written, "not a movement, as its conspiratorial critics would have it . . . [it is] a 'persuasion,' one that manifests itself over time, but erratically, and one whose meaning we clearly glimpse only in retrospect."[2] One uniting theme of neoconservative thought is a focus on economic growth, especially cutting taxes.

Two of the most prominent and influential neoconservative thinks tanks, the Heritage Foundation and the American Enterprise Institute, have developed a cottage industry for promoting tax cuts. Of course, not all tax cuts are equal. Members of these think tanks can and do criticize specific legislation promoted by the administration or Congress. On the 2001 tax rebates, Brian Riedl of the Heritage Foundation wrote:

> Washington borrowed billions from investors and then mailed that money to families in the form of $600 checks. This simple transfer of existing income had a predictable effect: consumer spending increased and investment spending decreased by a corresponding amount. No new wealth was created because the tax rebate was unrelated to productive behavior—no one had to work, save, or invest more in order to receive a rebate.[3]

Reidl argues that supply-side tax cuts, reducing marginal rates on business and workers, are effective because they "maximize long-run economic growth, which in turn raises income across the board."[4]

One aspect of the neoconservatives' economic policy represents an important break from their conservative predecessors:

> Neocons have abandoned the adherence to balanced budgets that had long been a cornerstone of conservative policy. To conservatives, the budget must be balanced, and the policies that government pursues

are limited by the need to be fiscally responsible, thus defined. Neocons elevated policy over budgets. As Irving Kristol puts it, "We should figure out what we want before we calculate what we can afford, not the reverse, which is the normal conservative predisposition."[5]

Indeed, the concern for balanced budgets that weighed so heavily on the minds of Republicans and Democrats during the 1990s has been thoroughly abandoned by neoconservatives. According to Stelzer,

> neoconservatives live quite comfortably with budget deficits, some because they believe that appropriate tax policies will shrink the deficits to manageable proportions, others because they believe deficits to be largely irrelevant to an economy's performance, and still others because they believe deficits prevent the adoption of expensive additions to an already-generous welfare state.[6]

The Triumph of Supply-Side Economics

As we saw in Chapter 3, the supply-side economic policies introduced by the Reagan administration did not result in boom times. Despite this, a national assumption that supply-side economics was the best method persisted. The possibility that tax cuts for the wealthy would benefit the middle class was not only too good to be true, it was irresistible as a political strategy: the middle class simply had to wait for the results, for prosperity was just around the corner. When the new effects didn't materialize for most of the middle class, the new solution was logical and direct: tax cuts were obviously not deep enough and not pervasive enough, so we needed more of the same thing.

The Effects of Tax Cuts

The results of the supply-side tax cuts and the fiscal policies that followed in the 1980s and early 1990s added further problems to the plight of the middle class. Federal tax rates shifted radically in the direction of providing substantial tax breaks for the already wealthy. But instead of watching the money roll in, the federal government ran record deficits and accumulated unprecedented levels of public debt. Tax receipts, never high as a percentage of GDP by international standards, dipped to a level just above Mexico's. Corporations in particular received huge tax breaks and in Washington the number of permanent lobbyists, most of them representing corporate interests, increased substantially.

The middle class saw very little of the Reagan tax cuts, and the effective tax rate change was close to zero for virtually all American taxpayers below the top 10 percent of income earners. By contrast, wealthy households in the

United States saw big drops in their effective taxation. Kevin Phillips describes the net effect of these tax cuts and other changes that came with them as a "capitalist heyday," comparable to the 1890s and the 1920s.[7]

Moreover, the so-called "supply-side miracle"—the increase in tax revenues that would follow from lowering tax rates—never materialized. What did materialize was a sea of government "red ink" (see Exhibit 6.1). The federal debt, about $930 billion in 1980, ballooned to $2 trillion by mid-decade and $4 trillion by the early 1990s, to $9 trillion on the eve of the 2008 recession (in spite of a robust economic expansion from 2003–2008 and the 2004 Bush tax cuts) and $16 trillion as of 2012, as the Obama administration dealt with the aftermath of the latest economic meltdown (see Chapter 7).[8]

Of course, plenty of evidence suggests that the United States was not on the side of the Laffer curve where reducing tax rates would increase tax revenues, producing a situation in which tax cuts pay for themselves. Some of this evidence comes from international comparisons, since the United States collects the lowest percentage of taxes as a percentage of total GDP of almost any other industrialized country.

The federal government's retreat from taxing the rich and its inability to curb budget deficits had another insidious effect on wealth distribution (see Appendix Exhibit 6.1). Saddled with a tight money supply, the United States

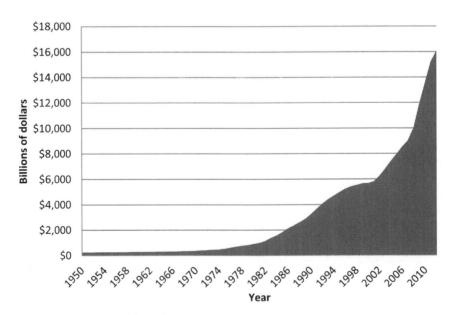

The National Debt Took Off in the 1980s and Keeps Rising

Exhibit 6.1 Annual Public Debt, 1950–2012

Source: TreasuryDirect.gov

began financing its government debt with investment income from wealthy Americans and foreign nationals, whose appetite for Treasury bonds selling at favorable interest rates seemed to be insatiable. The financial payouts from the bonds also went to the Americans who had Treasury bills in their investment portfolios, generally the very wealthy. As Kevin Phillips states:

> The underlying problem was the Reagan Administration's need to borrow huge sums of money at high interest rates to fund the 1981 tax cuts, the defense buildup, and 1981–1982 recession spending. To avert feared inflationary effects, the Federal Reserve Board in 1981 and 1982 raised U.S. interest rates to record high levels. With U.S. Bonds paying 15 percent while equivalent instruments in Germany and Japan were paying 5 percent or 6 percent, capital poured into the United States. As foreigners bought dollars to invest in U.S. debt, the dollar soared against other currencies.[9]

This investment boom in U.S. debt kept the government afloat, but it redistributed wealth to those who were already wealthy. The strong dollar threatened to and eventually did ruin the country's international trade position. The results of this for the manufacturing industry were especially devastating; as U.S. markets were flooded by inexpensive imports in industries like electronics and automobiles, factories that provided steady employment and middle class jobs were forced to lay off workers or shut down entirely.

The fervor for cutting taxes and the belief that such cuts would raise government revenues and benefit the middle class didn't subside, in spite of the wealth of evidence that the effects were slanted steeply in the direction of those already well off. Tax cutting by itself seemed to be gaining a momentum that was simply unstoppable, and states followed the federal government in cutting their own taxes. As each new piece of evidence suggesting that middle class incomes were stagnant and tax benefits were few appeared, the simple response by most politicians of both parties was that the benefits were "forthcoming."

The 1980s ushered in a long-term decline in the percentage of tax revenues taken from corporations (on corporate profits, generally a progressive form of taxation), and a gradual but steady increase in payroll taxes and individual income taxes as a percentage of federal revenues (see Exhibit 6.2). Further, a greater share of the federal tax burden was extracted using the regressive payroll tax to fund Social Security, a tax presently capped at $113,700 personal income. Taxation at the federal level thus shifted toward earned income and away from unearned income.

Evidence shows that corporate taxation was declining and that corporate tax avoidance was rising: corporate tax loopholes grew from $8.3 billion to $119.9 billion annually from 1970 to 1986. The overall effective tax rate for the

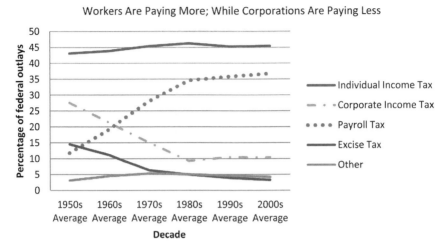

Exhibit 6.2 Composition of Federal Government Receipts by Source and Decade

Source: Office of Management and Budget, Budget of the United States

largest corporations in the United States dropped to 11.8 percent in 1982 before climbing back to 15 percent in 1984, and as of 2013, it stands at 12.6 percent.[10] This rate is far below the effective marginal income tax rate for high income earners, even with cuts in these top tax rates figured into the equation. Corporate taxes as a percentage of federal revenues declined to their lowest points since 1960 as corporate income tax receipts accounted for just 8.4 percent of all federal revenues in 2000. The long-term trend was unprecedented in any of the OECD countries. Since 1980, corporate income taxes as a percentage of GDP have been considerably lower in the United States than all other OECD countries.[11]

Despite the comparatively low corporate taxation rates in the United States, many companies avoid paying any taxes at all. One popular strategy is to set up shop in Bermuda or Barbados. In a process called corporate inversion, a company creates a subsidiary stationed in an offshore location like Bermuda, then transforms the subsidiary into the parent company. What would have originally been profits in the United States can then be drained out of the country as tax-deductible payments to the new parent company. As David Cay Johnston writes, "The tax savings from ostensibly moving a corporation's headquarters offshore are immense. Tyco estimated that it saved an average of $450 million each year after 1997, when it arranged to make Bermuda its tax headquarters while keeping its executive offices in the United States."[12] In the case of Tyco, not all the money ended up benefiting employees and shareholders: Tyco CEO Dennis Kozlowski and ex-Chief Financial Officer Mark Schwartz were convicted of stealing hundreds of millions of dollars from the company.

There also were changes in federal budget priorities (see Exhibit 6.3). The defense buildup from 1980 to 1990 was accompanied by cuts in the percentage of the federal budget devoted to education and social services (never a large

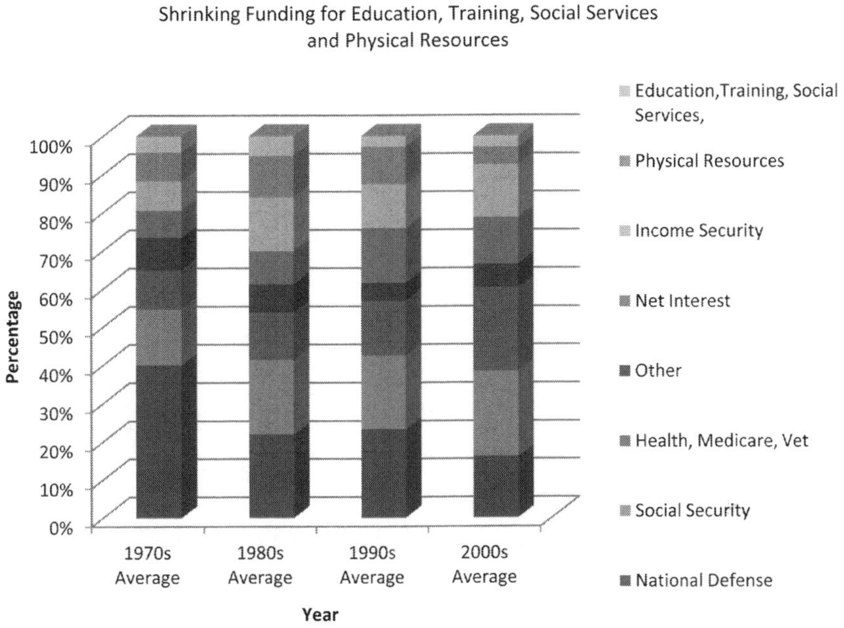

Shrinking Funding for Education, Training, Social Services
and Physical Resources

Exhibit 6.3 Federal Budget Breakdown by Decade

Source: Office of Management and Budget, Budget of the United States

percentage of the budget anyway) and income security. The amount of the federal budget devoted to servicing debt grew considerably, while the amount spent on physical resources like national infrastructure declined. In the 1990s and 2000s (as a result of economic expansion) these distributions shifted back toward the direction they were headed between 1970 and 1980, but the physical resources budget continued to decline, and spending on Social Security and income security rose again.

There was a largely unmeasured change in Washington as well, one that did not bode well for the prospects of those whose relative prosperity depended on earnings from a middle class job: the rise of a permanent lobbying class in Washington (see Exhibit 6.4).

Lobbyists relentlessly petition Washington for specific tax and regulatory breaks for corporations. In the 1980s, the door between lobbyists, corporations, and government officials was opened wider than at any time in recent memory as the Reagan administration granted unprecedented government access to corporate representatives.

The case of Edward C. (Pete) Aldridge, Jr., illustrates the conflicts of interest that emerge as a result of these close connections between government and industry. Mr. Aldridge (a former Air Force official) negotiated an expensive job contract with Boeing while overseeing Boeing business for the Air Force. Prior to that Mr. Aldridge had negotiated a lucrative $3 billion contract to build

Exhibit 6.4 Number of Political Action Committees (PACs), 1974–2011

Source: Howard W. Stanley and Richard G. Niemi, (various years) *Vital Statistics on American Politics*, Washington D.C.: Congressional Quarterly Inc.

Lockheed F/A 22 jets and then left the Air Force to join Lockheed's board of directors. Some of these actions come close to violating the law, but these types of career moves became pervasive in Washington from the 1980s onward.[13]

Despite the Clinton administration's attention paid to balancing the budget in the 1990s, and the need to continue cutting programs that helped the lower and middle classes, corporations still were able to finagle financial assistance. Jim Hightower describes one such subsidy designed to encourage U.S. firms to move jobs to Puerto Rico. The subsidy averages $27,000 per year for every job created, and it is based on profits rather than what the worker is paid (two to three times less than that). Drug companies have found these subsidies especially generous—Johnson and Johnson was given $50,000 per job moved to Puerto Rico, while Bristol Myers Squibb received $75,000 and Pfizer $156,000 per job per year. As Hightower states, "I realize this does not make sense, but I don't think it's intended to make sense.... [The entire program] costs us a total of a couple of billion bucks annually to subsidize our own job loss."[14]

The Reality for Everyone Else—Rising Taxes as a Percentage of Personal Income

While corporations and wealthy Americans saw their tax bills fall, average taxpayers (the median family income earner) saw theirs increase (see Appendix Exhibit 6.2). This increase was due to increases in Social Security payroll taxes and increases in state and local taxes, both generally regressive taxes.

Total taxes as a percentage of median family income in the United States have risen consistently since World War II, peaking at around 40 percent of family income in 1995 and declining slightly after that. That shift hides a much more serious shift in the sources of these taxes and the relatively progressive or regressive nature of the income source for federal, state, and local governments. Since 1955, the trend has been clear. Federal taxes on income, usually collected through a graduated income tax, have declined as a source of taxation on the nation's middle class. This decline has been more than offset by increases in payroll taxes (since 1955, from under 10 percent of total tax bills for median income earners to 20 percent) and sharp increases in state and local taxes as a percentage of total tax bills. Much of this state and local revenue is collected using sales and excise taxes that disproportionately extract income from the middle class and the poor.

In fact, state and local taxation usually is far more regressive in its effect than is taxation by the federal government. For example, the poor and middle class pay a larger percentage of their incomes to state and local governments in taxes than do the relatively well off. State and local sales and excise taxes explain most of this disproportion: while income taxes are generally progressively administered, the weight of sales and excise taxes falls disproportionately on the poor and middle class.[15]

Regressive taxes, which take a higher percentage of income from people with low incomes, are more burdensome on low-income individuals than on high-income individuals and corporations. Examples of regressive taxes are the Social Security payroll tax, which (as of 2013) is 6.2 percent on the first $113,700 of income and zero percent on any income over and above that. So, for example, someone who earns $113,700 a year owes $7,049 in Social Security payroll taxes, exactly 6.2 percent of her income, while another person making $200,000 still pays just $7,049, in this case only 3.5 percent of his total income.

Sales taxes on food and other essentials also take higher percentages of incomes for families and individuals with lower incomes because these people spend a greater percentage of their income on these items. The same is true of value-added taxes, which are paid by businesses that, in turn, pass costs on to consumers through higher prices.

Progressive taxes, on the other hand, take a larger percentage of income from those with higher incomes. For example, U.S. federal income taxes are progressive, taxing incomes at different rates depending on the size of income. As of 2013, the United States had seven income tax brackets (for single taxpayers):

Income: $1–$8,925   Tax bracket: 10%
Income: $8925–$36,250   Tax bracket: 15%
Income: $36,250–$87,850   Tax bracket: 25%
Income: $87,850–$183,250   Tax bracket: 28%

Income: $183,850–$398,350   Tax bracket: 33%
Income: $398,850–$400,000 and above   Tax bracket: 35%
Income: $400,000 and above   Tax bracket: 39.6%

The complicating factor is that individuals owe the U.S. Treasury the listed percentage of income *for each dollar within each range*, so someone making $45,000 would pay 10 percent on the first $8,925, 15 percent on the next $27,325, and 25 percent on the remaining $8,750 of income ($892 + $4,099 + $2,187 = $7,178 in federal tax, before deductions).

Of course, the relative fairness of state and local taxes varies greatly. The ten most regressive state tax systems tax their poorest citizens several hundred times the percentage of income they tax their wealthiest citizens, and many do the same to the middle class as well. Of these ten states, three—Illinois, Michigan, and Pennsylvania—are in the "rust belt"; one—South Dakota—is in the upper Midwest; one—Washington—is in the Pacific Northwest; and the remaining six—Florida, Texas, Tennessee, Louisiana, and Alabama—are in the South or Southeast. With the exception of California and Utah, the states with the most regressive sales taxes are all in the South, and almost all of these states collect sales taxes on groceries.

By contrast, the six states with the most progressive income taxes—California, New Mexico, Rhode Island, Vermont, Idaho, and Maine—tax the income of the poor relatively little and even allow tax credits to exceed the total amount of income tax owed (hence, they have negative effective tax rates). All of them have highly graduated tax rate systems.

This evidence overwhelmingly indicates a significant, long-term change in the nature of taxation in this country. We have switched from a system that taxes people on the basis of their ability to pay to a system that taxes unearned income from capital stock relatively little and earned income from work significantly more. Further, we've shifted the relative tax burdens toward earned income below the eightieth percentile of the earnings distribution and shifted tax burdens toward regressive sales taxes, excise taxes, and payroll taxes. The result is a government that does less for those who are not already wealthy, extracting more taxes from the have-nots, who don't represent the powerful political constituencies whose economic welfare most politicians care about (see Appendix Exhibits 6.3–6.5).

These policies flourished under the administrations of Ronald Reagan and George H.W. Bush, but Republicans have not been exclusively to blame for these trends. Bill Clinton thwarted Bush's reelection attempt in 1992 largely because of the faltering economy, which was in "jobless recovery" from the 1990–1991 recession. The budget deficit had risen to 4.2 percent of GDP, up from 2.8 percent in 1989; unemployment was at 7.3 percent.[16] James Carville's now famous rally cry for the Clinton campaign—"It's the economy, stupid!"—rang true with many Americans.

Clinton promised to ease the tax burden of the middle class and to make the rich "pay their fair share." However, this never really happened; instead, in 1996 Clinton and the Republican-controlled Congress turned their attention to cutting taxes on capital gains. Taking a page from the "voodoo economics" of Reagan, the Clinton administration argued that a capital gains tax cut— i.e., taxes on the increase of value of shares and real estate—would increase government revenue because many investors would cash in to take advantage of the lower rate, leading to a short-term increase in government revenues. Despite the negative long-term effects of cutting capital gains taxes, the idea was popular with politicians beholden to the interests of Wall Street and campaign finance, and there was widespread public support for the cut. Middle class Americans widely rallied with the wealthy to protect their common interest, leading Joseph Stiglitz to proclaim: "Ronald Reagan had had his ultimate victory. No matter that the capital gains tax cut saved the upper-income taxpayer $100 for every $5 that the middle-income taxpayer was spared.[17]

But Wait a Minute! Didn't the 2004 Bush Tax Cuts Do Better?

Of course one could argue that the effects of the Reagan-era tax cuts are past history. What about the tax cuts of the Bush administration, recently continued by the Obama administration? Is it possible that the tax cuts of the past and current tax cuts have not been structured the same way and won't have the same effects?

While this outcome is possible, it is doubtful, at least according to the Institute on Taxation and Economic Policy (see Exhibit 6.5). As with the tax cuts of the past thirty years, the latest round of tax cuts seems to be heading toward the same distributional consequences as those of the Reagan era—big tax cuts for the wealthy and tax increases for everyone else.

Looking at the change in total federal taxes resulting from the tax cuts, in 2012, the top 1 percent of income earners saw their share of federal taxes drop 5.6 percent, while everyone else but the top 20 percent will see their share drop 2.8 percent or less. Almost all of the 2004–2012 benefits from the tax cut accrue to the top 20 percent of all income earners, and all but 10 percent of those benefits to the already well-off go to the top 1 percent of income earners.

On top of this, a large percentage of taxpayers received under $100 in tax relief from the Bush tax cut program, and the share that received under $100 in tax relief grew to an average of 88 percent of all taxpayers by 2006. Ironically, the states with the highest numbers of taxpayers getting refunds of under $100 are Alabama, Arkansas, Louisiana, Mississippi, and West Virginia—all states that went to George W. Bush in the 2000 and 2004 elections, and McCain and Romney in the 2008 and 2012 elections. The five states with the fewest taxpayers that fall into the under-$100 category are

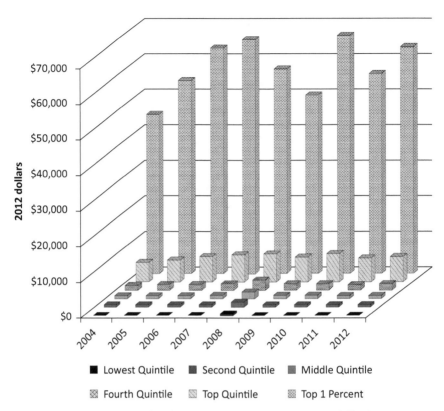

Exhibit 6.5 Average Value of Bush Tax Cuts per Household (2012 dollars)

Source: Center on Budget and Policy Priorities

Connecticut, New Hampshire, New Jersey, Vermont, and Wyoming; of these, only Wyoming and New Hampshire delivered their electoral votes to Bush, McCain, and Romney.

The effects are not evenly distributed across families in different circumstances, either. A large majority of taxpayers that received less than $100 from the 2003 tax cut are single, and the biggest beneficiaries are married parents. This outcome follows logically from the increase in income inequality between these groups generally.[18]

The Bush administration also brought back record-high budget deficits—a deficit of over $400 billion in 2006[19]—but was missing the tight money supply used by the Reagan administration to help pay off government debts. After the 2008–2009 recession, the Obama administration passed a large stimulus package to reinvigorate the economy and extended the 2003 Bush tax cuts, leading to record-high budget deficits (projected at $759 billion for 2013, down from $1.4 trillion in 2010) and sea of red ink for the U.S. government for the foreseeable future (see Appendix Exhibit 6.2).

Persistent Inflation and Benefit Declines for the Middle Class

Affording the Middle Class Lifestyle

In addition to these changes to federal, payroll, state, and local taxes, there are other, less obvious pressures on the indebted middle class. Persistent inflation on the big-ticket commodities consumers buy, increased prices for important services like healthcare and education, and declining employer commitment to providing healthcare and stable retirement options increase the uncertainty and volatility of their economic situation.

Let's start with the basics. Most Americans want to own homes, and for many, the unprecedented decline in home mortgage interest rates since the late 1990s has made owning a home a reality. But the effect of low interest rates has masked a rise in the price of new and existing homes: the median price of a new house in real dollars has risen almost 35 percent in ten years, from a 2011 inflation-adjusted median price of $197,000 in 1997 to $265,000 in 2007, on the eve of the 2008 recession. Median home prices took a serious dip after the real estate crash of 2008 and 2009, and median inflation-adjusted home prices dropped to a low of $222,000 in 2011 before inching back up to $256,000 in 2013. The sale price of existing homes rose as well, but less substantially, from an inflation-adjusted $133,000 in 1997 to $224,000 in 2007; it dropped precipitously with the 2008–2009 housing crash to $173,000 in 2010, and now stands at $206,000 in 2013 (see Appendix Exhibit 6.6).[20]

The real estate market expects average consumers to pay these astronomically higher prices with paychecks that have hardly changed a bit. The nominal dollar increases are much larger than that, and these are the "real" prices that people see in the real estate guides as they look for places to live. By this measure, the median sale price of new homes is close to $264,000 ($200,000 more than in 1980), and the median sale price of existing homes is $214,000 in current dollars.

The widely available streams of credit we discussed in Chapter 3 have made buying a house more affordable, in the sense that middle class Americans can now borrow money to achieve this American dream. But this same dream becomes less affordable when it comes to the sale price of the house. This situation has four effects on potential home buyers, and not all of these effects are bad:

1. Loan interest rates are low, so the amount of interest on a home loan for more expensive houses won't be any higher than it was for much more modestly priced homes in the late 1970s and early 1980s. (This is a good thing.)
2. The equity accrued in the home will be larger over the life of the loan as long as housing prices remain stable or inflate. (Another good thing.)
3. Payments on these costly homes will take a larger percentage from paychecks that are not increasing in real dollars. (Not good.)

4. Many new homes prior to 2008 were sold to buyers who used unconventional mortgages, with less money down and "balloon clauses" that allow interest rates to rise over the life of the loan. Further, the total value of the house depends on the continued rise in real estate prices that are fueled in part by low interest rates for home mortgages. The lack of confidence in the ability of buyers to pay their mortgages, and the generally high debt loads of middle class consumers, contributed to the 2008–2009 recession and housing crash, leaving millions of homeowners "upside down" on their mortgages (owing more for the home than the home was worth), record numbers of bankruptcies, record numbers of home foreclosures, and a loss of billions of dollars in middle class wealth (see Chapter 7). (Not good!)

In a prophetic speech in September 2005 to the American Bankers Association Annual Convention, Alan Greenspan (the chair of the Federal Reserve) expressed concern over the rise in unconventional mortgages in which buyers paid no money down, paid interest rates that changed over the life of the loan (Adjustable Rate Mortgages or ARMs), or bought houses using "interest-only" loans, with payments credited to the interest of the loan but not the principal. Unconventional mortgages were allowing buyers who barely qualified to purchase homes at inflated prices. Greenspan warned that a slump in price gains might lead to losses for both borrowers and lenders. The risk to the economy was magnified because consumers used about half the money they pulled from their homes upon refinancing for consumption or repayment of debts. Greenspan asserted that the abundance of interest-only loans and the introduction of "exotic" variable-rate mortgages were "developments that bear close scrutiny." [21]

Positive benefits of homeownership also depend on whether or not the homeowner has borrowed against the house's equity. Bill and Sheryl did so, and they have almost no equity in their house at all even though they've lived there for fifteen years. By the time they pay off their second mortgage and their regular mortgage, they'll be past retirement age, and chances are their home won't be paid off even then. On top of this, they've been cannibalizing all their savings to maintain their lifestyle in the house they currently own, and they're one missed paycheck away from falling behind on the payments and heading toward bankruptcy.

The High Cost of College Education

The middle class relies on public institutions of higher education as places of opportunity for their children. Traditionally, these institutions provide a high-quality education at a relatively modest cost. The difference in cost between a public and a private college education is considerable—conventionally, a private education costs about twice as much as a public education—and the differences in relative costs have risen steadily over the past 30 years.

What can Bill and Sheryl expect for their son Dillon, currently enrolled in college, and for their daughter Clara, just a few years away from starting? Let's begin by looking at real returns to education over time (see Exhibits 6.6 and 6.7).

Without a doubt, education pays dividends in terms of workplace earnings: the median income for men with at least a bachelor's degree has always been around $70,000 in real 2011 dollars for men, and the median earnings growth for women graduates has also been substantial, from $48,000 real 2011 dollars in 1990 to $55,000 in 2007 on the eve of the recession. (For women, these earnings gains are in real dollars that result from a variety of factors, including declines in labor market discrimination and the opening up of professional schools.)[22]

However, trends for males ominously reveal real declines in the value of education at levels below those who receive graduate and professional degrees. In fact, almost all of the rising earnings gap between college-educated and non–college educated men since the early 1970s result from declines in the real value of education below the college level, not increases in the value of a college education. This trend does not occur for women; instead, the gap between the earnings of the college educated and non–college educated is rising because returns of a college education are growing.

These figures hide another trend that is decreasing the value of college education, not to mention the value of graduate and professional degrees: growing earnings inequality within the traditional professions that college graduates aspire to enter.[23] As Michael Mandel and others have pointed out, a

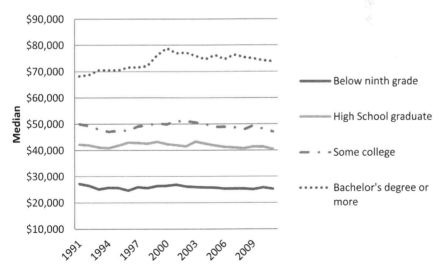

Exhibit 6.6 Male Median Earnings by Education Level, 1991–2011 (2011 Dollars)

Source: U.S. Census Bureau, Current Population Survey, Annual Social and Economic Supplements

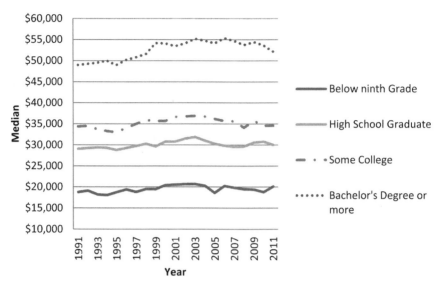

Exhibit 6.7 Female Median Earnings by Education Level, 1991–2011 (2011 Dollars)

Source: U.S. Census Bureau, Current Population Survey, Annual Social and Economic Supplements

college education has become increasingly like a lottery ticket: it is better to be in the lottery than not to have a ticket, but having a ticket does not guarantee winning.[24]

The same trend that has affected housing costs has also affected the costs of public higher education (see Exhibit 6.8). Average costs for public four-year colleges and universities have risen at a rate several times the rate of inflation, from around $6,000 per year to around $15,000 per year in real 2009 dollars.[25] The average annual cost for the 2012–2013 school year for students at public four-year universities was $17,857 for in-state students and $30,911 for out-of-state students.[26] These figures do not include additional expenses incurred by students—such as books and supplies, food, transportation, and basic living expenses. Although these costs are rarely factored in when estimating trends in the cost of higher education, they can add up and pose significant problems for students—even those with grant aid for tuition and fees: "It is not so much the prices charged by institutions, but the very real costs students incur by devoting their time to school and forgoing the income needed to support themselves and their families while in school that create the burden for these students."[27]

The rampant merger and acquisition (M&A) activity discussed in Chapter 4 has also found its way into the textbook publishing industry. The past few years have witnessed a flurry of M&A activity, led by private equity firms such as Apax Partners and the Apollo group, which has dramatically consolidated the industry.[28] When investors took on large debts to finance these transactions,

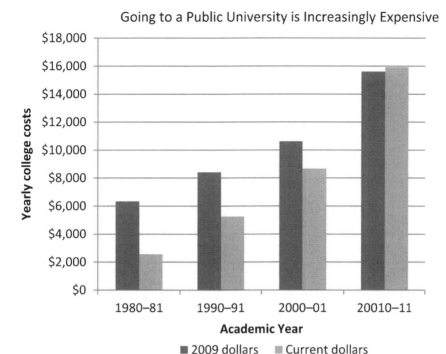

Exhibit 6.8 Public Four-Year College Tuition, Room and Board, 1980–2011 (Current and 2009 Dollars)

Source: U.S. Department of Education, National Center for Education Statistics

increased revenues were needed to finance the debt. It appears that raising prices on textbook and supplementary material has been the preferred way to try and generate this revenue; college textbook prices have risen 812 percent in the past three decades—with the steepest increase taking place since 2006.[29] At the same time, more and more students are choosing alternate ways of accessing course material to save money[30]—buying used books, renting, borrowing from friends, pirated online copies—which cut into the profit margins of publishers who then further increase prices to recoup those losses.

As we saw in Chapter 3, one mechanism for students to pay these increased costs has been for them to take on ever-larger amounts of student loan debt. In the late 1980s, student loans made up a small part of the debt owed by those in their twenties and thirties; in 2010, student loans are second only to mortgages for this age group.[31] Even though student loans may have relatively favorable interest rates, these loans add to the cumulative debt burden of the young would-be member of the middle class, and the federal government has increasingly made loans the preferred mechanism for supporting students pursuing higher education (see Appendix Exhibit 6.8 and 6.9). As with the other trends we've examined in this book, elites are loaning the middle class money rather than giving it to them.

Another trend tied to the decline of state and local investments in programs that benefit the middle class is the lessened contribution of state funding of public higher education. We see this in the increased percentage of public higher education costs that are funded by tuition, which has risen from 13 percent in 1980 to 19 percent in the 1990s, and came close to crossing the 50 percent threshold nationally in 2012![32]

For many students, the combination of going to classes and working part-time jobs to keep up with credit card payments can prove too much to handle. In 1998, an Indiana University administrator claimed, "We lose more students to credit card debt than academic failure."[33] For those that don't drop out, the seeds of middle class indenture are already sown by the time they leave college and enter the workforce. Graduates with high debt levels have trouble finding jobs because employers review credit reports. One interviewee was asked by a major Wall Street banking firm, "How can we feel comfortable about you managing large sums of money when you have had such difficulty handing your own credit card debts?"[34]

As discussed in the previous chapters, members of the middle class pay a higher share of their income in taxes to state and local governments and a higher percentage of their income to the federal government in payroll taxes, yet they receive little if any relief from the much-ballyhooed tax cuts of the past thirty years. Moreover, middle class Americans have seen subsidies for state activities like public higher education that benefit them cut, and the costs of a route to upward mobility increase.

Vanishing Benefits and the Costs of Working

Nearly eight out of ten Americans worry a fair amount or a great deal about the availability and affordability of healthcare.[35] And no wonder: especially in the past fifteen years, employers have reduced or eliminated their commitments to providing healthcare coverage for their employees. According to the Department of Labor, the percentage of the civilian workforce covered by employer-provided health plans dropped from 63 percent in 1992–1993 to 54 percent in 2010.[36] Almost all these plans require employee contributions for single and family coverage, and those contributions have risen considerably, from an average of $60.24 per month to $360 per month. Meanwhile, the cost of healthcare is rising much more quickly than the rate of inflation, and the number of Americans without any health insurance coverage or who rely on Medicare (for retirees) or Medicaid (for those with low incomes who can't afford any other type of medical coverage) has grown considerably. Unfortunately, for a large percentage of the middle class and most of the poor, our advice is, "Don't get sick" (see Appendix Exhibits 6.10–6.12).

For the growing number of two-income and single-parent families, another concern is the cost and availability of quality daycare. The average weekly price of daycare rose in real dollar terms by almost 30 percent from 1997 to 2011, from $143 a week to $181 (see Appendix Exhibit 6.13). While the upward trend is evident, the actual "average cost" masks significant variation in the amount families spend on childcare. National statistics on average costs include families using childcare a few hours a week as well as those using it full-time.[37] For families with two working parents, full-time daycare can easily cost between $8,000 and $10,000 a year *per child*.

The combined costs of healthcare and childcare, all taken from average paychecks that haven't increased, have taken a big bite out of the budget of the average middle class consumer. Even retirement pensions, which employees used to expect to receive after devoting long years of service to a company, are being attacked by employers and economic elite (see Exhibit 6.9). The number of workers with guaranteed pensions has not grown in proportion to the workforce. Increasingly, companies are setting up 401(k) plans for their employees, or have "optional" 401(k) plans that employees may contribute to out of their earnings. These plans often have vesting requirements and don't allow workers to determine where the money will be invested. For 32 percent of the workforce, funds are invested only in the employer's stock.[38] Combined with declines in the U.S. savings rate and in defined pension coverage in plans that guarantee a

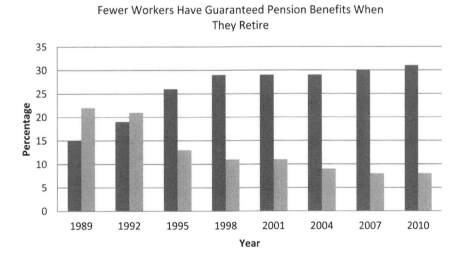

Fewer Workers Have Guaranteed Pension Benefits When They Retire

■ Defined Contribution Only   ■ Defined Benefit Only

Exhibit 6.9 Workers with Pensions

Source: Center for Retirement Research

payout at retirement, this means that Americans' retirement depends increasingly on Social Security or the whims of an undiversified "casino economy" stock portfolio that they do not control.

Retirement and the Collapse of Enron

Before Enron became synonymous with scandal, failure, and bankruptcy, it was the poster child for innovation and corporate success. The Texas-based company began with the merging of InterNorth and the Houston Natural Gas Company in 1985, and became the largest natural-gas pipeline company in the United States. By the late 1990s, the company had expanded into an energy trading company, buying and selling gas, electricity, metals, paper, financial contracts, and other commodities. Many viewed the company's meteoric rise and expansion—revenues grew from $4.6 billion in 1990 to $101 billion in 2000—as a testament to the new face of the post-industrial economy: diversified, complex, and aggressive.

However, much of Enron's success was fabricated through accounting practices that hid debts and artificially inflated profits. As a result, in December 2001, after filing for bankruptcy, Enron faced criminal investigation by the Justice Department. The collapse of Enron left over 4,000 employees, many of whom lost their entire life savings, out of work. Like many other companies, Enron had encouraged employees to invest in company stock as a part of their 401(k) plans and the company matched employee contributions with Enron stock. In Fall 2001, as Enron stock began to plummet, the company's retirement plan was in the process of being transferred to a different administrator and was in "lockdown"—meaning that participants could not change or sell their Enron stock during that period.[39]

Today, uncertainty surrounds even Social Security, a public benefit that working Americans have almost taken for granted since the 1930s. In 1935, President Roosevelt signed the Social Security Act, establishing two national social insurance programs to address the risks of old age and unemployment. Through a series of amendments in most decades since its creation, changes have expanded and redefined this program. For generations, working Americans have planned on receiving Social Security payments once they retire. Although for many these payments alone are not enough to provide a comfortable retirement, especially in the face of rising healthcare and prescription costs, the payments still provide much-needed income.

Political debates about the potential—and in the minds of many, the "inevitable"—insolvency of the Social Security program have driven recent discussions of the program. Estimates of its fiscal health vary widely depending on what assumptions—for example, the rate of economic growth or demographic changes—are made. In 2001, the president's Commission on Social

Security reported that payments from the program will begin to exceed revenue in 2016, and the trust fund will go broke in 2038. The Board of Trustees of Social Security put the date at 2041.[40] Meanwhile, the nonpartisan Congressional Budget Office stated that payments would exceed revenues in 2020, and in 2053 the program will no longer be able to pay the full benefits.[41] The stability of Social Security is obviously in jeopardy. One out of two Americans thinks that when he or she retires, Social Security will pay no benefits.

As we've shown in this chapter, the benefits that middle class Americans have come to depend on have been placed out of reach. But there is mounting evidence that the indebted middle class is running out of patience, and that the combination of private and public policies that have fueled economic stagnation have hardened and coarsened American public life.

Discussion Questions

- What are the most important differences between conservative and neoconservative policies?
- Do you think that we should adopt more regressive or progressive tax policies? Why?
- How do your college expenses compare to the national averages?

Notes

1. Paul Krugman, *The Great Unraveling: Losing Our Way in the New Century* (New York: W.W. Norton, 2003), 457.
2. William Kristol, "The Neoconservative Persuasion," in *The Neocon Reader*, ed. Irwin Stelzer (New York: Grove Press, 2004), 33.
3. Brian Reidl, "Ten Common Myths about Taxes, Spending, and Budget Deficits," *The Heritage Foundation Backgrounder*, June 13, 2003, 4.
4. Ibid.
5. Irwin Stelzer, "Neoconservatives and Their Critics: An Introduction," in *The Neocon Reader*, ed. Irwin Stelzer (New York: Grove Press, 2004), 21.
6. Ibid.
7. Kevin Phillips, *The Politics of Rich and Poor: Wealth and the American Electorate in the Reagan Aftermath* (New York: Random House, 1990), 32–51.
8. U.S. Department of Treasury Bureau of Public Debt, "Historical Debt Outstanding: 1950–2012," accessed July 23, 2013, http://www.treasurydirect.gov/govt/reports/pd/histdebt/histdebt.htm
9. Phillips, *The Politics of Rich and Poor*, 120.
10. Nelson D. Schwartz. "Big Companies Paid a Fraction of the Corporate Tax Rate," *New York Times*, July 1, 2013, accessed July 18, 2013, http://www.nytimes.com/2013/07/02/business/big-companies-paid-a-fraction-of-corporate-tax-rate.html?_r=0
11. Citizens for Tax Justice, "Corporate Income Taxes as a Percentage of GDP: The United States and Other OECD Countries," 2002, accessed www.ctj.org/images/oecd1.gif
12. David Cay Johnston, *Perfectly Legal: The Covert Campaign to Rig Our Tax System to Benefit the Super Rich—And Cheat Everybody Else* (New York: Portfolio Hardcover, 2003), 222.
13. Leslie Wayne, "Pentagon Brass and Military Contractors' Gold," *New York Times*, June 29, 2004.

14. Jim Hightower, *There's Nothing in the Middle of the Road but Yellow Stripes and Dead Armadillos* (New York: HarperCollins, 1997), 108.

15. Citizens for Tax Justice, *Who Pays? A Distributional Analysis of the Tax Systems in All 50 States* (Washington, D.C.: Citizens for Tax Justice and the Institute on Taxation and Economic Policy, 1996).

16. Joseph E. Stiglitz, *The Roaring Nineties* (New York: W.W. Norton, 2003), 39–41.

17. Ibid., 177.

18. U.S. Census Bureau, *Statistical Abstract of the United States* (Washington, D.C.: U.S. Government Printing Office, 2003).

19. Congressional Budget Office. *Historical Budget Data*, accessed August 12, 2013, http://www.cbo.gov/publication/42911

20. U.S. Census Bureau, *Statistical Abstract of the United States* (Washington, D.C.: U.S. Government Printing Office, 2003).

21. Alan Greenspan, "Remarks by Chairman Alan Greenspan to the American Bankers Association Annual Convention, Palm Desert, California" (September 26, 2005), accessed www.federalreserve.gov/boarddocs/ speeches/2005/20050962/default.htm

22. For more on this, see Kevin T. Leicht and Mary L. Fennell, *Professional Work: A Sociological Approach* (Oxford, UK: Blackwell, 2001).

23. Ibid., 61–81.

24. Michael Mandel, *The High-Risk Society: Peril and Promise in the New Economy* (New York: Times Business, 1996), 53–74.

25. U.S. Census Bureau, *Statistical Abstract of the United States 2005* (Washington, D.C.: U.S. Government Printing Office, 2006).

26. College Board, *Trends in College Pricing 2012*, accessed July 23, 2013, http://tren.collegeboard.org/college-pricing

27. Ibid., 8.

28. Barbara Quint, May 21, 2007. "Thomson Learning and Gale Under New Management Following Sale" Information Today, Inc. accessed June 13, 2013, http://newsbreaks.infotoday.com/NewsBreaks/Thomson-Learning-and-Gale-Under-New-Management-Following-Sale-36230.asp; Jeffrey A. Trachtenberg, November 26, 2012, "McGraw-Hill Sells Education Unit to Apollo" accessed June 13, 2013, http://online.wsj.com/news/articles/SB10001424127887323330604578143001164607408

29. Tyler Kingkade, "College Textbook Prices Increasing Faster Than Tuition and Inflation," *Huffington Post*, January 4, 2013, accessed July 23, 2013, http://www.huffingtonpost.com/2013/01/04/college-textbook-prices-increase_n_2409153.html

30. National Association of College Stores, "Student Spending on Textbooks Continues to Decline," 2012, accessed July 23, 2013, http://www.nacs.org/advocacynewsmedia/pressreleases/studentspendingontextbookscontinuestodecline.aspx

31. Caroline Ratcliffe and Signe-Mary McKernan, "Forever in Your Debt: Who Has Student Loan Debt, and Who's Worried," *The Urban Institute*, June 2013, 1.

32. Eric Kelderman, "States and Students Near a 50–50 Split on the Costs of Higher Education," *Chronicle of Higher Education*, March 6, 2013. http://chronicle.com/article/StudentsStates-Near-a/137709/.

33. Robert Manning, "Credit Card Debt Imposes Huge Costs on Many College Students," (Consumer Federation of America, 1999), 3, accessed www.consumerfed.org/pdfs/ccstudent.pdf

34. Ibid., 4.

35. Coleen McMurray, "Health Costs Dominate America's Health Concerns," *Gallup Poll Tuesday Briefing*, February 3, 2004 (Princeton, NJ: The Gallup Organization, 2004).

36. U.S. Department of Labor, Bureau of Labor Statistics, "National Compensation Survey: Employee Benefits in Private Industry in the United States, 2002–2003" (2003), accessed stats.bls.gov/newsrelease

37. Linda Giannarelli and James Barsimantov, "Child Care Expenses of America's Families," Occasional Paper Number 40, Assessing the New Federalism (Washington, D.C.: The Urban Institute, 2000).

38. U.S. Department of Labor, Bureau of Labor Statistics, "BLS Information," accessed July 24, 2013, www.bls.gov/bls/peoplebox7

39. For more on the precarious state of retirement planning, see Lauren Fox, *Enron: The Rise and Fall* (Hoboken, NJ: John Wiley and Sons, 2003); Stiglitz, *The Roaring Nineties*; and Mimi Swartz with Sheryl Watkins, *Power Failure: The Inside Story of the Collapse of Enron* (New York: Doubleday, 2003).

40. Martin Crutsinger, "Trustees: Social Security Broke in 2041," ABC News, March 23, 2005, accessed http://abcnews.go.com/Politics/wireStory?id=607878&page=1

41. Douglas Holtz-Eakin, "The Role of the Economy in the Outlook for Social Security" (CBO Testimony before the Subcommittee on Social Security Committee on Ways and Means, U.S. House of Representatives, June 21, 2005).

CHAPTER 7

The Great Recession of 2008–2009
The Illusion Exposed

What we have is socialism for them and capitalism for the rest of us. . . .
—Michael Harrington

Where is the morality in demanding the right to have one's ideas accepted regardless of how vague, contradictory, or unsupportable they may be? Who benefits from such a definition of morality? The answer is that it benefits ideologues, spin doctors, charlatans, and the cognitively diffuse. It benefits all who fail when their ideas are put to the test.

—Joan Huber

Our story so far has taken place in a context where the larger economy has been steadily growing, unemployment has been low, credit was easy to get, record profits were being made, and the United States was the dominant power in a triumphant world where neoliberal economic thinking was dominant and the "Washington consensus" was spreading to other parts of the world. The crisis of the American middle class was largely a hidden crisis from 1985 or so until 2008. The ability to hide stagnant wages, rising inequality, rising poverty rates, and a fraying social fabric seemed like it would never end as the seeds of American greatness were replaced by a political and economic culture more consistent with a South American military dictatorship. Then all of the sudden, right on the eve of the 2008 presidential election, the United States and then the global economy collapsed into the worst recession since the Great Depression of the 1930s. The consequences for the global economy were stark, but the consequences for the indebted American middle class were far worse.

The consequences of the recession continue to be felt even though we've officially left the recession and economic growth is happening again. In the aftermath, still more people (many of them members of the middle class) were and are being left behind to fend for themselves in a world of pessimism, diminished expectations, and even fewer opportunities. What happened?

The Financial Crisis: The Emperors Have No Clothes

In the United States and globally, the financial crisis and subsequent recession of 2008–2009 were truly gargantuan by any measure we care to use. Global markets lost $50 trillion in market value in 2008 alone, roughly $8,334 for every man, woman, and child on the planet. To spend just $1 trillion you would have to spend $34 million every day of your life for 80 years! So much money was lost that estimates are that it will take around 20 years to recover most of this wealth. The U.S. stock market lost over $11 trillion in value in just one year. In an eight-day period in October 2008 (one month before the 2008 election), the Dow Jones Industrial Average lost 22 percent of its value, falling from 10,851 to 8,451. But that drop masks a still larger drop from October 2007 to mid-October 2008—on October 7, 2007, the Dow stood at 14,164.[1]

By most accounts, there were three major stages to the financial collapse that led to the recession. First, from October 2007 until March 2008 the stock market started to go downward in a more or less orderly fashion—no big drops, no big gains, just a steady downward spiral. This is usually a signal from investors that a recession is coming. Investors pull their money out of the stock market and park it in more secure investments (like bonds and U.S. Treasury notes) to wait out what they see as an unstable investment environment. And none of this need directly affect the "real" economy where jobs and consumption actually occur.

Then, in mid-March 2008, Bear Stearns (a major Wall Street investment house) declared bankruptcy. At the time, this was the largest corporate bankruptcy in the history of the United States (the company had already written off almost $2 billion in devalued securities).[2] Investors were stunned but not totally rattled, so things remained relatively calm until around Labor Day, when Fannie Mae, Freddie Mack, AIG, and Lehman Brothers all declared bankruptcy over a ten-day stretch. Investors panicked and the Dow Jones fell 5000 more points between October 2008 and March 2009, as credit markets froze and fears of another Great Depression loomed. Worse still, from the standpoint of the average American, was the decline in real wealth held in mutual funds, whose value dropped from $6.5 trillion to $3.7 trillion in one year (January 2007–January 2008). Retirement savings accounts declined in value by 17 percent from October 2008 to October 2010 and have not recovered from the recession.

AIG and Lehman Brothers were private equity houses worth $712 billion and $639 billion respectively. AIG was a worldwide insurance company offering mortgage insurance and investment products to hundreds of thousands of customers. Its international division had invested heavily in credit default swaps, some $57 billion of which were designed to cover subprime loans issued to American consumers. The general collapse in confidence in subprime loans created a liquidity crisis in September 2008, and the U.S. Treasury offered to immediately cover AIG to the tune of $85 billion dollars. By the time the government support had ended, the Federal Reserve Bank had loaned $182 billion to AIG and received returns of $205 billion.[3] Lehman Brothers was an investment bank and financial manager, at the time the fourth largest in the United States. When the subprime mortgage market started to collapse early in 2008, Lehman Brothers lost 70 percent of its value and was left holding billions of dollars in worthless securities on delinquent home mortgages. Outside investors started to lose confidence in Lehman Brothers and started dumping stock, driving the overall value of the company down still further. By September 2008, when Lehman Brothers filed for bankruptcy, the company had liabilities of $613 billion. Unlike AIG, Lehman Brothers was allowed to go through an "orderly liquidation" (meaning that parts of the company were sold off in pieces to other investment banks) and U.S. Treasury bailout was applied. At the time, this was the largest commercial bankruptcy in U.S. history, and it led to a general crisis of confidence in financial markets in the fall of 2008.

Those were the big, visible financial houses at the leading edge of the 2008 financial crisis. But what about Fannie Mae and Freddie Mac, and who are they anyway? *Fannie Mae* is the shorthand name for the Federal National Mortgage Association in Washington, D.C., and *Freddie Mac* in the shorthand name for the Federal Home Mortgage Corporation in McLean, Virginia. Fannie Mae was created during the Depression era of the 1930s to stimulate mortgage lending to potential homeowners. Freddie Mac was created in the 1970s to provide some competition for Fannie Mae. Both enterprises buy mortgages from banks and other lenders so that those lenders can make more home loans. In September 2008, they held about $5.4 trillion in home mortgages, or about half of all outstanding U.S. home loans. Both are privately traded companies even though both were started by the federal government.

As with the private investment houses, Fannie Mae and Freddie Mac started to lose money as the value of home prices fell, beginning in 2007 and continuing into 2008. As the value of their holdings fell, their ability to borrow more money and continue normal operations (i.e., buying more mortgages from private banks and mortgage lenders) likewise fell. The government had to step in in September 2008 to guarantee debt issued by Fannie Mae and Freddie Mac to avert a far bigger catastrophe in the housing market. Both companies lowered the quality of loans they would buy and back, which increased their vulnerability to a financial meltdown as the housing market collapsed. In 2008 alone, Fannie and Freddie lost 80 percent of their traded value.[4]

How did this crisis affect average people? The average household lost $66,000 in on-paper wealth and almost $30,000 in real estate wealth as a result of the crisis. That's enough money to take a second mortgage on a house and finance all or part of a college education, save for retirement, buy several nice cars, or retire other debts from wages and earnings that don't grow. The federal government (and specifically the Treasury Department) spent roughly $501 billion on TARP (the Troubled Asset Relief Program), the major government program to bail out banks and investment houses (signed into law in September 2008 by President Bush and continued under President Obama). Of this, $205 billion went to the Capital Purchase Program (or CPP) to purchase direct stakes in banks to keep them afloat; $20 billion went directly to CitiGroup; $20 billion went to Bank of America; $70 billion went to AIG; $81 billion went to the domestic auto industry; $20 billion went to Term Asset-backed Securities Loan Facility (or TALF) to securitize new lending in the wake of the collapse of the private mortgage and asset-backed securities markets; $30 billion went to public-private investment partnerships (or PPIP) to buy up bankrupt and stressed subprime-backed securities; and $50 billion went to the Home Affordable Modification Program (or HAMP) to forestall massive home foreclosures by subsidizing the rewriting and renegotiations of mortgages that became delinquent or "underwater" as housing prices collapsed (more on underwater mortgages shortly). The financial bailout of Fannie Mae and Freddie Mac cost taxpayers $157 billion directly.

As a result of the financial crisis, consumers stopped spending, companies stopped hiring and investing, and investors stopped investing as well, leading to serious drops in the national GDP. The GDP fell by 5.4 percent in the last quarter of 2008, and by 6.4 percent in the first quarter of 2009. Job losses for that twelve-month period ran at 5.5 million U.S. jobs, costing an average of $5,800 per U.S. household. The value of American family homes for that twelve-month period dropped an average of $30,300 per household, or almost $3.4 trillion dollars. Total lost wages from underemployment and job loss are estimated at $3,250 per household, and (as we've extensively shown already) job quality and earnings were not keeping up with the rest of the economy before all this started (see Chapter 3).[5]

The credit market collapse was tied to problems with the subprime mortgage market and the aftermarket for mortgage-backed securities. There is plenty of blame to go around regarding the collapse of these markets, and at least some evidence that the entire downturn was avoidable.[6]

Betting the House and Losing

Subprime mortgages are mortgages advanced to those would otherwise not qualify for conventional mortgages due either to poor credit histories or insufficient incomes. The availability of subprime mortgages was (partially) responsible for the housing bubble of 2004–2006, though the generally easy availability of credit for everyone else (the major theme of this book) also played a major role. We've discussed in Chapter 5 where all the credit came from, and the ability to originate loans and sell them on the securities market, and then do more lending, generated profits that were large and almost impossible to resist.

As housing prices rose, more people had an incentive to get into the housing market, and those already in it had big incentives to "trade up" and buy newer, fancier, and larger homes. Subprime mortgages offered loans that, in the short term, had easier terms with adjustable interest rates (and low introductory rates for the first few years of the mortgage), interest-rate balloons (low rates of interest followed by higher market-based rates later on), low or zero down payments, and no closing costs. Buyers were lured by these easy initial terms and the hope that they could refinance their mortgages at easier terms in the near future while still maintaining the rising home equity that came from the inflated home values caused by the housing bubble. Between 2005 and 2007, housing prices were moderating and interest rates for home refinancing were rising, making it more difficult to refinance out of subprime loans before the ARM interest rates ballooned.

When these easy initial terms expired, mortgage defaults and foreclosures started to go up (see Exhibit 7.1). By 2006, 23 percent of all mortgages originated in the United States were subprime, and a vast majority of those were securitized in the mortgage-backed securities market. Once defaults and foreclosures started, banks and investors started losing money. They lost faith in the soundness of mortgage- and other asset-backed securities, the securitization

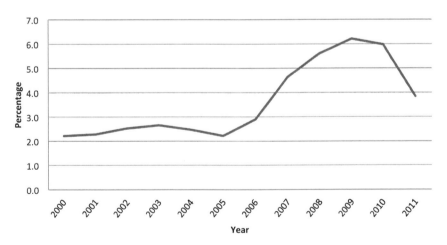

Exhibit 7.1 Foreclosures per 1,000 Owner-Occupied Dwellings, 2000–2011

Source: Federal Reserve Bank of New York

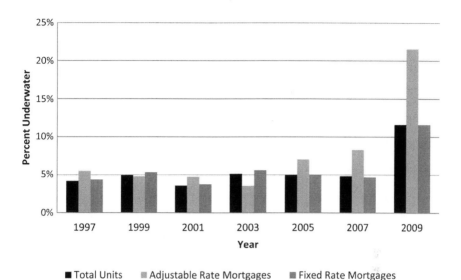

■ Total Units   ■ Adjustable Rate Mortgages   ■ Fixed Rate Mortgages

Exhibit 7.2 Percent Housing Units with Negative Equity ("Underwater"), Total Units and by Mortgage Type, 1997–2009

Source: U.S. Census Bureau, 1997–2009 American Housing Survey

market collapsed, and business and consumer credit markets dried up. The resulting foreclosures and falling prices meant that by September 2010, fully 23 percent of all U.S. homes were worth less than their original mortgage loan (or were "upside down," in the language of the housing industry). An *upside-down mortgage* occurs when the homeowner owes more money to the bank in mortgage principal (the purchase price of the home) than the house is currently worth on the open market. In this case, the owner of the house is literally "stuck" in the house, unable to sell it without owing the difference between the sale price and the amount of money originally borrowed to buy it (see Exhibit 7.2).

As we discussed in Chapter 3, mortgage securitization has been around since the 1970s. What happened in the 1980s and 1990s was a vast expansion of this market, as financial deregulation, the general desire for homeownership in the United States, and bank incentives for quick profits on loans increased incentives to loan money to riskier clients and then to sell the loans as asset-backed securities to investors. The securities are valued on the basis of housing prices and mortgage payments to investors. Anything that interferes with rising housing prices or the ability of consumers to pay their mortgages affects the securities market, and that (in a nutshell) is precisely what happened in 2008.

Analysts and experts claim that the following factors contributed to the housing bubble and subsequent financial crisis that followed. They may emphasize one of these more than others, but most refer in some way or another to all four.

1. *The general push toward homeownership in the United States.* Most Americans value homeownership, and the desire to own a home for non-owners, and to have a bigger and better home for those who are already in the market, is as American as apple pie. The general rise in housing prices in the early and mid-2000s, and the generally easy availability of credit that we've already discussed, made home buying easier than it has ever been in the United States. Mortgage applications were easier to fill out, and in many cases, proof or verification of income was unnecessary. Credit checks were done but loans often were not based on them. Traditional mortgage lending and payment limits seemed to be thrown out the window.[7] One could get a mortgage from a variety of sources, from conventional banks to specialized mortgage lenders that operated outside of the conventional banking system. It all seemed so easy, and the almost automatic increase in home values increased the on-paper wealth of millions of Americans, many of whom used their houses like ATMs to cash in on the rising value of their houses to pay bills, consolidate debt, or buy still more consumer goods (see Chapter 5).

   The subsequent market crash would leave many of these homeowners with massive piles of debt.

2. *Government policies and lack of adequate regulation.* Here (as with everywhere else in our market crash scenario) there are sins of omission and commission. Since the end of World War II, virtually every U.S. presidential administration has supported and encouraged homeownership, and the Clinton (1992–2000) and Bush (2000–2008) administrations were no different in this regard. The deregulation of the financial industry, including the repeal of the Glass-Steagall Act in 1999, which separated commercial and investment banks; the 1982 Alternative Mortgage Transactions Parity Act, which allowed non–federally chartered housing creditors to write adjustable-rate mortgages; and the Housing and Community Development Act of 1992, which created an affordable housing loan purchase mandate for Fannie Mae and Freddie Mac, all increased the overall dynamism of the market for single-family homes. HUD mandates began at 30 percent of both entities' loan purchases and rose to above 50 percent during the Bush administration.[8]

   On top of these issues there is considerable evidence that government regulators were not keeping up with developments in the newly deregulated financial markets. Budgets for regulatory agencies were slashed, many regulators had significant ties to the Wall Street banks they were overseeing (the revolving door we discussed in Chapter 6), and the overall growth of financial activities not tied to the regulated banking sector meant that nobody was minding the store. The growth of financial activities not tied to banks is often referred to as the "shadow banking system," since most bank regulations only address banks that take individual consumer deposits. Federal Reserve chair Tim Geithner referred to this as "19th-century regulation of 21st-century financial activity."[9]

3. *The incentives faced by bankers and mortgage lenders.* The ability to securitize mortgage debts (basically selling mortgages to investors where the returns are tied to housing prices and timely payments on mortgages) meant that profits and still more lending could occur if mortgages were offloaded onto investors. Investors had an interest in buying asset- and mortgaged-backed securities and assumed that the housing market would continue to increase in value well into the future. Because these loans were offloaded by those who had originally issued them, loan originators paid less attention to the creditworthiness of those they loaned money to (this has traditionally been referred to as *fiduciary responsibility*, the traditional duty of financial advisors to make sure that financial transactions are in the best interest of their employers and consumers). After all, the investor was going to be left holding the bag, not them. And as long as housing prices were rising, foreclosure was an option for loan originators who could repossess a house, resell it on the open market, and make good their commitment to investors.

4. *Investors and investment banks.* Investors loved asset- and mortgage-backed securities and often borrowed money to purchase them using loopholes in government regulation to take on highly leveraged positions (i.e., buying lots of investments with borrowed money). As long as lenders were lending and mortgage payments were being made at some level (and there was considerable evidence that mortgage payments were paid first), housing prices would continue to rise and mortgage-backed securities would be good investments.

But there was an additional investment vehicle that added volatility and moral hazard to the role of investors, and that was the spread of the credit default swap market. *Credit default swaps* allow investors to insure themselves against losses incurred in the mortgage-backed securities market. But even those not investing in mortgage-backed securities could buy credit default swaps and essentially "bet" that investments would go down. So investors could cover themselves whether these securities paid out or didn't, and plenty of speculators bet that the MBO market would collapse. The Financial Crisis Inquiry Commission of 2011 stated that credit default swaps made a significant contribution to the 2008 financial crisis and the collapse of credit markets because they made it virtually impossible to tell what the obligations of different financial institutions were or what financial positions they held.[10]

Once there was any indication that housing prices were not rising or that mortgage holders were having trouble making the payments, the entire system froze up and collapsed under the weight of its own paper. Government regulators (and politicians) were stunned. But (from our standpoint) the worst problem of all was that the U.S. real estate market collapsed.

From our perspective, all of these problems were caused by the same underlying dynamic. U.S. middle class consumers were loaned money they could not afford to pay back in order to fuel the profits driven by a consumer economy that (until the middle of the 1970s) was fueled by rising wages and earnings. But, as we've seen, median earnings and the earnings of most Americans have gone essentially nowhere for at least two decades. In the absence of rising incomes to rely on, easy credit seemed to be the only way to drive consumption forward and secure record financial profits. Once lenders could offload the risks of consumer lending onto investors and the financial markets, the interaction of the longstanding American desire for homeownership combined with the ability to write and dispose of loans and make instant profits was irresistible. Homeowners would benefit from steadily rising housing values as new buyers were continually available. Investors would be assured that housing prices would continue to rise and mortgages would be paid. The government would see the benefits of a deregulated financial market generating profits and tax revenues. What was not to like?

As we'll see, the results for middle class Americans have been still more job loss, more income decline, and declines in real assets and wealth. As of 2013, corporate profits have recovered, but the middle class isn't even back to where it was in 2007, before the recession started.

How bad did the housing situation get? In parts of the United States where there was the most subprime lending (Arizona, California, Florida, and Nevada), and in surprising places in the rust belt (like Cleveland, the home of Bill and Sheryl), home values collapsed, foreclosures rose to catastrophic levels, and vacancy rates for existing homes rose massively. In most of these places, homes lost around 50 percent of their value, and almost as many homeowners were "underwater" on their mortgages.

The impact of these types of financial losses are far from academic. Bill and Sheryl (in Cleveland) were leveraged to the maximum to begin with, to put their son Dillon through Ohio State University. The resulting housing downturn put them seriously underwater on their mortgage, so much so that they might be better off leaving their house than staying in it. The inability to figure out what do combined with the continued mortgage payments keeps them in their home and in Cleveland, when they may have been better off selling at a loss (or letting foreclosure go forward) and resettling somewhere else where job prospects were better. But since they're underwater they don't really have a clean opportunity to do this, and they aren't in so much financial distress that they can declare bankruptcy. So in the meantime, they sit tight and hope things will improve. If current trends continue, however, it will take thirteen years for housing values to return to where they were in 2006.

The same problems affect David and Monica in Tampa. They have remained employed (a blessing in itself, as we will see in the next section), but their house has lost around 40 percent of its value over the past two years. The real estate market in Tampa has probably bottomed out, but if either one of them lost their job or they were forced to move, they would be in serious trouble. They went from having dubious control of a few financial assets, big debts, and flat wages to holding the bag on a financial asset that is worth less than they owe, and still more big debts and flat wages. The American consumer's faith in the housing market has clearly been shaken by these events.

Unemployment, Job Loss, and Collapsing Demand: The New Poor

But far more things went wrong than just the decline in housing values. The credit market for employers and consumers in other realms also dried up, job losses started to mount, the unemployment rate rose to levels not seen since the recession of the early 1980s, and wages remained flat or declined in real value from their already dubious position.

One of the long-term problems that reared its head again for the average indebted member of the middle class was the rise in bankruptcies (see Exhibit 7.3). Bankruptcies declined significantly in the aftermath of bankruptcy reform legislation passed by Congress,[11] and there is considerable debate about whether bankruptcy reform legislation met its intended goals. Just prior to the recession, bankruptcy filings hit record highs, and even after the legislation took effect, bankruptcy filings started to climb again. Recent research suggests that the biggest determinants of bankruptcy filings are unexpected medical expenses and job losses, and that bankruptcy filers are typical Americans living typical lives, not spendthrifts attempting to make a quick buck or avoid their financial responsibilities.[12]

But the most serious outcome of all has been the near collapse of the U.S. job market (Exhibits 7.4 and 7.5). The unemployment rate prior to the 2008 recession was very low (just over 4 percent, almost to the level where economists

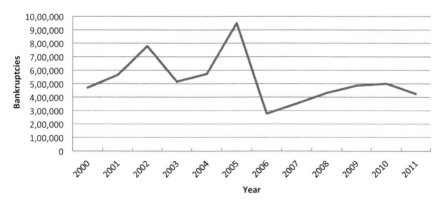

Exhibit 7.3 Number of Consumer Bankruptcies, 2000–2011

Source: American Bankruptcies Institute

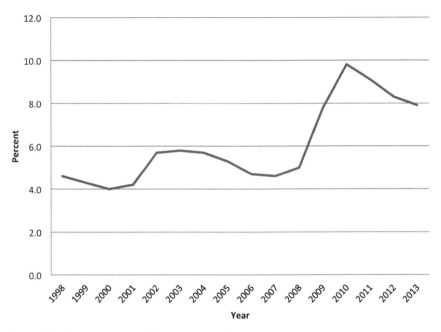

Exhibit 7.4 Unemployment Rate, 1998–2013

Source: Bureau of Labor Statistics, Current Population Survey

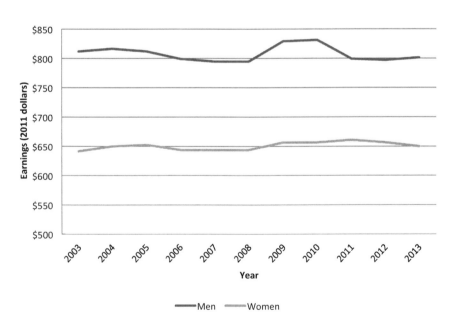

Exhibit 7.5 Median Weekly Earnings, Full-Time, Men and Women, 2003–2013 (2011 Dollars)

Source: Bureau of Labor Statistics, Current Population Survey

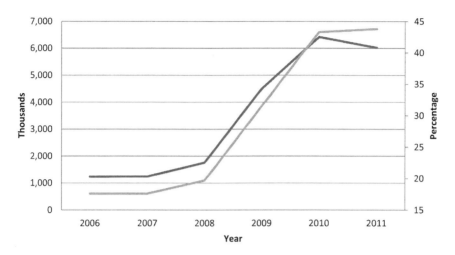

Exhibit 7.6 Long-Term Unemployed, 2006–2011

Source: Bureau of Labor Statistics, Current Population Survey

and other policy analysts declare that we've met "full employment" goals), but it almost immediately skyrocketed in late 2008 and 2009, as credit markets, investment, and consumer spending dried up. Unemployment in early 2010 actually rose above 10 percent, and the percentage of unemployed who were out of work for six months or longer reached record-high levels (Exhibit 7.6). Worse, there has been considerable evidence that the long-term unemployed have become "discouraged workers" who have left the labor force entirely (there were well over a million such workers in 2012). People who stop actively looking for work are not counted in unemployment statistics even if they have looked for work for over six months and have given up looking for a job.

Worse still, evidence from the Bureau of Labor Statistics suggests that that the recession created a serious jobs shortage relative to the number of people looking for work.[13] In December 2000, there was just over 1 job seeker per job available, a quite favorable job-to-job-seeker ratio, and on the eve of the 2008 recession, the ratio was still under 2 seekers per job. But by July 2009, the ratio had ballooned to almost 7 job seekers per job, and it currently stands at 3.3 job seekers as of May 2013. The bureau estimates that at the current rate of job creation, it will take between three and six years to get back to 2007 levels of employment. And (needless to say) all of this is happening in an economy where the median real weekly wage and the hourly wage have fallen to levels not seen since 1999 (Exhibit 7.5).

What does all this suggest? Our argument is that the indebted middle class has needed ongoing help and support for decades, at least since the early 1980s if not before. But now the situation is even more dire than it was when we began our analysis. Billions of dollars in personal wealth have disappeared. The ability to find a good, steady job is more elusive than ever and, if you manage to find one, your wages, earnings, and benefits will be a fraction of what they were in the 1970s.

All of this would suggest that millions of Americans needed help. Did they get it? No. But the banks and investment houses sure did.

Socialism for the Banks, Capitalism for the Rest of Us: Government Policy Responses

In case you hadn't noticed, we spent a lot of time talking about the federal government's stabilization of the banking and financial system in the early part of this chapter. Depending on what is counted, the federal government spent around $700 billion immediately bailing out banks and shoring up the financial system. The big banks and the mortgage lending system were viewed as "too big to fail," and the prevailing and not-unfounded fear was that problems created by housing would spread to other parts of the economy.

To their credit, many politicians in Washington and policy analysts were distressed that the federal government had to step in and do these things to keep the financial system afloat. They did not want to bring about a repeat of the entire financial meltdown sometime in the future. One major proposed solution was the Dodd-Frank Wall Street Reform and Consumer Protection Act, passed in May 2010. Billed as the biggest piece of comprehensive financial legislation since the Glass-Steagall Act of the 1930s (the act that separated investment banking from consumer banking), the legislation has many parts to it. The legislation created and authorized the Consumer Financial Protection Bureau with an independent budget and an independent director to oversee consumer-lending products like subprime loans and credit cards. Banks are prevented from using depositors' money to invest in hedge funds and other risky investments solely for the bank's benefit. The bill creates a financial oversight council that monitors the entire financial industry, recommends when companies need to increase their capital reserves to cover their investments and loans, and allows for more general oversight of hedge funds and other formerly unregulated parts of the "shadow banking system." Credit default swaps were to be overseen by the Securities and Exchange Commission instead of existing in an unregulated no man's land. And the legislation authorized the Government Accountability Office to monitor the Federal Reserve's use of bailout funds and prohibited the rescue of specific companies. The Federal Reserve must also publish the names of companies accepting bailout funds.[14] Though the legislation was passed and signed by President Obama, there has been unprecedented lobbying pressure from Wall Street to keep hedge funds and other exotic financial instruments unregulated, and there has been considerable resistance to the creation of the Consumer Financial Protection Bureau by Republicans and Wall Street.[15]

So the financial markets have been extensively subsidized and protected from themselves. Corporate profits (as we have seen) have returned to their pre-recession levels. What have the rest of us gotten?

In a word, not much. If banks and investment houses have been deemed too big to fail, perhaps the rest of us have been deemed too little to succeed. The 2008 Troubled Asset Relief Program (TARP) passed the U.S. House and Senate almost immediately once the crisis was apparent. That's the part that bailed out banks and kept the financial system afloat. The 2009 American Recovery and Reinvestment Act (signed into law in February 2009) increased the length and size of unemployment benefits and job training; provided a one-time $300 rebate to Social Security recipients; and authorized infrastructure spending on roads, bridges, education, scientific research, and law enforcement. The 2010 Tax Relief, Unemployment, and Job Creation Act extended the early 2000s Bush tax cuts for two more years (they have been further extended since then) and provided a tax cut for employee contributions to Social Security and Medicare. Finally, the Home Affordable Refinance Program (or HARP) is designed to subsidize the renegotiation and refinancing of home mortgages so that owners who are underwater or in danger of foreclosure can lower their payments, stay in their homes, preserve wealth, and keep the real estate market afloat.

Unlike TARP, almost all of these programs designed to get average Americans working, saving, and consuming have met with serious obstacles. The Dodd-Frank Wall Street Reform and Consumer Protection Act is stalled in its implementation; a permanent director for the Consumer Financial Protection Bureau Richard Cordray was not confirmed until July 2013, and lobbyists actively interfere with the implementation of most of the Wall Street oversights in the law. The extension of the Bush tax cuts has had the same effect now as we described earlier, and was used as a "bargaining chip" to get the U.S. House and Senate to pass one-time payroll tax relief for average workers (worth $934 to the average family).[16] Much of the infrastructure spending in all of the new legislation has been held up by politicians worried about budget deficits and threatening government shutdowns. HARP was originally not designed to help homeowners whose mortgages were underwater (some 40 percent of all home loans during the recession), but the new and improved "HARP 2.0" is designed to help homeowners who are, though mortgage companies are still obstructing these deals. As of April 2013, only about 14 percent of home refinancing applications were for HARP.[17]

You would be forgiven for noticing that there is a pattern here—instantaneous bailouts of large Wall Street banks, the restoration of profitability, and the continued growth of income inequality accompanied by obstruction and half-hearted measures for the rest of us. There seems to be little relief for the indebted middle class in sight. Although, in a speech delivered at Knox College in July 2013, President Obama identified many of the threats to the middle class that we've documented in the preceding pages:

I'll lay out my ideas for how we build on the cornerstones of what it means to be middle class in America, and what it takes to work your way into the middle class in America: Job security, with good wages and durable industries. A good education. A home to call your own. Affordable health care when you get sick. A secure retirement even if you're not rich. Reducing poverty. Reducing inequality. Growing opportunity. That's what we need.[18]

These recommendations are consistent with the the the analysis that we have developed in the preceding pages. Additionally, President Obama goes on to suggest that rising inequality is fraying our social fabric. This is the subject of Chapter 8.

Discussion Questions

- In what ways did the government bailouts reveal the power and influence of Wall Street?
- Do you think the recovery following the 2008 Great Recession will lead to greater or lesser economic inequality? Why?
- Do you agree with President Obama's assessment of what it means to support the middle class?

Notes

1. Tim Paradis, "The Statistics of the Great Recession," *Huffington Post*, October 10, 2009, accessed July 28, 2013, http://www.huffingtonpost.com/2009/10/10/the-statistics-of-the-gre_n_316548.html. For further reading on the Great Recession, see also: David B. Grusky, Bruce Western, and Christopher Wimer, Eds., *The Great Recession* (New York: Russell Sage Foundation, 2011); Paul Krugman, *The Return of Depression Economics and the Crisis of 2008* (New York: W.W. Norton & Company, 2009); Kevin Phillips, *Bad Money: Reckless Finance, Failed Politics, and the Global Crisis of American Capitalism* (New York: Penguin Group, 2008); Joseph Stiglitz, *Freefall: America, Free Markets, and the Sinking of the World Economy* (New York: W.W. Norton & Company, 2010); Richard A. Posner, *A Failure of Capitalism: The Crisis of '08 and the Descent into Depression* (Cambridge, MA: Harvard University Press, 2009).
2. Gary Shorter, "CRS Report for Congress: Bear Stearns; Crisis and 'Rescue' for a Major Provider of Mortgage-Related Products," March 26, 2008, Congressional Research Service.
3. Phillip Swagel, "The Costs of the Financial Crisis: The Impact of the September 2008 Economic Collapse," Briefing Paper #18, Pew Charitable Trust Economic Policy Groups, March 2010.
4. Alana Semuels, "Understanding the Two Loan Giants," *Los Angeles Times*, September 8, 2008, accessed July 27, 2013, http://articles.latimes.com/2008/sep/08/business/fi-qanda8
5. Swagel, "The Costs of the Financial Crisis."
6. Sewell Chan, "Entire Financial Crisis Was Avoidable, Inquiry Finds," *New York Times*, January 25, 2011, accessed July 27, 2013, http://www.nytimes.com/2011/01/26/business/economy/26inquiry.html?_r=1&adxnnl=1&adxnnlx=1375103395-UzufaeedXJ2AoRZbZCUq8g
7. See Kevin T. Leicht, "Political Environments and Labour Market Opportunities as Contributors to Housing Indebtedness: A U.S. State-Level Analysis," *Cambridge Journal of Regions, Economy and Society* 5 (2012): 61–75, and Leicht, "Borrowing on the Brink: Consumer Debt in America," in *Broke: How Consumer Debt Bankrupts the Middle Class*, ed. Katherine Porter and Elizabeth Warren, 195–217 (Palo Alto, CA: Stanford University Press, 2012).
8. James Gwartney, "The Economic Crisis of 2008: Causes and Aftermath," accessed www.com monsenseeconomics.com

9. See note 6 above.

10. Ibid.

11. See Katherine Porter, "Driven by Debt: Bankruptcy and Financial Failure in American Families," in *Broke: How Consumer Debts Bankrupts the Middle Class*, ed. Katherine Porter, 1–24 (Palo Alto, CA: Stanford University Press, 2012).

12. Ibid.; Elizabeth Warren and Deborah Thorne, "A Vulnerable Middle Class: Bankruptcy and Class Status," in *Broke: How Consumer Debts Bankrupts the Middle Class*, ed. Katherine Porter, 25–39 (Palo Alto, CA: Stanford University Press, 2012).

13. Lawrence Mishel, Josh Bivens, Elise Gould, and Heidi Shierholz, "Still Not Enough Jobs for Too Many People," (Ithaca, NY: Economic Policy Institute, ILR Press, 2013).

14. United States Senate Committee on Banking, Housing, & Urban Affairs, "Brief Summary of the Dodd-Frank Wall Street Reform and Consumer Protection Act," accessed July 27, 2013, http://www.banking.senate.gov/public/_files/070110_Dodd_Frank_Wall_Street_Reform_comprehensive_summary_Final.pdf

15. Public Citizen. "Report: Wall Street's Opposition to Dodd Frank Echoes Its Resistance to New Deal Safeguards," July 12, 2011, accessed July 27, 2013, https://www.commondreams.org/newswire/2011/07/12–0

16. Chuck Marr and Nathaniel Frentz, "Expiration of Payroll Tax Cut Is Biggest Tax Change for Most People in 2013," Center for Budget and Policy Priorities, April 11, 2013, accessed July 27, 2013, http://www.cbpp.org/cms/?fa=view&id=3151

17. Tara Siegel Bernard, "Hope and Frustration in U.S. Effort to Help Homeowners," *New York Times*, May 25, 2012, accessed http://www.nytimes.com/2012/05/26/your-money/mortgages/harp-2–0-stirs-hope-and-frustration-for-homeowners.html?pagewanted=all&_r=0

18. Megan Slack, "President Obama Lays Out a Better Bargain for the Middle Class," *The White House Blog*, July 24, 2013, accessed July 27, 2013, http://www.whitehouse.gov/blog/2013/07/24/president-obama-lays-out-better-bargain-middle class; Jackie Calms and Michael D. Shear, "Obama Says Income Gap Is Fraying U.S. Social Fabric," *New York Times*, July 27, 2013, accessed July 27, 2013, http://mobile.nytimes.com/2013/07/28/us/politics/obama-says-income-gap-is-fraying-us-social-fabric.html?from=homepage

CHAPTER 8

The Consequences of
Middle Class Meltdown

Don't talk about the majority of bums who live in tin huts. They shouldn't even vote. . . . Anyone who goes on welfare should lose their right to vote. They are parasites.
> —Michael Savage, AM Talk Show Host, April 18, 2002

Well, what if you said something like—if this happens in the United States and we determine that it is the result of extremist, fundamentalist Muslims, you know, you could take out their holy sites?[1]
> —Rep. Tom Tancredo (U.S House of Representatives,
> Colorado) on a Florida Radio Talk Show

Next time your liberal friends talk about the separation of Church and State ask them why they're Nazis.[2]
> —Glen Urquhart, the Tea Party–backed 2010
> Republican candidate for the Delaware Senate

For everyone who's a valedictorian, there's another 100 out there that weigh 130 pounds and they've got calves the size of cantaloupes because they're hauling 75 pounds of marijuana across the desert.[3]
> —Rep. Steven King (U.S. House of Representatives, Iowa)
> referring to Mexican immigrants, 2013

Our analysis thus far has provided a description and explanation of the American middle class, whose indebtedness and economic instability at the hands of elites has rendered them politically powerless, living from one paycheck to the next, one misstep away from economic disaster.

The deterioration of the middle class has not affected only its own members; changes in the economic standing and plight of the middle class have had broad implications for the overall coarsening of American life. The middle class was the bedrock on which an advanced consumer economy was built. The rules of the middle class game defined not only how to economically get ahead, but in a broader sense, what many people defined as right and wrong.

Several authors have analyzed the sociological impact of changes to the middle class.[4] We focus on four important economic and social consequences that emerged well before the 2008 Great Recession.

1. The record number of bankruptcies and overall tightness of the middle class budget leave most consumers with little to fall back on when job losses, health crises, divorces, or general misfortunes strike.
2. The cultural contradictions of American politics have become increasingly visible as the unbridled commitment to free-market capitalism tugs at the very fabric of the social order that most members of the middle class rely on.
3. The result of these problems and contradictions is declining confidence in public institutions and the fraying of community ties that were once major components of middle class life.
4. A hardening of public discourse and a general politics of displacement encourage an "us versus them" mentality, combined with a form of identity politics that divides Americans.

While each of these trends poses significant challenges to the middle class, taken together they make it unlikely that middle class Americans will recognize important economic commonalities and act on them.

Most members of the middle class remember the old rules for getting ahead, which can be summarized by one simple idea: if I work hard, things will work out fine. The middle class ethic was built on the concept of self-sufficiency: good, responsible people take care of themselves. They work. They marry and stay together. They raise children. They contribute to the economy as workers and consumers. They pay their bills.

Granted, there were exceptions to this ethic. For example, one of the biggest tax breaks in the federal tax code is the mortgage interest deduction. While this allows millions of Americans to buy houses that they might not otherwise be able to afford, it is a subsidy to the housing industry and a substantial benefit for homeowners. Until very recently, the Social Security system was paying out far more money in benefits to recipients than they and their employers had ever contributed. Likewise, the interest payments for most of the student loans that so many rely on to pay for college expenses are subsidized by the federal government. Adding up the costs of these "benefits," it is difficult to say that most members of the middle class were standing *completely* on their own; still, the perception is important and generally true.

As far as norms are concerned, it is clear that the middle class understanding of how life works has changed. The job instability of the past thirty years flies in the face of the idea that good, steady work is rewarded with long-term commitments from employers. Moreover, wages from average jobs have not increased, but the expenses and taxes that the middle class pay have either stayed the same or risen. Such middle class markers as home and car ownership have become much more difficult to attain, and consumption is fueled by debt—the same mechanism that fueled dependency in the feudal and sharecropping systems of a prior age.

From the standpoint of control and independence, the middle class has surrendered much of its independence, or had its independence expropriated, by elites who have replaced earned income from jobs with credit and debt. This credit and debt allows employers to dictate the terms and conditions of employment to employees who must work harder, and who are in poor bargaining positions because of looming insolvency and bankruptcy. Union membership is now at its lowest level since 1916,[5] which further weakens attempts at collective bargaining to secure wage increases and workers' benefits. Further, the wealthy and business classes now dominate political life through political action committees and privileged access to politicians who skew the tax system and government regulation to serve their interests. Those in the middle class suspect that something is wrong and that the system is rigged against them, but coherent political action to combat these trends is beyond their reach.

"A Pox on Both Their Houses": Examples of Middle Class Alienation from Politics and Community

Scott Clark and Robert Boyer, two harried members of the middle class interviewed by the *Washington Post*,[6] provide real-life examples of this political alienation. Scott, fifty-one, worked for a circuit board factory from the mid-1970s until Lucent Technologies bought the company in 2001, closing the plant. After his plant closed, Scott started doing deliveries as a driver for hire, working thirteen-hour days delivering office mail for four different companies with no vacation or benefits. Scott doesn't have much patience for politicians:

> When Sen. John F. Kerry (Mass.), the Democratic presidential nominee, comes on the radio to talk about the economy, proclaiming, "I believe in building up our great middle class," Clark sneers, "Yeah, right." When President Bush's voice echoes through the cab a little later, Clark dubs him "a liar."

He's not the only one angry with politicians and pundits. Robert Boyer, one of Scott's ex-coworkers, fumes, "When these guys get on the boob tube and say there's jobs out there, you just gotta go out there and get them, it makes me want to go out there and grab them by the throat and say, 'Where? Where are the jobs at?'"

The cynicism that Scott and Robert have toward politics is understandable, but beyond expressing their displeasure by grumbling, they may not have the time to muster the energy for civic engagement in other venues. The ever-increasing efforts they need to make to simply maintain the lifestyle that the middle class has expected in the United States has taken a serious toll on their ability to engage in the activities that maintain communities.

Some of the middle class Americans interviewed by sociologist Alan Wolfe as part of the Middle Class Morality Project echoed these concerns.[7] One respondent described community life by saying, "It's almost as if we set up our own islands. It's a street full of islands. And, you know, we would love to have a great relationship and great neighbors and that sort of thing, but it has just never evolved." Another said, "We don't know who those people are or how they spend their time. We pass them on the street. We talk across the fence, but socially we don't do things with our neighbors to speak of." Rachel Benjamin, a dentist from Brookline, Massachusetts, provides a concise explanation for why middle class Americans feel so disconnected from one another: "People just have less time. . . . When you look at the number of hours people spend at work now, the whole issue of living in the suburbs has cut time off people's days. Having dual-career families cuts time out of the day."[8]

In addition to finding it extremely difficult to build and maintain supportive communities, members of the middle class see little support from politicians and other elites, believing that they don't understand the realities of everyday life. The economy may be humming along, but that means little to Scott Clark, who is forced to work long hours with little job security to make ends meet. If he or any of our protagonists found time to read the newspaper, they would be reminded of just how out of touch some of our elected officials are. Take the following examples,[9] starting with this one from 1997: House Speaker Newt Gingrich stated, "'I'm not a wealthy man. . . . I'm a middle class guy,' to explain why despite his $171,500 salary, he needed a loan from former Sen. Bob Dole to pay an Ethics Committee fine." Gingrich's salary alone was a four times the median income in the United States at the time. The prior year, Fred Heineman, former Republican Congressman from North Carolina, said that he had a "lower middle class" salary of $183,500. He added that when someone is making anywhere from $300,000 to $750,000, "that's middle class."[10]

During the 2012 presidential election, both the Democratic nominee Barack Obama and the Republican nominee Mitt Romney repeatedly defined the "middle class" as families with incomes below $250,000. Because candidates must appeal to a broad swath of voters and claim that their policies will help the middle class, it is not surprising that this definition of middle class incomes was higher than the figure typically used by researchers. More telling was Romney's response to George Stephanopoulos's interview question, asking whether $100,000 was middle income; Romney responded, "No, middle income is $200,000 to $250,000 and less."[11]

The lower limit of middle class income in Romney's view was *four times* the median household income. What would Bill and Sheryl or David and Monica have to say about that? Here is another politician claiming to want to help the broad middle class, but defining the middle class in a way that excludes over 95 percent of households!

Of course, not all politicians have such outlandish views on how much middle class Americans make. Still, each high-profile quote just confirms what many middle class Americans already suspect: the decision makers are out of touch with the realities of middle class life. This disconnect can and does lead to alienation and pent-up anger for many middle class Americans. But before turning to these political and cultural outcomes, let's first look an important economic consequence of the middle class squeeze.

Record Numbers of Bankruptcies

In 2005, after eight years of trying and three failed attempts, the credit card industry finally got the bankruptcy changes they'd been lobbying for. The new bankruptcy law, which took effect on October 17, 2005, prohibited some people from filing for bankruptcy at all, made it more difficult for consumers to arrange manageable payment plans, and had fewer protections from collection efforts than the prior bankruptcy laws in effect since 1978.[12]

One change the new bankruptcy law put into effect bars those with above-average incomes from filing for Chapter 7 bankruptcy, in which debts can be wiped out entirely. Those who pass a "means test" that suggests they have at least $100 a month left after paying certain debts and expenses will have to file a five-year repayment plan under the more restrictive Chapter 13 bankruptcy laws. People who file for Chapter 7 also will be required to get professional credit counseling. These changes made it more difficult for the middle class to file for bankruptcy when faced with unexpected job losses or medical expenses, which has led to a decrease in the number of Chapter 13 filings; these now account for one-fourth of consumer bankruptcies.[13]

The groundbreaking Consumer Bankruptcy Project (CBP), conducted in 1991, 2001, and 2007, has changed the way that scholars understand consumer bankruptcy.[14] The data from these studies reveal that families going through bankruptcy are not very different from the rest of us, and more importantly, that bankruptcy is a decidedly middle class phenomenon. As Katherine Porter writes, "Consumer debt has become one of the most common shared qualities of middle class Americans, usurping the fraction of the population that owns a home, is married, has graduated college, or attends church regularly."[15] High debt loads, stagnant wages, and declining benefits conspire to put middle class households at risk of bankruptcy. Often all it takes to push families over the precipice is an unexpected layoff or illness. This economic precariousness explains why about 90 percent of households in bankruptcy are middle class households (see Figure 8.1).[16]

Teresa A. Sullivan, Elizabeth Warren, and Jay L. Westbrook's book *The Fragile Middle Class* analyzes the myriad reasons why Americans have been filing up to 1 million bankruptcy claims per year, including job and income loss, sickness and injury, divorce, homeownership (mortgage payments that are too high), and too much credit. Of these, the effects of credit and homeownership are (or appear to be) voluntary, while the effects of job loss, sickness, and divorce are less so. The book concludes that the cause of this epidemic of bankruptcies is the lack of a viable back-up plan for people who suffer misfortunes. There is little financial "slack" in most late twentieth- and early twenty-first-century middle class budgets, so slight changes in economic circumstances often lead to financial disaster.

Elizabeth Warren and Amelia Warren Tyagi's *The Two-Income Trap* makes a similar argument, claiming that one reason the American middle class is having so much trouble is because two incomes are now needed to cover what one income used to pay for, and that unregulated credit markets have allowed Americans to pile up huge amounts of debt. As our Chapter 3 shows, debt now equals 100 percent of most family income, if not more.

The Two-Income Trap also suggests that there is now no reliable public or private "safety net" for members of the middle class. While the public safety net that exists for the middle class—unemployment insurance and Social Security—can offer modest protection for some, the majority of middle class

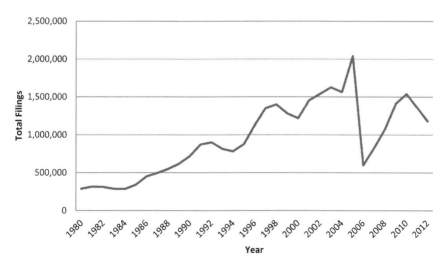

Figure 8.1 U.S. Personal Bankruptcy Filings, 1980–2012

Source: American Bankruptcies Institute

families don't qualify for these limited public programs. Whom can these people call on for assistance as they struggle to stay afloat? Historically, housewives and stay-at-home moms have provided a private safety net; because the financial situation of the household was not predicated on their paid labor, in hard times they could enter the workforce and bring in extra income. This private safety net is disappearing, however, because more and more families are now two-earner families to begin with; there is no "reserve worker" to step up when things get tight.

Warren and Tyagi argue that most of the money that the second earner is bringing in goes toward buying suburban houses in neighborhoods with good schools, and that the premium on these houses drives the costs of homeownership upward. They also rail against changed provisions in bankruptcy laws that claim bankruptcy is an "automatic way out for irresponsible spenders" and other "freeloaders" who are abusing the financial system.

Of course, as Warren and Tyagi point out, the problem is further exacerbated by the high divorce rate and the growing presence of single-parent families in the United States. These families have few prospects in an economic poker game that requires two incomes just to ante up. And many of the problems associated with time, money, and affordability of the lifestyle of the middle class are unreachable by single parents, let alone married and cohabiting parents attempting to get by on two incomes that don't grow and jobs that don't last.

Thus, the indebted middle class increasing ends in financial insolvency and bankruptcy. Granted, much of the spending associated with accumulating debt is voluntary, but the banking industry and others have spent millions of dollars peddling their wares—money available through credit and the "good life" it brings—to virtually anyone who will listen, and some of this plight is caused by unstable jobs and healthcare expenses that aren't covered. Is this really the best we can do?

The Cultural Contradictions of American Politics

Politicians routinely appeal to voters by trumpeting "traditional family values" and "free markets" and decrying "big government." The combination of these catchphrases has long proved successful for conservative politicians, but as Anthony Giddens argued in *Beyond Left and Right: The Future of Radical Politics* (1994),[17] the conservative movement (or "neoliberal" movement, in his terminology) is driven by a fundamental contradiction. The support of unbridled free markets and global capitalism is supposed to be founded on a bedrock of traditional family values, but these same traditional family values, and the cultural and community traditions they foster, are the very things that unbridled free markets attack. As we've shown throughout this book, markets and their activities are radically de-traditionalizing influences on the social fabric.

The present neoconservative movement in the United States pays lip service to traditional family values, but only as long as they don't cost anyone money or productivity. Many champion traditional family values (in effect the values of the 1950s, complete with subordinate women in nuclear families, neighborhood segregated schools, and one-earner households) as the ideal that will lead society to happiness once and for all. Yet the conservative movement does precious little to make their dreams a reality. The very trends we discuss are (in part) the product of changes the conservative movement has championed, regardless of whether specific political decisions or policies were responsible for bringing them about.

In a speech for the American Enterprise Institute, Charles Kessler offers a sympathetic critique of the conservative movement: "American conservatives have always been more confident of what they were against than what they were *for*. Sparked by their opposition to President Clinton's health care plan, for example, right-wing Republicans won an enormous electoral victory, capturing the House of Representatives and the Senate in 1994."[18] But, as Kessler points out, a clear assertion of conservative principles was not forthcoming. A similar pattern emerged in 2011, when President Obama's proposed American Jobs Act—which an independent firm estimated would add 1.3 million jobs to the economy—was blocked by Republicans in Congress,[19] and continued into 2013, as efforts to expand preschool education and improve infrastructure have been stymied by Republicans in the House of Representatives.[20]

The neoconservative movement has been successful in promulgating the idea that people who play by the rules should be rewarded for doing so, and that those who don't play by the rules deserve no rewards. Their policies thus fuel resentment while making the goals of the old rules unattainable; they've shown almost no inclination to act on their broad portrayals except through the politics of cultural resentment. Their policies imply that if only more repression was directed at those who don't follow the rules, such as minorities, the poor, gays and lesbians, immigrants, and the urban underclass, then those who do play by the rules would succeed. At the same time, those bigwigs who don't play by the rules at all—who stuff their pockets full of stolen Monopoly money—are completely ignored in the neoconservative mindset.[21]

So a significant portion of the middle class believes that if only they vote for the right people, they will benefit from tax cuts, and those who don't play by the rules will be punished. But with each round of elections, the tax cuts benefit those already well off instead, more taxes are excised from the middle class, wages remain flat, and the values the neoconservative movement claims to champion become more untenable.

This may be a transient formula for electoral victory, or a formula for fomenting cultural resentment and hatred. But it is certainly *not* a formula for reinvigorating the middle class.

Of course, conservatives and neoliberals are not exclusively to blame for the plight of the middle class. The American left has shown little or no connection to the values of the middle class and in some cases openly despises them. Worse still, the Democratic Party, as the world's second most enthusiastic capitalist party[22] ignored the economic interests and cultural concerns of the middle class. In their 2000 study of white working-class Americans—who make up about 55 percent of the voting population, and the majority of whom face the same economic realities as the middle class—Ruy Teixeira and Joel Rogers identify the persistent challenges facing "America's forgotten majority": stagnant wages, lack of health insurance, disappearing pensions, and the costs of childcare and education. These factors have meant that "resolving the tensions between work and family life is becoming more daunting with every passing year. Competing in a global economy is making it harder, not easier, to ensure one's family a decent standard of living."[23] Importantly, many of these voters are convinced that neither the Democrats nor the Republicans have their best interests in mind and are resentful of both political parties and their records over the past twenty-five years. In this context, it's no wonder that Scott Clark and Robert Boyer are mad.

The Fraying of Community

The challenges facing the indentured middle class over the past decades have had consequences for the fraying of community life. In 1985, Robert N. Bellah, Richard Madsen, William M. Sullivan, Ann Swidler, and Steven M. Tipton's *Habits of the Heart: Individualism and Commitment in American Life* was a bellwether of the fraying of community that resulted from the precarious state of the middle class. This research project involved focus groups and surveys among representative samples of Americans, all of whom were asked to discuss their aspirations for life and their conceptions of goodness. What came through in their interviews was that most aspirations were individual and intimate; national life and community life were rarely if ever mentioned. "[T]hough the nation was viewed as good," they wrote, "'government' and 'politics' often had negative connotations. Americans, it would seem, are genuinely ambivalent about public life, and this ambivalence makes it difficult to address the problems confronting us as a whole."[24]

Using National Election Studies data, Teixeira and Rogers show the dramatic decrease in the public's trust of government from 1964 through the mid-1990s. In 1964, nearly 80 percent of respondents said they trusted the government in Washington to do the right thing "most or all of the time," but by 1980, just above 25 percent agreed, and in 1996, slightly less than 30 percent did.

Our discussions have suggested some good reasons for this decline, both before and after 1985. The deindustrialization of the 1980s and the corporate downsizing of the 1990s tore the fabric of the middle class, and little evidence suggests that government at any level has done much to stop these activities; indeed, the government has not indicated that it intends to do anything about the current crisis of exporting white-collar service jobs to India and other English-speaking parts of the developing world.[25] Small wonder the middle class doesn't trust government. What has it done for them lately?

In addition to doing little to preserve the jobs that provide the earnings that make middle class life possible, federal and state governments radically altered their fiscal and taxation policies in favor of the wealthy and those with unearned income (see Chapter 6). The real, and unresolved, issue for political sociologists and other observers is how helping the poor came to be defined as a social experiment that failed, while the massive government-aided redistribution of wealth to the rich was labeled as unleashing free-market capitalism.

In 2000, Robert Putnam published his groundbreaking *Bowling Alone: The Collapse and Revival of American Community*,[26] which discusses what Putnam considers to be an alarming decline in *social* capital, the interactive activities that make communities and neighborhoods better places to live. Putnam documents declines in civic participation of all kinds, from voting to church attendance to membership in local civic organizations. Along with this, he documents declines in mutual trust, honesty, and reciprocity across the twentieth century, trends that seemed especially pronounced in the 1980s and 1990s.

Putnam blames television, increased working hours, and non-standard working hours for these trends. But could they be due instead to changes in the economic life of the middle class? The middle class is struggling to financially stay afloat, feeling political alienated and struggling to make sense of the "new rules" of middle class life; could this be the main reason we see less participation in the activities and groups that once formed the fabric of American community life?

People are more likely to volunteer, get involved in their communities, and make a difference in the lives of children, the elderly, the poor, and others if they have a stable economic base. Increasingly, the indebted middle class does not have that base, and volunteerism and a sense of community suffer as Putnam describes. People spend more time commuting to work, more hours at work, and more hours as a family working, all for earnings that don't increase in value.

This situation is especially ironic considering the political messages of the past twenty years. In George H. W. Bush's 1988 presidential campaign, Americans were told to embrace a "thousand points of light," to develop a new public spirit, civic awareness, and sense of volunteerism and community. While Bush's appeal may have been sincere, the economic policies he embraced were eroding the base from which such civic spirit must grow. Our "thousand points of light" requires electricity to work, and stable jobs with reasonable working hours, good wages, healthcare benefits, and some prospects for retirement are the power plant.

*Political Alienation and Anger: The Hardening of Public Discourse
and the Politics of Displacement*

Imagine that you are a new arrival in a strange land called the United States of America. You've been told that this country is "world's greatest democracy," a country where each person has the right to speak his or her own mind and to participate fully in the political process. This political process, in turn, creates the laws and policies that shape and govern the nation. You imagine that people all across this land must be continuously engaged in reflection and debate on important issues. Surely, in this land of democracy and opportunity, people will be actively engaged in the political process; they will yearn for greater understanding of the problems they collectively face; they will revel in new knowledge and strive to share this knowledge with others with the hopes of creating a better society for all. So to learn more about this process, you start by looking at the Declaration of Independence and the Constitution; clearly these are bedrock documents. But you decide that they are pretty old and stuffy and probably won't tell you a lot about what the people here and now care about. To really get a sense of the political discourse, you turn to the mass media: cable television and the popular press.

Spend a few minutes watching MSNBC or FOXNews, and the coarsening of American politics quickly becomes apparent. Political "debate" and "commentary" shows, like *Crossfire* (cancelled in 2005, it returned to the air in September 2013), *Hardball*, *Hannity and Colmes*, and *The O'Reilly Factor* (with an average of 4.5 million daily viewers, it has consistently ranked as the number one cable news show for the past ten years),[27] provide simplistic, caustic, and often highly partisan glimpses of complex issues. This is not political discourse; it is simply a form of political theater. It is stylized name-calling that gives the illusion of reasoned debate. As comedian Jon Stewart said during a now-famous appearance on *Crossfire*, calling that show a "debate show" is "like saying pro wrestling is a show about athletic competition."[28]

In the realm of popular press, there seems to be no end to new non-fiction works about current events and politics. Unfortunately, we once again find evidence of a polarized and coarse debate, pitting "us" against "them." Take, for example, the opening lines of syndicated columnist and bestselling author Ann Coulter's book *Treason: Liberal Treachery from the Cold War to the War on Terrorism:* "Liberals have a preternatural gift for striking a position on the side of treason. . . . Everyone says liberals love America, too. No they don't. Whenever the nation is under attack, from within or without, liberals side with the enemy. This is their essence."[29] Clearly these are not the opening lines of a book seeking to find common ground.

Of course, controversial and antagonistic writing is not limited to conservative authors. Jim Hightower begins his *Thieves in High Places: They've Stolen Our Country—And It's Time to Take It Back* with the following:

klep-to-crat na-tion (klep′te krat ná′ shen), *n.* **1.** a body of people ruled by thieves **2.** a government characterized by the practice of transferring money and power from the many to the few **3.** a ruling class of moneyed elites that usurps liberty, justice, sovereignty, and other democratic rights from the people **4.** the USA in 2003[30]

The quotes from Coulter and Hightower represent a tendency to use name-calling and boundary-making to make a political point. This tendency is most prevalent on the AM dial: the most popular form of talk radio has been the vitriolic ranting of Rush Limbaugh and a series of similar commentators. In 1980, there were about 75 commercial talk stations in the United States; by 2003, there were about 1,300.[31]

Okay, you might say, these shows and books may be a bit caustic, but they're just entertainment. The tone is different within the hallowed halls of Congress, right? Unfortunately, we also witness this coarseness of public debate among our elected officials.

Pointing out this changing tone of debate in Washington, Paul Krugman notes that Senator Phil Gramm "declared that a proposal to impose a one-time capital gains levy on people who renounce U.S. citizenship in order to avoid paying taxes was 'right out of Nazi Germany.'" This comparison was denounced by others, including the ranking Republican on the Senate Finance Committee, Charles Grassley. Yet as Krugman notes, a few week prior, Grassley himself had also used a Hitler analogy to get his political point across: "I am sure voters will get their fill of statistics claiming that the Bush tax cut hands out 40 percent of its benefits to the top 1 percent of taxpayers. That is not merely misleading, it is outright false. Some folks must be under the impression that as long as something is repeated often enough, it will become true. That was how Adolf Hitler got to the top."[32]

The Bush administration's strident unilateralism after the attacks of September 11, 2001, and during the buildup to the war in Iraq told the world and Americans who disagreed with this course of action, "You are either with us or against us." In an "us versus them" world, there is no middle ground.

The divisive rhetoric claiming that the enemy is anyone who holds different views had tragic consequences in January 2011, when U.S. Representative Gabrielle Giffords was the target of an assassination attempt that left six dead and a dozen injured. Prior to the shooting, political commentator and former vice-presidential nominee Sarah Palin had "produced an online map during the elections targeting districts of liberal lawmakers, including Giffords' District 8, with the cross hairs of a rifle scope. The ex-Alaska governor fired up her followers, saying, 'Don't retreat; reload.'"[33]

Several commentators have discussed the growth of alienation and cynicism in the American electorate.[34] Kevin Phillips's *Boiling Point: Republicans, Democrats, and the End of Middle Class Prosperity* documents how during the

1980s, Washington turned to a "soak the middle class" strategy to fuel the latest capitalist heyday, mirroring the capitalist heydays of the 1920s and 1890s. The combination of government debt, changed government funding priorities, and the growth of "one world" economic ideologies placed the middle class in a position in which prosperity was sacrificed for a "rentier class" of capitalists who don't make anything and don't employ anyone, and do little but look to Washington for additional tax and deregulation favors.

Thomas Byrne and Mary D. Edsall's *Chain Reaction* (1992) highlights a process that is still all too familiar in American politics: the association of government action with high taxes in the name of race and civil rights, and the ability of conservative politicians to exploit these connections to garner votes and political power. The Edsalls blame the Democratic Party for abandoning, or appearing to abandon, their original working-class constituency to garner votes from minority groups. The resulting misgivings about trends in government programs and the economic instability of the 1970s provided a window of opportunity for the Republican Party to regain electoral stamina by drawing connections between high taxes and "social experiments" that did little for the average voter—or worse, that provided minorities with superordinate sets of "rights" (through affirmative action and zealous civil rights enforcement) that could be used against whites in the workplace and public institutions.

Why would the embattled middle class latch onto the "race, rights, and taxes" framework as a viable political action strategy? Our research provides several possible reasons:

1. The tax system is biased against the middle class, and to some extent the poor, and taxes have shifted from progressive sources (income taxes) to regressive sources (payroll taxes and state and local sales taxes). The lion's share of the taxes that pay for the welfare state are extracted from the people just above welfare recipients—a formula for resentment and hatred.

2. Our embattled member of the middle class has no reason to choose another political course of action, given that the Democratic Party seems unable to articulate a coherent politics of the middle class that can compete with the right's focus on social pathology, high taxes, and "violating the rules."

3. The middle class is faced with two sets of "middle class rule violators," one visible—the poor and minority groups, as portrayed by conservatives and media—and one that is beyond their control—the wealthy, who have paid themselves handsomely from the productivity gains the middle class have helped produce. It is far easier for the middle class to express resentment over the workings of the system by insisting on control over the visible, subordinate group.

And Please! Let's Fight about Anything *but Money. . . .*

Finally, philosopher Jean Bethke Elshtain, in her provocative book *Democracy on Trial* (1995), suggests that much of what we call public life and public discourse has been coarsened and hardened by identity politics—the belief that there is no public sphere and that all arguments come down to the affirmation of personal identities. She faults academics, activists, and others for turning the pursuit of individual rights into an unbridled war of "us versus them," in which group boundaries are created through non-negotiable and unchangeable personal identities that reflect the sum total of all that is necessary to wage war in the political arena.

In political life, battles over personal identities and the ensuing culture wars eliminate common obligations and public spheres of political discourse about shared problems. Elshtain refers to this predicament as the "politics of displacement," where "private identity takes precedence over public ends or purposes; indeed one's private identity becomes who and what one is *in public,* and public life is about confirming that identity."[35] Elshtain blames feminists, environmentalists, gays and lesbians, and representatives of racial minority groups for engaging in the "politics of displacement." But it is time to ask some other, harder questions about the "politics of displacement" as a consequence of the plight of the middle class. For example, what are we to make of the millions of listeners who regularly tune into hate radio and other talk radio media that do little but ridicule those who aren't like "the rest of us"? What are we to make of negative campaign ads and the growing obsession with the "other" that this form of communication implies? These forms of public discourse involve the same dynamic now pervading middle class life in the United States. The indebted middle class is made up of the people who play by the rules—they are the "us," and those who don't play by the rules are "them." "Our" virtues are defined by "their" vices.

More insidiously, the politics of displacement is routinely played out in our legislative bodies any time proposals for tangible improvements to middle class life reach the limelight. Does someone want to talk about healthcare for all? Sidetrack the discussion by bringing up the abortions and stem cell research that "they" want. Does someone want to talk about family-friendly social policies like family leave and childcare subsidies? Rant instead about gay marriage, cohabiting partners, and how these benefits shouldn't apply to "them." Does someone want to discuss why American corporations export jobs overseas and hire illegal immigrants here at home? Sidetrack the discussion by mentioning how much unemployment an increase in the minimum wage would bring. What about improvements to the public schools? Propose that school prayer and vouchers that aren't large enough to pay for real school choice are the answer.

The list goes on, but the important point is that a politics of displacement operates at multiple levels of the American political system, diverting attention from the economic problems of the middle class. These diversionary tactics have become more pervasive as the problems of the middle class have worsened, and the media outlets that convey these messages portray the topics of these tactics as the real issues.

Of course, stem cell research, abortion, gay marriage, and school vouchers are important issues that deserve public debate; they are important both for those directly affected and for the country as a whole. But by allowing our political discourse to focus solely on these issues, politicians divert the collective attention of the middle class from the issues that can unite us. The rules of middle class life have been eroded and in many cases violated, but the middle class has not yet found the political will to demand better. We might be the policy wonks that Robert Boyer complains about, but we are willing to bet our upper-middle class salaries that engaging in the politics of displacement will *not* create a better economic life for Boyer and his compatriots.

The alienation and anger resulting from the violations of the norms of middle class life are pervasive. Rising bankruptcies, the growing cultural contradictions of American politics, the fraying and straining of communities, and the growing politics of displacement are cultural manifestations of the economic plight of the embattled middle class. Identifying these manifestations helps explain why significant portions of the middle class have apparently resigned themselves to peonage.

Will this continue? Is there any hope for change? In our final chapter, we revisit our arguments and then conclude by offering a "manifesto for the middle class" that provides some individual and collective possibilities for change.

Discussion Questions

- Do you think it should be easier or harder to file for personal bankruptcy?
- What are some ways that you can get involved on campus and/or in your community?
- In what ways can identity politics have a positive impact on society?
- Do you think that more or less effort should be put into finding common ground within the middle class?

Notes

1. Associated Press. 2005. "Colorado lawmaker: U.S. could 'take out' Mecca," accessed August 2, 2005, http://www.nbcnews.com/id/8616677/ns/politics/t/colorado-lawmaker-us-could-take-out-mecca/#.UfPRAW3RKRM

2. Brian Montopoli, 2010, "Delaware GOP Candidate: Ask Liberals Why They're Nazis," CBS News, accessed July 1, 2013, http://www.cbsnews.com/8301-503544_162-20016873-503544.html

3. "Rep. Steve King earns bipartisan condemnation for saying there are 100 drug dealers for every dreamer success story," *Houston Chronicle*, July 23, 2013, accessed July 25, 2013, http://blog.chron.com/txpotomac/2013/07/rep-steve-king-earns-bipartisan-condemnation-for-saying-there-are-100-drug-dealers-for-every-dreamer-success-story/

4. These analyses include Teresa A. Sullivan, Elizabeth Warren, and Jay L. Westbrook, *As We Forgive Our Debtors: Bankruptcy and Consumer Credit in America* (Washington, D.C: Beard-Books, 1999), and Sullivan, Warren, and Westbrook, *The Fragile Middle Class: Americans in Debt* (New Haven: Yale University Press, 2000); Elizabeth Warren and Amelia Warren Tyagi, *The Two-Income Trap: Why Middle Class Mothers and Fathers Are Going Broke* (New York: Basic Books, 2003); Robert N. Bellah, Richard Madsen, William M. Sullivan, Ann Swidler, and Steven M. Tipton, *Habits of the Heart: Individualism and Commitment in American Life* (Berkeley: University of California Press, 1985); Robert D. Putnam, *Bowling Alone: The Collapse and Revival of American Community* (New York: Simon and Schuster, 2000); and Jean Bethke Elshtain, *Democracy on Trial* (New York: Basic Books, 1995).
5. Steve Greenhouse, "Share of the Work Force in a Union Falls to a 97-Year Low, 11.3%," *New York Times*, January 23, 2013. http://www.nytimes.com/2013/01/24/business/union-membership-drops-despite-job-growth.html.
6. Griff Witte, "As Income Gap Widens, Uncertainty Spreads," *Washington Post*, September 20, 2004. http://www.washingtonpost.com/ac2/wp-dyn/A34235-2004Sep19?language=printer.
7. Alan Wolfe, *One Nation, After All* (New York: Viking, 1998).
8. Ibid., 251.
9. Sam Roberts, "Another Kind of Middle Class Squeeze," *New York Times*, May 18, 1997. http://www.tenant.net/Alerts/Guide/press/nyt/sr051897.html.
10. Ibid.
11. Steve Peoples, "Romney: 'Middle-Income' is $200K to $250k and Less," Associated Press, September 14, 2012. http://www.knoxnews.com/news/2012/sep/14/romney-says-middle-income-between-200-and-250k/.
12. Associated Press, "Changes in Law Spurs Bankruptcy Filings," September 24, 2005.
13. Katherine Porter, "Bankruptcy and Financial Failure in American Families," in *How Debt Bankrupts the Middle Class*, ed. Katherine Porter (Palo Alto, CA: Stanford University Press, 2012), 17–54.
14. Sullivan, Warren, and Westbrook, *As We Forgive Our Debtors: Bankruptcy and Consumer Credit in America* (New York: Oxford University, Press, 1989), and *The Fragile Middle Class: Americans in Debt* (New Haven, CT: Yale University Press, 2000); Elizabeth Warren and Amelia Warren Tyagi, *The Two-Income Trap: Why Middle Class Mothers and Fathers Are Going Broke* (New York: Basic Books, 2003); Elizabeth Warren and Deborah Thorne, "A Vulnerable Middle Class: Bankruptcy and Class Status," in *How Debt Bankrupts the Middle Class*, ed. Katherine Porter, 25–39 (Palo Alto, CA: Stanford University Press, 2012); Katherine Porter, "Methodology of the 2007 Consumer Bankruptcy Project," in *How Debt Bankrupts the Middle Class*, ed. Katherine Porter, 235–244 (Palo Alto, CA: Stanford University Press, 2012).
15. Katherine Porter, "Bankruptcy and Financial Failure in American Families," in *How Debt Bankrupts the Middle Class*, 5.
16. Elizabeth Warren and Deborah Thorne, "A Vulnerable Middle Class: Bankruptcy and Class Status," in *How Debt Bankrupts the Middle Class*, 38.
17. Anthony Giddens, *Beyond Left and Right: The Future of Radical Politics* (Stanford, CA: Stanford University Press, 1994), 9.
18. Kessler, Charles. 1998. "What's Wrong with Conservatism." *Speech for the American Enterprise Institute for Policy Research*, June 8. Accessed February 9, 2002 www.aei.org/publications/pubID.16662.filter.all/pub_detail.asp.
19. Paul Krugman, "Obstruct and Exploit," *New York Times*, September 9, 2012.
20. "Better Off with Barack? The President Revives a Favorite Tune," *The Economist*, July 27, 2013.
21. Paul Krugman, *The Great Unraveling: Losing Our Way in the New Century* (New York: W.W. Norton, 2003).
22. Kevin Phillips, *Boiling Point: Democrats, Republicans, and the Decline of Middle Class Prosperity*, 72–77 (New York: Random House, 1993).
23. Ruy A. Teixeira and Joel Rogers, *America's Forgotten Majority: Why the White Working Class Still Matters* (New York: Basic Books, 2000), xi.
24. Bellah et al., *Habits of the Heart*, 250.

25. Steve Lohr, "Cutting Here, but Hiring over There," *New York Times*, June 25, 2005, accessed http://www.nytimes.com/2005/06/24/technology/24blue.html?_r=0; John Helyar, "Outsourcing: A Passage out of India," *Bloomberg Businessweek*, March 15, 2012, accessed http://www.businessweek.com/articles/2012–03–15/outsourcing-a-passage-out-of-india

26. Robert D. Putnam, *Bowling Alone: The Collapse and Revival of American Community* (New York: Simon and Schuster, 2000).

27. International Business Times. http://www.ibtimes.com/bill-oreilly-re-signs-fox-10-controversial-quotes-factor-host-693072

28. For a transcript of this October 15, 2004, episode of *Crossfire*, see http://transcripts.cnn.com/TRANSCRIPTS/0410/15/cf.01.html. For video, see http://www.ifilm.com/ifilmdetail/2652831, accessed.

29. Ann Coulter, *Treason: Liberal Treachery from the Cold War to the War on Terrorism* (New York: Crown Forum, 2003), 1.

30. Jim Hightower, *Thieves in High Places: They've Stolen Our Country—And It's Time to Take It Back* (New York: Penguin Group, 2003), xiii.

31. Thom Hartmann, "Turn Your Radio On—The Unions' Answer to Right-Wing Static," Common Dreams News Center, August 11, 2003, accessed http://www.commondreams.org/views03/0811-02.htm

32. Paul Krugman, *The Great Unraveling: Losing Our Way in the New Century* (New York: W.W. Norton, 2003), 183.

33. James Gordon Meek, "Sara Palin Now in 'Cross Hairs': Gabrielle Giffords' Husband Blames Rhetoric for Arizona Shooting," *New York Daily News*, January 10, 2011, accessed http://www.nydailynews.com/news/national/sarah-palin-cross-hairs-gabrielle-giffords-husband-blames-rhetoric-arizona-shooting-article-1.149234#ixzz2a4NRJr1i

34. See, for example, Larry Bartels, *Unequal Democracy: The Political Economy of the New Gilded Age* (Princeton, NJ: Princeton University Press, 2010); Thomas Byrne and Mary D. Edsall, *Chain Reaction: The Impact of Race, Rights, and Taxes on American Politics* (New York: W.W. Norton, 1992); Kevin Phillips, *Boiling Point: Democrats, Republicans, and the Decline of Middle Class Prosperity* (New York: Random House, 1993); Jeffrey C. Goldfarb, *The Cynical Society: The Culture of Politics and the Politics of Culture in American Life* (Chicago: University of Chicago Press, 1991); and Thomas Frank, *What's the Matter with Kansas? How Conservatives Won the Heart of America* (New York: Metropolitan Books, 2004).

35. Elshtain, *Democracy on Trial*, 53.

CHAPTER 9

What Can We Do? A Manifesto
for the Middle Class

Most people want to live in a capitalist economy, not a capitalist society.
— Juliet Schor[1]

A world of difference separates an economy that loans money to consumers and one that pays them. In the first case, consumers earn adequate wages, pay cash, and use credit reasonably, planning their futures and preparing for the uncertainties of the present. In the second, consumers borrow because they can't save cash and have inescapable debts, stifling their financial growth and forbidding planning for the future. On the surface, consumers in these different economies may seem the same because they spend money on the same goods and services. But in one case the consumer is in control, and in the other financial institutions and investors in consumer debt hold the reins.

The dilemma of the middle class is not easily solved, but since prosperous economies depend on the middle class as consumers, some changes are essential. We know that there are no magic beans we can plant in the middle class garden to grow a beanstalk that reaches to wealthy elites and their pots of gold. Entrenched and powerful interests, global economic trends, advancing technology, long-held cultural beliefs, corporate actions, and governmental policies come together to shape the distribution of rewards in our economy and society. Challenging and transforming these institutions and trends will take time, but reestablishing the security and stability of the American middle class is within our reach.

Clearly, doing so requires concerted collective action, but that doesn't mean that we should not also address our own particular situations and individual needs.

Individual Responses: Avoiding the Trap of Middle Class Indebtedness

The social, economic, and political structures that have produced the middle class meltdown are too big to be combated effectively by individuals. This does not mean, however, that there is nothing that you can do to reduce your chances of falling victim to these forces. Not all of the measures necessary to avoid indebtedness are easy. Worse, not all of them are in your control—for example, sudden joblessness or illness may be inevitable. For the decisions within your control, we offer a few practical suggestions guided by the premise that middle class aspirations and the American dream are perfectly legitimate desires in our society.

Credit Is a Good Servant but a Bad Master

The post-industrial, deregulated American economy provides seemingly inexhaustible ways to accumulate debts. Since the early 1980s, the most popular way of doing so has been through credit cards.

The array of interest rates and fees built into credit cards is bewildering. Many have annual fees; some accumulate interest from the date of purchase; some calculate interest based on the amount owed, using recondite formulas; some offer low interest rates at the start that balloon to much higher rates after six months or a year; many include "universal default" clauses that allow companies to automatically raise interest rates, even if payments are made on time, if other loans default or if the lender determines that the cardholder has too much overall debt. Still, nobody can deny that credit cards are convenient and an almost necessary part of American economic life.

Here are three suggestions on how to protect yourself from sinking into the credit quagmire.

1. *Get a credit card that is also a debit card*. Debit cards allow you to deduct charges automatically from a checking account. The advantage is that, in effect, you are writing a check for purchases using funds you already have rather than slowly accumulating debts that you have to pay off later. If you use the debit side of your credit card for some of your purchases, you avoid accumulating interest charges and you pay for purchases out of your current funds. You'll have less money at the end of the month, but fewer debts—and you won't have to carry large amounts of cash or go through the hassle of writing checks for your purchases. One drawback to debit cards is although they have the same legal protections against fraud and theft that credit cards offer, unauthorized withdrawals from your checking account can have a more immediate impact on your finances than unauthorized credit card transactions.

2. *Be a ruthless credit card shopper*. Look for and keep cards with no annual fees and low interest rates—they're out there, but it takes some effort

to find them. Don't assume that your local bank, or a nationally visible bank that issues hundreds of thousands of credit cards, has the best deal. Read the fine print on credit agreements, and don't be sweet-talked into low short-term interest rates in exchange for higher long-term ones.

As we mentioned earlier, Americans receive many credit card offers each year. Those credit card companies must really want our business! Why not shop for the best deal? They're only taking our money, after all.

3. *Develop a "weight-loss clinic" philosophy toward credit card debt. If you don't put it there in the first place, you don't have to go on a "diet" to take it off.* Granted, this is easier said than done. But consumers who use credit cards that are also debit cards and who comparison shop for the best interest rates and low annual fees can also keep track of how much they charge, and put themselves on a payment program that pays down their debts rather than builds them. Be particularly wary of minimum payments that do little else but allow interest to accumulate on your purchases. The best practice with credit cards is to pay your balance off completely every month. Barring this, the best practice is to make payments so that the balance on the credit card shifts downward each month.

Credit is both an opportunity and a cost. The right decisions will keep credit from turning you into an indentured servant whom employers can strong-arm into extra hours and whom credit sharks can milk for assets and cash.

Buy the Big-Ticket Items You Want, and Don't Lease or Rent Them

On its surface, leasing or renting a luxury item such as a couch, stereo, or microwave oven might seem a good idea, but as we've discussed, the costs of doing so often become overwhelming. Whether you buy or lease a car, for example, depends a good deal on your personal circumstances and tastes. When seeking a deal that's right for you, keep the following in mind.

1. *Renting to own is always a bad deal.* Regardless of what you want to buy, it is always better to buy that item using cash, a credit card, or available credit from stores than it is to rent the item in anticipation of owning it. The interest rates on most rent-to-own deals are several hundred percent a year. Many stores offer much better six- to twelve-month "same as cash" deals; consider setting up a payment plan that pays off your purchase in the "same as cash" window before interest starts to accumulate.

2. *Don't lease cars; buy them instead.* If you have a good job, not much in savings, and a very old car that's suddenly broken down, leasing a car might be a viable short-term strategy to keep you moving until you decide what you want to do for your next car. Outside this one circumstance, buying cars is a better deal because you get to keep the car longer, and provided

you keep up the car's maintenance, the time you drive the car after it is paid off drastically reduces your overall costs. When you lease a car, you never free yourself from a cycle of payments: you first make lease payments during the terms of the lease, then either turn the car in and lease another one or buy the car you just leased and start paying a car loan that eventually leads to ownership of the car. In either case, you are paying for your car far longer than you would if you'd simply taken out a four-, five-, or even six-year loan to make the car payments.

If you want a luxury or sports car, you can take advantage of the growing auto leasing market. Consider buying a car someone else leased for two years. The original lessee has absorbed much of the depreciation in the car you'll want to buy, the car has usually been well maintained (otherwise, the original lessee would owe the car dealership a lot in closing costs for the lease), and the price is often one-half to two-thirds the cost of a comparable new car. Moreover, people tend to lease popular luxury cars so you should be able to find a good deal on an almost-new car.

Saving Money Is a Habit That Starts Small

Regardless of their economic circumstances, most people don't make a habit of saving money. As we showed in Chapter 3, the U.S. savings rate is low for several reasons, but the number of people with no savings at all is alarming. Our advice here is simple.

1. *Start saving early, and start small.* Considering the evidence we've presented on flat wages, high taxes, higher prices, and job instability, it's clear that people don't have a lot of money to save. But saving a little money is better than not saving any at all. Financial analysts will tell you that people who end up with big nest eggs when they retire often started by saving small amounts when they weren't making very much money.
   a. Putting ten dollars a month in a money market account is a good place to start. Money market accounts generally pay higher interest rates than passbook savings accounts (which pay as low as 0 percent interest) yet still provide liquidity (that is, you have access to this money without having to pay penalties). As your nest egg grows, look into putting some of your savings into short-term certificates or other investment products, which pay higher interest rates but do not provide the same level of liquidity.
2. *Make saving a habit.* Doing so eventually makes saving relatively painless: once you start putting away a fixed amount of money at regular intervals, you start not to miss it. If you put money in an account regularly and pretend it isn't there, you eventually build up a reserve fund that will be there when you need it. This makes saving for the future easier as well.

When the Time Comes, Buy a House You Can Afford

No doubt, owning a house is far better than renting in the United States. Owning provides cumulative financial advantages over time and tax advantages that accrue relatively early in the term of the mortgage. But this assumes that you buy a house you can afford to pay for, not one you can barely afford, and only if your economic circumstances remain the same or improve. As Elizabeth Warren and Amelia Warren Tyagi point out in *The Two-Income Trap*, purchasing a house that requires two high and rising incomes to make the payments has "bankruptcy" written all over it.[2] Purchase a more modest home you can afford rather than an expensive, trendy home that the bank or mortgage company will eventually foreclose on.

Obviously, we're making some assumptions here that for many are simply not true. Real estate where you live might be unaffordable for members of the middle class regardless of the interest rates available on mortgages. You might live in a part of the country where real estate prices go through boom and bust cycles—California and New England seem especially susceptible to this problem—in which case the type of house you can afford depends on what phase of the cycle the area is in. And in parts of the country where housing values are stagnant or declining, you may be faced with having little to no equity built up when it comes time for you to sell your current home.

Assuming you can buy a house in the first place leads to our second piece of advice. *Build up the equity in your house and don't borrow against it.* Don't be tempted by the tax advantages to borrow against the equity in your home to pay off debts and to finance big-ticket purchases; almost none of these advantages are as good as the long-term advantage of building equity in the home. If you *do* borrow against the equity in your home, doing so to improve the home makes the most sense, and then through a home equity loan rather than a home equity line of credit. Be wary of home equity lines of credit that issue "credit cards" that draw funds from the equity in your house.

Collective Responses: As a Nation, We Can Do Better Than This

We can put our own economic houses in order, but the long-term solution to the problems facing the twenty-first-century American middle class involves collective action. Collective action will be necessary to work toward an American society that links capital accumulation with the financial well-being of the middle class; that invests in families by providing stable jobs, good wages, healthcare, and pensions; and that acknowledges the corrosive effects of extreme inequality and the political influence that the wealthy can buy. Stagnant incomes, rising debts, higher taxes, productivity gains expropriated by others, the politics of anger . . . as a nation, we can do better than this!

Collectively, there is an array of things we could do. Many of these require political courage we haven't yet mustered. Some will require changes in how we perceive ourselves. Let's start with the key perception.

Reevaluating the Successes of the Past

To confront our modern dilemma, we must finally admit that the middle class prosperity of the 1950s and 1960s was an accident. The United States emerged from World War II as the world's foremost economic and political power. Low fertility rates during the Depression, relatively low levels of immigration in the decades following the 1924 Immigration Act, and the push for women to return from the labor force to the homestead created a boom in jobs for males. The industrial economy had broken free from the Depression through the stimulus of wartime production. The economies of our opponents (the Germans and Japanese) and even our allies (France and Britain) lay in ruins; years would pass before they were economically competitive with us again. Moreover, consumers had a pent-up demand for items such as cars and refrigerators that were not widely available during the war. Under these conditions, it would have been a miracle if the middle class *hadn't* prospered.

The 1970s saw the beginning of a globally competitive marketplace. Since then, easy profits and productivity gains have slowly vanished, and with them the more or less automatic pay raises, job stability, and long-term commitments of 1950s and 1960s middle class life. The goods once produced here are now produced elsewhere and shipped here, then sold to consumers at lower prices.

The coherent rules that once governed middle class life have not been replaced by equally coherent updated rules. And as fond as many are of recalling the middle class heyday of the 1950s and 1960s (conservatives recall strong family values, while liberals recall strong economies with lower economic inequality and rising wages), we cannot return to this era by simply rolling back the clock. Collectively recreating those cultural conditions is not only impossible, but given the levels of discrimination toward women and racial minorities during that period, it is also not desirable in many respects.

It seems that the middle class got it right once in our nation's history. If returning to our past is impossible, what can we do instead?

Reconnecting Capital Accumulation to Middle Class Prosperity

One hidden virtue of the industrial economy of the 1950s and 1960s was that the social classes needed each other. Investment occurred in tangible ways and tangible places. Work occurred at fixed worksites where employers and investors made extensive commitments. Investors and employers often lived in the same communities as average workers. In spite of the labor strife that this era is often remembered for, the classes needed each other and had to deal with each other if each was to prosper.

One reason for the plight of the middle class is that capital accumulation is divorced from the economic prosperity and health of the middle class. The middle class of a prior age fueled the consumer economy by spending the rising wages received from work. The middle class fuels the consumer economy by borrowing money from the same financial elites who accumulate capital through financial manipulations, capital flight, and expropriating productivity gains.

Given the power that voters have in an electoral representative democracy, the question is whether or not we're willing to acknowledge that policies that benefit the wealthy do not trickle down to the rest of us. This leads to a broader question, one we must ask in an era in which massive assets can be accumulated through the manipulation of markets, financial instruments, and tax loopholes: Under what conditions do we want capital to accumulate, and how will we reward those who follow those rules? Under the present circumstances, there are few if any rules, and the rules that do exist are not respected by people protected by extensive legal staffs, campaign contributions, and political action committees.

What should these rules be? We could start our answer with a very simple idea. In order to accumulate wealth in the United States, you have to take some of us with you as employees. There are currently almost no rewards for creating steady jobs that pay well—in fact, there are financial *penalties* for doing so. Would it be too much to ask that government provide a substantial tax credit to corporations that employ a lot of people for long periods of time without laying them off? Given everything else you can get a tax break for, this sounds reasonable.

To help define what is acceptable, let's define what is *not* acceptable: the unbridled accumulation of wealth through market and tax manipulations that involve the relentless buying and selling of companies, laying off of workers, cutting of wages, elimination of benefits, and paying CEOs and investors from productivity gains that the overworked, downsized, perpetually frightened workforce produces. Simply acknowledging that this is not what we want would be a start.

If We Value Families, We Should Put Our Money Where Our Mouths Are

Much of what passes for "family values" rhetoric is a classic example of the politics of displacement. (You don't see the connection between teenage abstinence from sexual activity and falling middle class wages? We don't either.) However, elements of our current cultural unrest about the state of the American family are not the manipulative invention of unscrupulous politicians. The divorce rate really is high, and child welfare, bad schools, and quality daycare and supervision for kids really are problems.

But just as we can't go back to the 1950s and 1960s, the political right can't do so either. In fact, as Giddens would point out,[3] exactly the opposite has to occur. If we value families, traditions, and communities, they must be sheltered from global market forces, not left to their mercy. A collective response that truly promotes family values is not merely rhetorical, and it will have an economic cost. No amount of religious fundamentalism, personal transformation, sexual abstinence, forced marriages, or complaining about those who don't follow the rules will help people make the choices that promote the long-term health of families. These things won't work because the economic base is not there.

If we truly want to support the American family—in all its forms—we must provide the economic base. Here are three suggestions for altering the rhetorical discussion concerning family values:

1. *Good jobs at good wages are a family value.* The turmoil that ravages modern families is often driven by economics. Couples fight over money, and fight harder over money when they're in debt and they don't have any money. When both parents have to work longer hours for lower wages, children are not supervised. Children who are not supervised get into trouble. When parents have to work non-standard hours, the problem is worse.

   a. Many on the political right claim that the problems of American families are caused by cultural decline. This decline, to the extent there is one, would be leveled by offering middle class parents stable jobs, offered by employers that are rewarded for providing them; ready access to healthcare; affordable childcare; family leaves; reasonable work hours; and paid vacations. The present political system does not view this social experiment as worth the effort, and no politician is currently willing to make this the centerpiece of a political campaign.

2. *All types of work must be treated with dignity and respect.* As other commentators have suggested,[4] working poverty needs to be legislated out of existence, even at the cost of slightly higher unemployment. The tax system must provide those who earn income with some of the same tax breaks as those who make unearned income. Or, more rightly perhaps, the tax system should treat both types of income the same way. The rhetorical claim that investment income is somehow tied to the prosperity of the middle class has not been true for the post-industrial economy of the past thirty years. Hence the tax breaks that favor all types of unearned income are not justified. Worse, from a cultural standpoint, such provisions of the tax law penalize—and degrade—work. In short, if we're really interested in stopping cultural decline, those who work should not be poor. We should promote the work ethic for everybody.

3. *The government must provide national healthcare and a viable, portable pension system.* These would not only restore the basic dignity of work but would also reduce the anxiety of job instability. Pensions and mandatory contributions by employers and employees should be universal and portable. Employees should not be forced to invest 401(k) plans only in company stock, but should have control over retirement funds. These funds should be administered by responsible third parties to which employers don't have access.

A viable national healthcare system would eliminate healthcare crises caused by skyrocketing out-of-pocket expenses, a major source of bankruptcy among the middle class. The Patient Protection and Affordable Care Act signed into law by President Obama in 2010 is a major step toward expanding healthcare to all Americans. There have been legal challenges to the act and various attempts to derail its implementation. Even if fully implemented, it will not provide the level of national coverage that exist in other countries. Every other industrialized nation in the world has national healthcare, so why can't we?

Finally, We Need to Acknowledge That Inequality Is a Social Problem

The issue of income and wealth inequality is much more fundamental than the old question of whether inequality motivates people to pursue economic opportunities. In the past few years, a national dialogue has begun on these issues—as protestors (The Occupy Movement) and Nobel Prize–winning economists (e.g., Joseph Stiglitz, in *The Price of Inequality*) help shape public understandings of economic inequality as a social problem. We aren't arguing that inequality at any level is bad, but how much of it do we need to promote the economic activities that make our economy prosperous?

Three major problems arise for a society with high and rising levels of economic inequality:

1. *Those who have privileged access to wealth can buy political influence with it.* This access guarantees access to other forms of wealth accumulation and deprives those with less political clout of economic opportunities. The tax and wealth redistribution of the past thirty years and the relative weighing of the tax system toward earned income and away from unearned income provides substantial evidence that this has happened.

2. *The rest of us lose faith in the system.* As we discussed in Chapter 8, an economically harried, unstable, one-step-from-bankruptcy middle class is not a group on which peace and social harmony can be built. Not only will government not function well, but virtually all other areas of civic life are damaged as well. Economically stable people are generous and giving; economically unstable people might still give and might still pay,

but they won't like it, and the system gives them no reason to like it. None of this would matter, of course, if private organizations and private volunteering really did pick up the slack created by declines in government services. But the same money the middle class pays in taxes that don't provide these services is earned from unstable working hours and jobs in distant suburbs that leave no room for voluntary activities.

3. *Extreme levels of inequality eliminate the possibility that we might think, "There but for the grace of God go I."* The wealthy and the superrich increasingly buy their way out of the social and personal problems they produce, hiring lawyers to extricate them from legal trouble, living in gated communities to shield themselves from urban decay, sending their children to private schools when public schools go downhill, hiring private physicians to attend to their healthcare needs and nannies to take care of their children. They hire employees in developing countries for 50 cents an hour and fire them without looking them in the face. Some can even buy helicopters and airplanes to avoid commuting gridlock, and install water purifiers and private sewer systems in their homes. What exactly are the connections between these elites and the rest of us?

For a long time, the only political message we heard was that we should all aspire to be like them. Change is possible, but first we must see through the illusions and rhetoric and recognize that the plight of the indebted middle class is real, and that as a nation we can—and must—do better.

Discussion Questions

- What other recommendations do you have for individual responses to these problems?
- What other recommendations do you have for collective responses?
- What groups or organizations could you join to get involved?
- What do you think is the single most important issue that we need to address in order to strengthen the American middle class?

Notes

1. Juliet Schor, personal communication, October 1, 2010.
2. Elizabeth Warren and Amelia Warren Tyagi, *The Two-Income Trap: Why Middle Class Mothers and Fathers Are Going Broke* (New York: Basic Books, 2003), 123–62.
3. Anthony Giddens, *Beyond Left and Right: The Future of Radical Politics* (Palo Alto, CA: Stanford University Press, 1994), 22–50.
4. Theda Skocpol, *The Missing Middle: Working Families and the Future of American Social Policy* (New York: W.W. Norton, 2000), 140–71.

Appendix: Exhibits

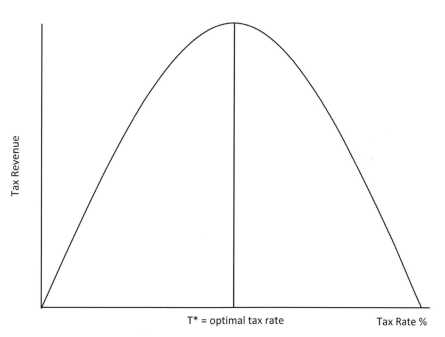

Appendix Exhibit 3.1 Taxing Less and Getting More—The Laffer Curve in Supply-Side Economics

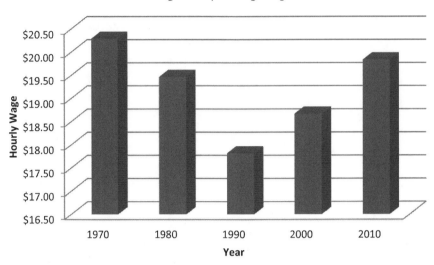

Appendix Exhibit 3.2 Average Hourly Earnings of Non-Farm Workers, 1970–2010 (2011 Dollars)

Source: Bureau of Labor Statistics

Appendix Exhibit 3.3 Ratio of the Middle Fifth Share of Income to the Top Fifth

Source: U.S. Census Bureau, Current Population Survey, Annual Social and Economic Supplements

The Growing Gap Between the Mean and Median Family Income
Indicates that Income Inequality is Rising

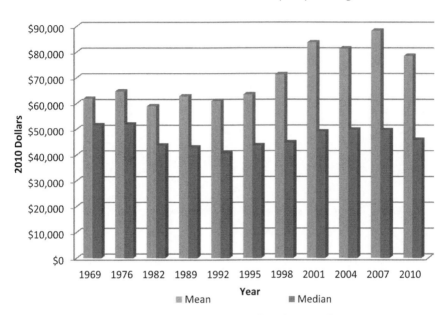

Appendix Exhibit 3.4 Difference between Mean and Median Family Income, 1969–2010

Source: Federal Reserve Bulletin, various years

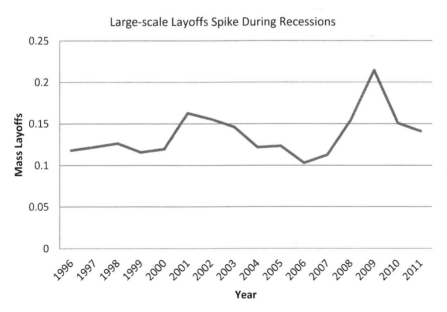

Appendix Exhibit 3.5 Mass Layoffs per 1,000 Workers, 1996–2011

Source: Bureau of Labor Statistics

The U.S. Balance of Payments Declines Significantly; We Buy More for the Rest of the World than we Sell to Them

Appendix Exhibit 3.6 U.S. Balance of Payments, 1970–2010

Source: U.S. Census Bureau, Division of Foreign Trade

Appendix Exhibit 3.7 Index of Aggregate Work Hours

Source: Bureau of Labor Statistics

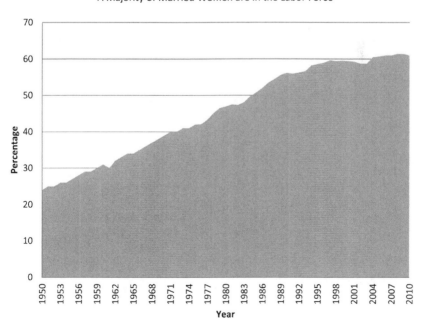

Appendix Exhibit 3.8 Percentage of Married Women in the Labor Force, 1950–2010

Source: U.S. Census Bureau, Statistical Abstract of the United States

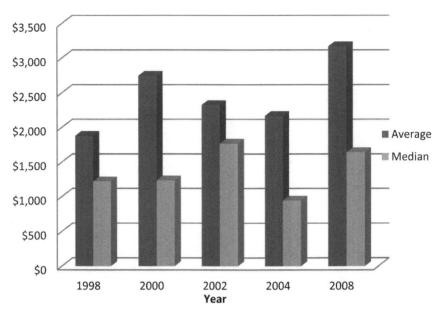

Appendix Exhibit 3.9 Average and Median Credit Card Debt per College Student, 1998–2008

Source: Sallie Mae, 2012

Productivity, the relationship between production output and the resource inputs used to generate that output, is usually expressed as the ratio of output per unit of input over time. For labor inputs, productivity is usually measured as outputs per person-hour worked.

The *National Income and Product Accounts* (NIPA) provide a national-level view of usages of the nation's output and income derived from production. The two most widely used measures from the NIPA are gross domestic product (GDP) and gross domestic income (GDI). The NIPA was revised in 1999 and again in 2003.

Economies of scale represent the increase in efficiency that results from producing more goods. Generally, average costs per unit decline as production increases because fixed costs—the costs of plants, buildings, equipment, and materials—are spread over a larger number of finished products.

Reinvestment refers to taking profits from specific activities and (usually) investing them in those same activities or businesses to improve efficiency and remain competitive.

In the abstract, productivity measures are divided into *single-factor* and *multi-factor productivity*. Single-factor productivity measures usually have focused on labor productivity and are measured as *output ÷ hours worked*.

"Output" in this context varies from one industry to another and even from one workplace to another. In some service-related and high-technology firms, discrete units of output might not exist at all. But this indicator has the advantage of easy measurement, and data of this kind are generally collected by almost all workplaces for internal purposes. The downside of measures like this is that they don't measure the contribution of labor alone. Virtually all changes that increase the efficiency of the production process are "credited" to labor and appear as productivity change.[1] More importantly from our standpoint, non-labor contributions to productivity can deteriorate, and this will appear as declines in labor's contribution to productivity.[2]

The development of the specific measure of productivity favored by the U.S. Department of Labor resulted from the economic and political environment surrounding the adoption of Keynesian economics during the Roosevelt administration of the 1930s.[3] Specifically, economists and policy analysts at the Works Progress Administration (WPA) and other federal agencies were convinced that wages lagged behind productivity gains in the 1920s, and that the resulting "underconsumption" was a drag on the U.S. economy. But at the time there was no statistical mechanism for measuring aggregate productivity in the economy, so convincing arguments that wages lagged behind productivity relied solely on speculation.

Economists developing measures of productivity had another problem on their hands: output units were unique to specific industries (for example, tons of steel, number of cars assembled, and reams of paper manufactured) and were thus incomparable. Though productivity within industries over time could be compared, doing so provided policy-makers with little useful information on how aggregate productivity was changing across the economy. No measure of productivity could deal with the different capital inputs and changes in the organization of work that affected aggregate, single-factor productivity measures in ways that had little to do with whether labor inputs improved.

Beginning in 1947, the U.S. government published the National Income and Product Accounts,[4] introducing the measure of gross national product (or GNP) that converted the measurement of output from physical inputs (tons of steel, for example) to dollar values. The Bureau of Economic Analysis furthered the development and use of GNP measures by publishing them by industry, tying the production of national output to shares contributed by various sectors of the economy. This virtually eliminated any attempt at measuring physical outputs, instead measuring output in dollars.

This measurement, however, often reflects the "deflation" problem: as output is more efficiently made, the price may drop faster than unit labor costs drop, making productivity look artificially low. Most output measures attempt to measure output in real (inflation adjusted) dollars to take this change into account. Inflation adjustment can adjust for deflation (actual drops in the price of goods and services) as well as for other increases in prices.

Multifactor productivity measures try to avoid some problems of single-factor productivity measures by taking into account combined inputs (for example, capital, labor, energy, raw materials, and purchased services).[5] But the problems here are no less daunting than the problems of using single-factor productivity measures. Figuring out what the relevant inputs are and assigning the correct values to them are serious challenges. Further, most policy analysts and some economists are interested in the relative contributions of different inputs for increasing productivity.

William Nordhaus proposes that we use a "chain-weighted index" of sectoral productivity growth in place of the standard output-per-hours-worked measure of productivity that is part of NIPA.[6] This method says that mathematically, output and productivity in one sector of the economy is critically bound to productivity in other sectors. Further, the productivity in the entire economy changes as investment grows in one sector of the economy and not another—industries with slow investment growth usually have slow productivity growth, and vice versa. And productivity changes as employment shares shift from high (or low) productivity industries and sectors to low (or high) productivity industries or sectors. Our current aggregate measures of productivity bottle up all these changes and attribute them to changes in output per hour worked.

For reasons that Nordhaus explains, from a social welfare standpoint, the traditional measure of productivity needs to be supplemented by the addition of changes due to changing expenditure shares on productivity across industries. If capital investment increases at different rates across industries, then productivity will lag. This second component of a productivity measure places emphasis on increased capital inputs in addition to standard output per unit input.

Current productivity measures do not represent differences in inputs across industries well, so including these two factors while excluding the portion accounted for by shifts in employment is justified. The level of productivity (as opposed to changes in productivity) varies by a factor of over 100 across industries.[7] Capital intensive and human capital (educated) sectors of the economy have high levels of productivity. Labor intensive and low-skilled areas of the economy (private household workers, for example) have low levels of productivity. In practice, relative productivity levels almost never move, but industries do change their ability to convert inputs into outputs. That change in ability is what newer measures of productivity try to capture.

How effective are new capital investments at increasing productivity, and do these investments pay off in terms of increased efficiency? If new capital investments don't produce their intended results unless work routines are reorganized, then capital investments by themselves may do relatively little to boost aggregate productivity. If work routines are changed but workers are required to use antiquated equipment that breaks down frequently and requires extensive maintenance, then increased worker inputs won't yield the expected efficiency gains. Without those efficiency gains, the division of the economic pie between investment, profits, and compensation is a fight over who will get theirs at the expense of others. Such confrontations rarely lead to long-term harmony.

Appendix Exhibit 4.1 Productivity: An Elusive Concept

[1] Manser, "The Bureau of Labor Statistics (BLS) Productivity Programs."

[2] Bluestone, Barry and Bennett Harrison. 1982. *The Deindustrialization of America: Plant Closings, Community Abandonment, and the Dismantling of Basic Industry.* New York: Basic Books, 25–48.

[3] Block and Burns, "Productivity as a Social Problem." 768–72.

[4] Ruggles, Richard. 1983. "The United States National Income Accounts, 1947–1977: Their Conceptual Basis and Evolution" in *The U.S. National Income and Product Accounts*, ed. Murray F. Foss. Chicago: University of Chicago Press, pp. 15–104.

[5] Manser, "The Bureau of Labor Statistics (BLS) Productivity Programs."

[6] Nordhaus, "Alternative Methods for Measuring Productivity Growth," pp. 1–20.

[7] University of Michigan. 2004. "More Jobs Unable to Offset Higher Inflation and Interest Rates." Retrieved from www.sca.isr.umich.edu.

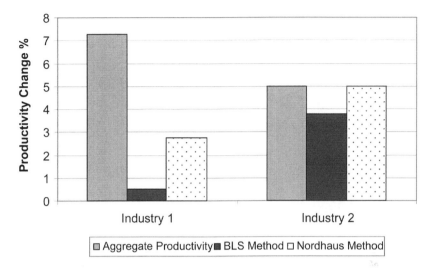

Appendix Exhibit 4.2 Hypothetical Differences in Productivity in Two Economies—
One with Shifts toward Employment and One with Shifts in Output Shares

Source: William Nordhaus. 2001. "Alternate Methods for Measuring Productivity Growth" Working
Paper 8095. National Bureau of Economic Research

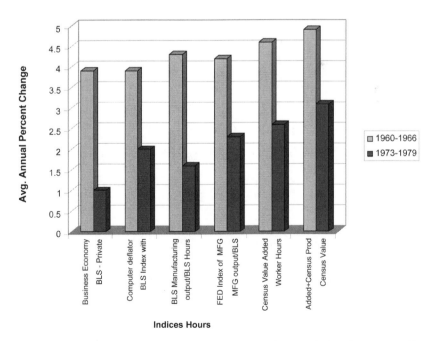

Appendix Exhibit 4.3 Alternative Productivity Indices Calculated Using Different
Sources, 1960–1979

Source: Fred Block and Gene Burns. 1986. "Productivity as a Social Problem: The Uses and Misuses of
Social Indicators" *American Sociological Review* 51(6)

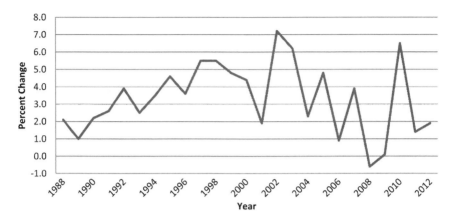

Appendix Exhibit 4.4 Manufacturing Productivity: Annual Change in Output per Person, 1987–2012

Source: Bureau of Labor Statistics

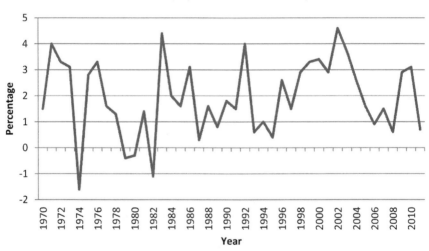

Appendix Exhibit 4.5 Non-Farm Business Productivity: Annual Percentage Change in Output per Hour

Source: Bureau of Labor Statistics

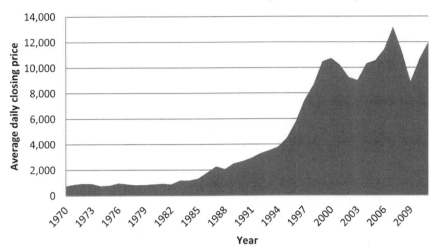

Appendix Exhibit 4.6 Dow Jones Industrial Average, 1970–2010

Source: *2012 Economic Report of the President*, U.S. Government Printing Office

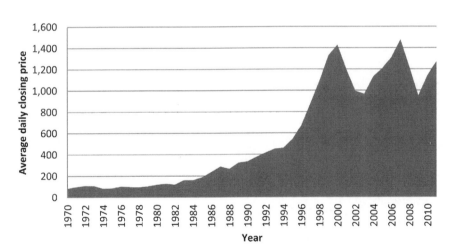

Appendix Exhibit 4.7 Standard & Poor's Composite Index, 1970–2010

Source: *2012 Economic Report of the President*, U.S. Government Printing Office

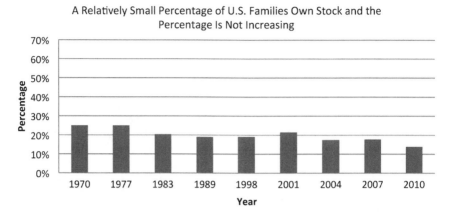

Appendix Exhibit 4.8 Percentage of U.S. Families That Own Stock

Source: Survey of Consumer Finances, Federal Reserve Bulletin, various years

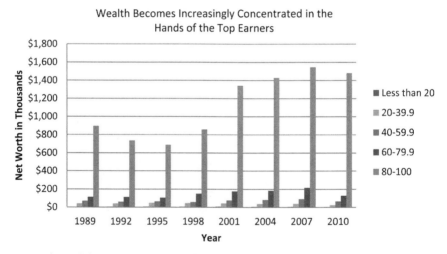

Appendix Exhibit 4.9 Median Family Net Worth by Income Quintiles, 1989–2010 (Thousands of 2010 Dollars)

Source: Survey of Consumer Finances, Federal Reserve Bulletin, various years

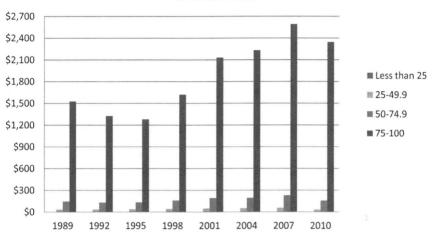

Appendix Exhibit 4.10 Median Family Net Worth by Wealth Quartiles, 1989–2010 (Thousands of 2010 Dollars)

Source: Survey of Consumer Finances, Federal Reserve Bulletin, various years

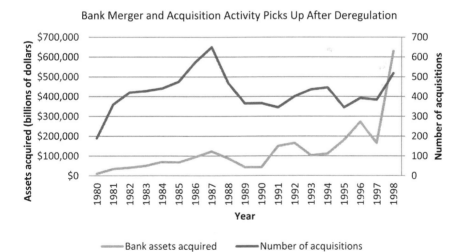

Appendix Exhibit 5.1 Bank Mergers and Bank Assets Acquired, 1980–1998

Source: Federal Reserve Board

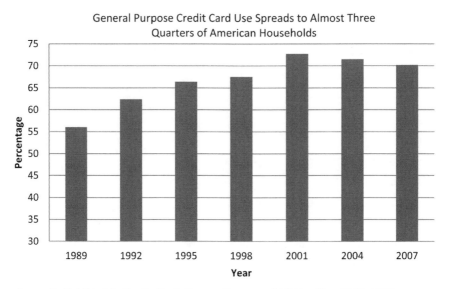

Appendix Exhibit 5.2 Credit Card Users as Percent of All Families, 1989–2007

Source: U.S. Census Bureau, Statistical Abstract of the United States

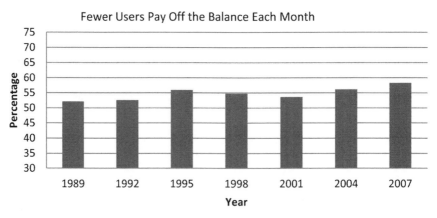

Appendix Exhibit 5.3 Percent of Credit Card Users Carrying a Balance, 1989–2007

Source: U.S. Census Bureau, Statistical Abstract of the United States

Appendix Exhibit 5.4 Percentage of Households Leasing Vehicles, 1989–2001

	1989	1992	1995	1998	2001
All Households	2.5	2.9	4.5	6.4	5.8
Household Income					
Less than $10,000	(z)	(z)	(z)	(z)	(z)
$10,000 to $24,999	(z)	(z)	1.5	4	1.8
$25,000 to $49,999	(z)	3.3	3.4	5	5.3
$50,000 to $99,999	6.1	4.1	9.4	9.5	7.6
$100,000 and over	5	9.6	14.2	14.8	12.9

(z) = Ten or fewer observations

Source: U.S. Census Bureau, Statistical Abstract of the United States

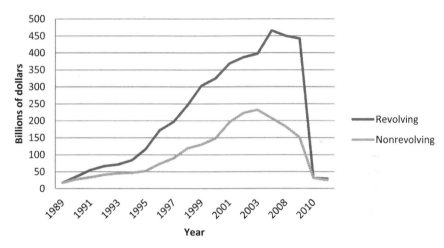

Appendix Exhibit 5.5 Consumer Credit Outstanding, Pools of Securitized Assets, 1989–2011

Source: Federal Reserve Board

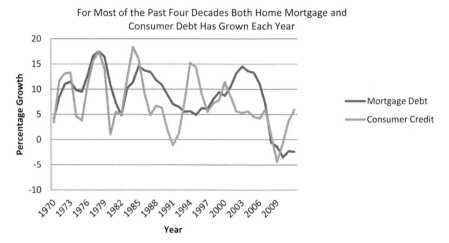

Appendix Exhibit 5.6 Percentage Growth in Home Mortgage and Consumer Debt, 1970–2011

Source: Board of Governors of the Federal Reserve System, Flow of Funds Accounts

Appendix Exhibit 6.1 Top Marginal Federal Income Tax Rate

Source: U.S. Census Bureau, Foreign Trade Division

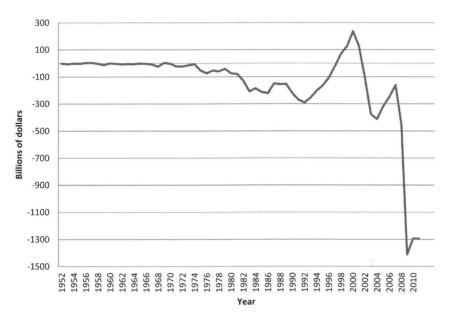

Appendix Exhibit 6.2 Federal Deficit 1950–2012

Source: Internal Revenue Service

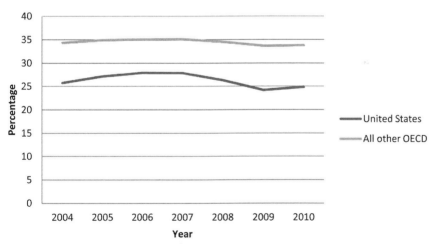

Appendix Exhibit 6.3 Total Taxes as a Percentage of GDP: The United States in Comparison with OECD Countries

Source: Organization for Economic Co-Operation and Development, Tax Statistics

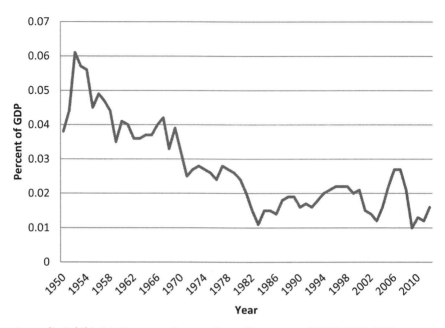

Appendix Exhibit 6.4 Corporate Income Tax as Percentage of GDP, 1950–2012

Source: Office of Management and Budget, Budget of the United States

Appendix Exhibit 6.5 Average Federal and Payroll Tax Rate Paid for Median, Four-Person Family, 1955–2013

Source: U.S. Census Bureau; U.S. Treasury Department; Tax Policy Center

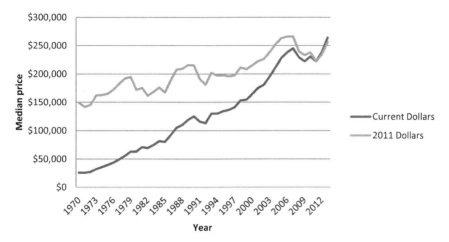

Appendix Exhibit 6.6 Median New Home Sale Prices (Current and Constant 2011 Dollars)

Source: U.S. Census Bureau

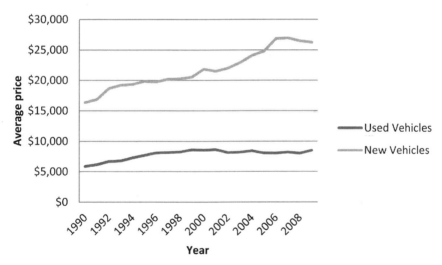

Appendix Exhibit 6.7 Average Price of New and Used Passenger Vehicles (Current Dollars)

Source: U.S. Census Bureau, Statistical Abstract of the United States

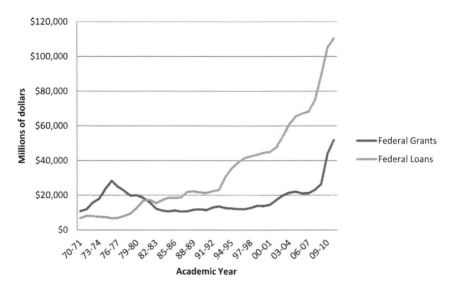

Appendix Exhibit 6.8 Trends in Federal Grants and Loans for Student Aid (in Current Dollars)

Source: The College Board, 2012

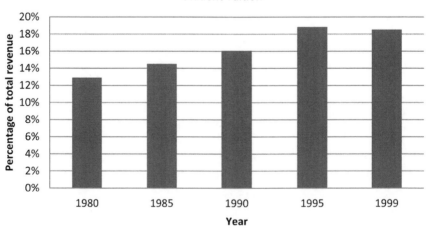

Appendix Exhibit 6.9 Percentage of Public Higher Education Costs Funded by Tuition and Fees, 1980–1999

Source: The College Board, 2012

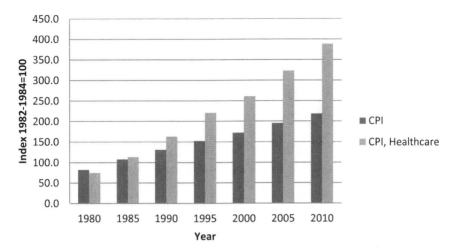

Appendix Exhibit 6.10 Change in the Price of Healthcare Relative to the Consumer Price Index, 1980–2010

Source: U.S. Census Bureau, Statistical Abstract of the United States

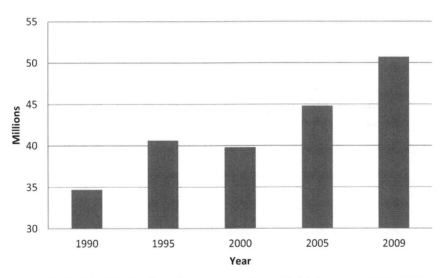

Appendix Exhibit 6.11 Number of Americans without Health Insurance, 1990–2009

Source: U.S. Census Bureau, Statistical Abstract of the United States

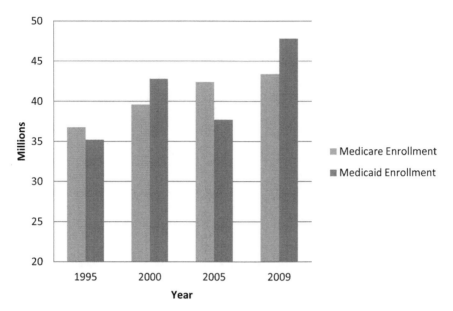

Appendix Exhibit 6.12 Number of Medicare and Medicaid Recipients, 1995–2009

Source: U.S. Census Bureau, Statistical Abstract of the United States

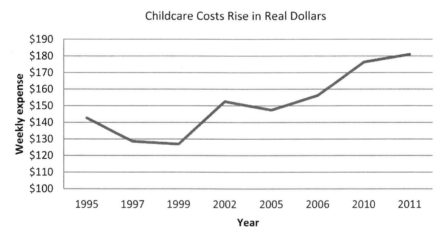

Appendix Exhibit 6.13 Average Weekly Childcare Expense for Children under Five Years Old (2011 Dollars)

Source: U.S. Census Bureau, Survey of Income and Program Participation

Index

Page numbers in italics refer to tables and figures.

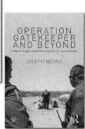

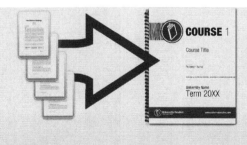